THE NEW CAMBRIDGE SHAKESPEARE

GENERAL EDITOR
Philip Brockbank, *Director, The Shakespeare Institute, University of Birmingham*

ASSOCIATE GENERAL EDITORS
Brian Gibbons, *Professor of English Literature, University of Zürich*
Bernard Harris, *Professor of English, University of York*
Robin Hood, *Senior Lecturer in English, University of York*

Romeo and Juliet, edited by G. Blakemore Evans
The Taming of the Shrew, edited by Ann Thompson
Othello, edited by Norman Sanders
King Richard II, edited by Andrew Gurr
A Midsummer Night's Dream, edited by R. A. Foakes
Hamlet, edited by Philip Edwards
Twelfth Night, edited by Elizabeth Story Donno
All's Well That Ends Well, edited by Russell Fraser

ALL'S WELL THAT ENDS WELL

Christine de Pisan composing her *Cent Balades*

ALL'S WELL THAT ENDS WELL

Edited by
RUSSELL FRASER

Austin Warren Professor of English Language and Literature,
University of Michigan

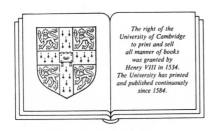

The right of the
University of Cambridge
to print and sell
all manner of books
was granted by
Henry VIII in 1534.
The University has printed
and published continuously
since 1584.

CAMBRIDGE UNIVERSITY PRESS

Cambridge
London   New York   New Rochelle
Melbourne   Sydney

Published by the Press Syndicate of the University of Cambridge
The Pitt Building, Trumpington Street, Cambridge CB2 1RP
32 East 57th Street, New York, NY 10022, USA
10 Stamford Road, Oakleigh, Melbourne 3166, Australia

First published 1985

Printed in Great Britain by the
University Press, Cambridge

Library of Congress catalogue card number: 85–4167

British Library cataloguing in publication data

Shakespeare, William
All's well that ends well – (New Cambridge Shakespeare)
I. Title   II. Fraser, Russell
822.3′3   PR2801.A2

ISBN 0 521 22150 1 hard covers
ISBN 0 521 29365 0 paperback

UP

THE NEW CAMBRIDGE SHAKESPEARE

The *New Cambridge Shakespeare* succeeds *The New Shakespeare* which began publication in 1921 under the general editorship of Sir Arthur Quiller-Couch and John Dover Wilson, and was completed in the 1960s, with the assistance of G. I. Duthie, Alice Walker, Peter Ure and J. C. Maxwell. *The New Shakespeare* itself followed upon *The Cambridge Shakespeare*, 1863–6, edited by W. G. Clark, J. Glover and W. A. Wright.

The New Shakespeare won high esteem both for its scholarship and for its design, but shifts of critical taste and insight, recent Shakespearean research, and a changing sense of what is important in our understanding of the plays, have made it necessary to re-edit and redesign, not merely to revise, the series.

The *New Cambridge Shakespeare* aims to be of value to a new generation of playgoers and readers who wish to enjoy fuller access to Shakespeare's poetic and dramatic art. While offering ample academic guidance, it reflects current critical interests and is more attentive than some earlier editions have been to the realisation of the plays on the stage, and to their social and cultural settings. The text of each play has been freshly edited, with textual data made available to those users who wish to know why and how one published text differs from another. Although modernised, the edition conserves forms that appear to be expressive and characteristically Shakespearean, and it does not attempt to disguise the fact that the plays were written in a language other than that of our own time.

Illustrations are usually integrated into the critical and historical discussion of the play and include some reconstructions of early performances by C. Walter Hodges. Some editors have also made use of the advice and experience of Maurice Daniels, for many years a member of the Royal Shakespeare Company.

Each volume is addressed to the needs and problems of a particular text, and each therefore differs in style and emphasis from others in the series.

PHILIP BROCKBANK
General Editor

For MARY AND RALPH GESUALDI

CONTENTS

ILLUSTRATIONS

PREFACE

This edition draws on the labour of most of Shakespeare's editors who have preceded me, beginning with Rowe in 1709. Sir Arthur Quiller-Couch and John Dover Wilson, who began *The New Shakespeare* in 1921, are conspicuous among these predecessors. The *New Cambridge Shakespeare* in which the present volume appears does not depend on their work, and is a completely new edition. Shakespeare's critics, beginning with Meres in 1598 and coming down to the present, are represented in this edition as their critical comments seem pertinent. I have often had G. K. Hunter's work in mind, and his Arden edition (1959) deserves special mention. No particular school or point of view gets primacy, however.

I have had the good fortune of being able to depend on the extraordinary resources of the University of Michigan libraries, and I am grateful for this. The Rackham School of the University and my own department helped me financially, not least by enabling me to engage Brian Foley as my assistant. He did all the typing, checked all the collations, and his help in these and other ways has been indispensable throughout.

The section on Recent Years in the Introduction has been contributed by the General Editor.

R. F.

University of Michigan

ABBREVIATIONS AND CONVENTIONS

Shakespeare's plays, when cited in this edition, are abbreviated in a style modified slightly from that used in the *Harvard Concordance to Shakespeare*. Other editions of Shakespeare are abbreviated under the editor's surname (Evans, Hunter) unless they are the work of more than one editor. In such cases, an abbreviated series name is used (NS, Var. 78). When more than one edition by the same editor is cited, later editions are discriminated with a raised figure (Rowe[3]). References to Abbott's *Shakespearian Grammar* are to paragraph numbers. All quotations from Shakespeare, except those from *All's Well*, use the text and lineation of *The Riverside Shakespeare*, under the general editorship of G. Blakemore Evans.

1. Shakespeare's plays

Ado	*Much Ado about Nothing*
Ant.	*Antony and Cleopatra*
AWW	*All's Well That Ends Well*
AYLI	*As You Like It*
Cor.	*Coriolanus*
Cym.	*Cymbeline*
Err.	*The Comedy of Errors*
Ham.	*Hamlet*
1H4	*The First Part of King Henry the Fourth*
2H4	*The Second Part of King Henry the Fourth*
H5	*King Henry the Fifth*
1H6	*The First Part of King Henry the Sixth*
2H6	*The Second Part of King Henry the Sixth*
3H6	*The Third Part of King Henry the Sixth*
H8	*King Henry the Eighth*
JC	*Julius Caesar*
John	*King John*
LLL	*Love's Labour's Lost*
Lear	*King Lear*
Mac.	*Macbeth*
MM	*Measure for Measure*
MND	*A Midsummer Night's Dream*
MV	*The Merchant of Venice*
Oth.	*Othello*
Per.	*Pericles*
R2	*King Richard the Second*
R3	*King Richard the Third*
Rom.	*Romeo and Juliet*
Shr.	*The Taming of the Shrew*
STM	*Sir Thomas More*
Temp.	*The Tempest*
TGV	*The Two Gentlemen of Verona*

Tim.	*Timon of Athens*
Tit.	*Titus Andronicus*
TN	*Twelfth Night*
TNK	*The Two Noble Kinsmen*
Tro.	*Troilus and Cressida*
Wiv.	*The Merry Wives of Windsor*
WT	*The Winter's Tale*

2. Other works cited and general references

Abbott	E. A. Abbott, *A Shakespearian Grammar*, 1869, reprinted 1966
Addis	John Addis, '*All's Well That Ends Well*', *N&Q* 10 (1866), 446
Alexander	Peter Alexander (ed.), *Works*, 1951
Brigstocke	W. Osborne Brigstocke (ed.), *All's Well That Ends Well* (Arden Shakespeare), 1904
Cam.	William George Clark, J. Glover and William Aldis Wright (eds.), *Works* (Cambridge Shakespeare), 1863–6
Capell	Edward Capell (ed.), *Works*, 1768
Case	Arthur E. Case (ed.), *All's Well That Ends Well* (Yale Shakespeare), 1926
Collier	John P. Collier (ed.), *Works*, 1842–4
Collier MS.	in Perkins's Second Folio, 1632 (Huntington Library)
conj.	conjecture
Craig	W. J. Craig (ed.), *Works*, 1891
Daniel	Peter A. Daniel, *Notes and Conjectural Emendations of Certain Doubtful Passages in Shakespeare's Plays*, 1870
Delius	Nicholaus Delius (ed.), *Works*, 1854–60
Dyce	Alexander Dyce (ed.), *Works*, 1857
Dyce²	Alexander Dyce (ed.), *Works*, 1864
E&S	*Essays and Studies*
EIC	*Essays in Criticism*
ELH	*ELH: A Journal of English Literary History*
Evans	G. Blakemore Evans (ed.), *The Riverside Shakespeare*, 1974
F	*Mr William Shakespeares Comedies, Histories, and Tragedies*, 1623 (First Folio)
F2	*Mr William Shakespeares Comedies, Histories, and Tragedies*, 1632 (Second Folio)
F3	*Mr William Shakespeares Comedies, Histories, and Tragedies*, 1664 (Third Folio)
F4	*Mr William Shakespeares Comedies, Histories, and Tragedies*, 1685 (Fourth Folio)
Globe	William George Clark and William Aldis Wright (eds.), *Works* (Globe Shakespeare), 1864
Glover	John Glover (*see* Case, *above*)
Hanmer	Thomas Hanmer (ed.), *Works*, 1743–4
Harrison	G. B. Harrison (ed.), *Works* (Penguin Shakespeare), 1937–56
Heath	Benjamin Heath, *A Revisal of Shakespear's Text*, 1765
HLQ	*Huntington Library Quarterly*
Hunter	G. K. Hunter (ed.), *All's Well That Ends Well* (Arden Shakespeare), 1959

JEGP	*Journal of English and Germanic Philology*
Johnson	Samuel Johnson (ed.), *Works*, 1765
Kittredge	George L. Kittredge (ed.), *Works*, 1936
Knight	Charles Knight (ed.), *Works*, 1838–43
Lowes	John L. Lowes (ed.), *All's Well That Ends Well* (Tudor Shakespeare), 1912
Malone	Edmond Malone (ed.), *Works*, 1790
MLQ	*Modern Language Quarterly*
N&Q	*Notes and Queries*
Neilson	William A. Neilson (ed.), *Works*, 1906
NS	John Dover Wilson and Arthur Quiller-Couch (eds.), *All's Well That Ends Well* (New Shakespeare), 1929
OED	*Oxford English Dictionary*, 1884–1928
Onions	C. T. Onions, *Shakespeare Glossary*, 1911
PMLA	*Publications of the Modern Language Association*
Pope	Alexander Pope (ed.), *Works*, 1723–5
Pope²	Alexander Pope (ed.), *Works*, 1728
Rann	Joseph Rann (ed.), *Works*, 1786–94
RES	*Review of English Studies*
Riverside	*See* Evans, *above*
Rowe	Nicholas Rowe (ed.), *Works*, 1709
Rowe²	Nicholas Rowe (ed.), *Works*, 1709
Rowe³	Nicholas Rowe (ed.), *Works*, 1714
SB	*Studies in Bibliography*
SD	stage direction
SH	speech heading
Singer	S. W. Singer (ed.), *Works*, 1826
Singer²	S. W. Singer (ed.), *Works*, 1856
Sisson	Charles Sisson (ed.), *Works*, 1953
SQ	*Shakespeare Quarterly*
S.Sur.	*Shakespeare Survey*
Staunton	Howard Staunton (ed.), *Works*, 1858–60
STC	*A Short-Title Catalogue of Books Printed in England, Scotland, & Ireland, and of English Books Printed Abroad, 1475–1640*, compiled by A. W. Pollard and G. R. Redgrave, 1956, first published 1926; 2nd edn, rev. W. A. Jackson, F. S. Ferguson and Katherine F. Pantzer, 1976–
subst.	substantively
Tannenbaum	S. A. Tannenbaum, 'Removing a scar from *All's Well* (IV.ii.38–39)', *Shakespeare Association Bulletin* 18 (1943), 133–6
Theobald	Lewis Theobald (ed.), *Works*, 1733
Theobald²	Lewis Theobald (ed.), *Works*, 1740
Thirlby	Dr Styan Thirlby (see John Nichols, *Illustrations of the Literary History of the Eighteenth Century*, 8 vols., 1817–58, pp. 189–647)
Thiselton	A. E. Thiselton, *Some Textual Notes on All's Well That Ends Well*, 1900
TSLL	*Texas Studies in Language and Literature*
Tyrwhitt	Thomas Tyrwhitt, *Observations and Conjectures upon Some Passages of Shakespeare*, 1766
Var. 73	Samuel Johnson and George Steevens (eds.), *Works*, 1773
Var. 78	Samuel Johnson and George Steevens (eds.), *Works*, 1778
Var. 93	George Steevens and Isaac Reed (eds.), *Works*, 1793

Walker, W. S.	William S. Walker, *A Critical Examination of the Text of Shakespeare*, 1860
Warburton	William Warburton (ed.), *Works*, 1747
White	Richard Grant White (ed.), *Works*, 1857

All quotations from the Bible are taken from the Geneva version, 1560.

INTRODUCTION

Date

The first indisputable mention of *All's Well That Ends Well* occurs in the Register of The Stationers' Company, which on 8 November 1623 licensed the play for printing in Shakespeare's Folio. Some, however, have suspected an earlier allusion in a commonplace book, *Palladis Tamia: Wit's Treasury*, published in 1598 by the literary clergyman, Francis Meres. Commending Shakespeare's comedies, Meres lists six, including the apparently lost or misnamed play, 'Love labours wonne'. In 1764 Bishop Percy, the antiquarian, suggested in a letter to the Shakespeare scholar Richard Farmer that *Love's Labors Wonne* (as he called it) was perhaps 'some play that we now have under another title', very possibly *All's Well That Ends Well*. Farmer endorsed this conjecture in his *Essay on the Learning of Shakespeare* (1767), and was followed by Edmund Malone in the 1778 Variorum edition. Subsequently Malone changed his mind and assigned the play to 1606.

The opinion that *All's Well* was early work, however, persisted in a modified form. John Payne Collier in his 1842–4 edition of the *Works* detected in the play two strata of form and content and argued that an early version, from the same period as *Love's Labour's Lost*, was revised in 1605. Collier saw himself as developing a case first put forward by Coleridge, but for evidence we depend upon his own imperfectly reliable reports of Coleridge's lectures.

A bookseller's account book for 1603 (discovered by T. W. Baldwin in 1957) lists, among other plays, 'Love's Labor Won'. This evidence would confirm the existence of a play of that name but does not affect the speculative nature of its connection with *All's Well*.

Attempts to date the play from its company history have proved indecisive. The part of Lavatch, for example, has often been ascribed to Robert Armin, who appears to have replaced Will Kemp as clown in Shakespeare's company (the Chamberlain's Men) in 1599. Kemp had created the earlier clowns, like Launce in *The Two Gentlemen of Verona*, Peter in *Romeo and Juliet* and Dogberry in *Much Ado*, and Armin's greater sophistication has been thought to inform the role of 'wise fools' like Touchstone in *As You Like It* and Feste in *Twelfth Night*. Leslie Hotson, however (in *Shakespeare's Motley*, 1952), sees in Lavatch the crude style of Kemp and settles for an early date. On the other hand, G. K. Hunter (1959) compares Lavatch with Thersites in *Troilus and Cressida*, the fool in *Lear* and Apemantus in *Timon*, which would point to a date between 1603 and 1606.

The case for revision continues to rest essentially on stylistic evidence and is endlessly arguable. For instance, the rhyming letter addressed by Helena to the Countess in 3.4 is sometimes adduced as exemplifying Shakespeare's early style, artificial, 'romantic'. Like the first interchange between Romeo and Juliet, it is written in sonnet form. The effect and presumably the intention are decisively different, however. Helena's language (and not hers only) is often gnomic, simple but not simplistic, suggesting and corroborating a tone or psychology beyond realism. This tone is not backward-looking. It looks forward to the last plays.

The dating of the play therefore becomes a critical exercise, and our response to Shakespeare's art may test our maturity as well as his. Rhyming couplets are conspicuous in *All's Well*, but underneath the facile surface deeper tides are moving:

> He that of greatest works is finisher
> Oft does them by the weakest minister:
> So holy writ in babes hath judgement shown,
> When judges have been babes; great floods have flown
> From simple sources; and great seas have dried
> When miracles have by the great'st been denied. (2.1.132–7)

Shakespeare in these lines is asking us to search the springs of memory, recalling how the Red Sea parted its waters before the children of Israel, and how Moses struck the rock and brought the water forth; and perhaps he is asking us to remember 1 Corinthians 1.27: 'God hath chosen the weak things of the world, to confound the things which are mighty.' For this kind of reminiscence, not irrational but not open to reason, we want the recurring rhyme and metronomic beat. The apparent innocence of the language is consistent with its authority, reminding us that 'judges have been babes'. Helena, like the Duke in *Othello* (1.3.199), speaks 'to lay a sentence'.

All's Well makes a coherence ('howsoever, strange and admirable'), and rationality participates in it. Sometimes rational utterance is displaced by incantation:

> Ere twice the horses of the sun shall bring
> Their fiery torcher his diurnal ring,
> Ere twice in murk and occidental damp
> Moist Hesperus hath quenched her sleepy lamp,
> Or four and twenty times the pilot's glass
> Hath told the thievish minutes how they pass... (2.1.157–62)

Much of the poetry in *All's Well* is, like some passages in *Macbeth*, casting an appropriate spell. When Helena vows to free the King from his illness, the cure she proposes is like no cure in nature. That is what the poetry says.

Blank verse in *All's Well* is often tortuous, obscure, elliptical, and this bespeaks the 'old' poet. I think we hear late Shakespeare in passages like these:

> He lasted long,
> But on us both did haggish age steal on,
> And wore us out of act. (1.2.28–30)

> Yet in this captious and intenible sieve
> I still pour in the waters of my love
> And lack not to lose still. (1.3.174–6)

> Good alone
> Is good, without a name; vileness is so.   (2.3.120–1)

> I will throw thee from my care for ever
> Into the staggers and the careless lapse
> Of youth and ignorance.   (2.3.154–6)

> Let's take the instant by the forward top;
> For we are old, and on our quick'st decrees
> Th'inaudible and noiseless foot of time
> Steals ere we can effect them.   (5.3.39–42)

Mostly, however, it is the baldness of much of the diction, bordering as in *Pericles* on the archaic, that declares the lateness of this play, anyway for this reader:

> What dar'st thou venter?
>   ...my maiden's name
> Seared otherwise; ne worse of worst – extended
> With vilest torture.   (2.1.166, 168–70)

Shakespeare is often pious, and a homiletic manner is not beneath him. In this, he shows his difference from intellectuals like Chapman and Marlowe. In *All's Well*, however, the mumbler of old proverbs gives himself scope:

> All's well that ends well; still the fine's the crown.
> Whate'er the course, the end is the renown.   (4.4.35–6)

What does this mean? Partly it means that the end is the end. But 'end' itself is a complex word, with meanings ranging from the final consummation of an objective to mere petering out. Shakespeare's meanings encompass this range.

In *All's Well* 'telling' takes precedence over 'showing'. This appears in the play's high incidence of saws and sayings, and in the respect with which Shakespeare treats the old styles of worldly wisdom. Where, for example, he looks awry at Polonius's advice to Laertes in *Hamlet*, he allows to the Countess when she admonishes Bertram (1.1.49–58) the full dignity and authority of a tradition which goes back to classical times. The proverb which yields the play's title is elaborately recalled in the dialogue (4.4.35–6, 5.3.322–3, Epilogue 2), and we are made to pay more than usually close attention to apparently facile observations. The greatest passage in the play has for its context the easy commonplaces vented by First and Second Lord, and we feel the prosy context is right.

> FIRST LORD How mightily sometimes we make us comforts of our losses!
> SECOND LORD And how mightily some other times we drown our gain in tears!...
> FIRST LORD The web of our life is of a mingled yarn...   (4.3.55–60)

This penchant for telling us rather than showing us sometimes betrays itself in the cursory handling of exposition. 'And I was about to tell you', says old Lafew (4.5.54), casually informing us that his daughter is now proposed as a match for Bertram. The resort to simple statement, amounting to negligence, anticipates the enfeebled theatre of *Henry VIII*, where First and Second Gentlemen report the joys and sorrows which earlier Shakespeare would have put before us; or the expository narrative distributed among First, Second and Third Gentlemen in the winding up of *The Winter's Tale* (5.2); or the second scene of *The Tempest*, where Prospero fatigues Miranda and incidentally ourselves with his tale that might cure deafness. The fatigue is Shakespeare's, though. He is disinclined to bother much with theatre 'business' any more, and anxious to get on to other things. 'In the mean time', says First Lord, 'what hear you of these wars?' (4.3.31). He answers his own question. Alarms and excursions are gratuitous now.

Though the war as violent business does not engage Shakespeare, his demonstrative treatment of the war is nevertheless theatrical. It focuses on the farewell parting of the nobles on different sides, on the war's 'physic' for a gentry 'sick/For breathing and exploit' (1.2.16–17), also on the victory parade (3.5). The telling is far from inept, for example in Helena's speech concluding 3.2; and the showing is precise and vivid in the unmuffling of Parolles (4.3). For this late play, however, the preferred mode is telling.

There are different styles in *All's Well*, as in *Measure for Measure*, where, for example, the tetrameter couplets which conclude Act 3 make a curious amalgam with the randy discourse of Lucio and Pompey. But the differences in both plays are, in my opinion, meditated, and do not attest composition at separate periods. In *All's Well*, the playwright is estimating his material with a realistic eye. At the same time he is evoking a pattern of significance that is not obvious and not discerned in the narrative material that comes to Shakespeare from Boccaccio or from his English translator, William Painter. *All's Well*, like the 'web of our life', is 'of a mingled yarn'. On my reading, this mingling is appropriate and adds to the expressiveness of the play. It does not indicate separated periods of composition and revision.

Affinities in tone and idea with *Hamlet* and *Measure for Measure* are often remarked, and since these plays date ascertainably from the early years of the seventeenth century, it seems reasonable to locate *All's Well* in that period, too. Both *Hamlet* and *All's Well* begin with mourning for departed fathers, and we have already had occasion to notice Polonius and the Countess schooling Laertes and Bertram in the occupation of courtier. *Measure for Measure* and *All's Well* have in common a sexually irresponsible hero tricked into bed with his proper partner by a resourceful heroine. There are important differences, however, and critics frequently argue from these differences that *All's Well* was written first. For example: Isabella grows and changes; Helena goes on undeflected to the end. (This is not a fault in Helena but a function of plot and perhaps of psychology.) The reformation of Angelo is more or less believable; Bertram executes a mere volte-face.

But the argument cuts both ways. *Measure for Measure*, customarily dated 1604, is more hopeful in its treatment of character, and the dénouement follows logically on the access of charity in Isabella. Shakespeare, like Duke Vincentio, seems willing in *Measure for Measure* to express some confidence in the human resources of his characters and in the play's outcome. In the dénouement of *All's Well*, human agency does not participate much, and the logic of experience gives place to the playwright's beneficent contriving. *All's Well* is not so thick with physical fact as *Measure for Measure*, and its connections with the world of human realities are not so firmly

established. This is generally true of the late romances when put against the tragedies
they appear to redact. I take *All's Well* to present a sceptical recension of the same
material which Shakespeare has been deploying in *Measure for Measure*, or a second
look at the material, refined to the point of abstraction, making it the more radical
case. I follow Collier and Malone and date the play about 1605.

Sources

The healing of the king and the performance of an impossible task by a virgin heroine
are staple elements of folklore. Variations on the theme are endless, and whether some
of them reached Shakespeare through oral tradition remains an open question.[1] Their
quickening presence in his imagination, however, conscious or unconscious, seems
beyond dispute. Similar recollections haunt earlier plays. The history of Prince Hal
and his disappointed father, for example, reached Shakespeare through the chronicles
and through an old play, but behind it looms the Biblical story of Absalom and David.

Behind Shakespeare's Helena is the virginal heroine of folklore, rejuvenating the
realm through the person of its ruler. In this rejuvenating role, she has a pattern in
the medieval writer Christine de Pisan (1365–?1430) (see frontispiece). The story of
this ardent and resourceful feminist, at once historical and fabulous, was translated
by Caxton in 1489 and several times reprinted in the sixteenth century.[2] Christine,
widowed at twenty-five, discovered like Helena that her remedies lay in herself. The
important string on which she harps is the right of her sex to a place in the scheme
of things. Like the Helena of the 1920s imagined by William Poel in his revival of
All's Well, she pleaded 'for the removal of class barriers where the affections between
men and women were in question'.[3]

This pleading is fortified by nature and art. Christine de Pisan is the type of the
active woman who 'derives her honesty and achieves her goodness' (1.1.34–5). From
her father the physician and astrologer Thomas of Pisano, whose fame as a magus
had spread as far as Hungary, she acquired her wide knowledge of philosophy and
science and the literatures of Latin, French and Italian. She owed him her skill in
mathematics and in divining the secret influence of the stars. But the sovereign remedy
of which Helena boasts, 'That's able to breathe life into a stone' (2.1.69), evidently
eluded both father and daughter.

In 1365, Thomas came to Paris at the invitation of the newly crowned king,
Charles V. A mysterious fistula afflicted the king, and the congregated college of
physicians had given him up for lost. For sixteen years, Thomas laboured for his
restoration but in the end mortality proved too much for his knowledge, and he failed
to ransom nature from her incurable estate. Shakespeare's heroine has better fortune.
(This is where art redresses nature.) She cures the French king, but fails to appease

---

[1] For analogues in story to *All's Well*, see W. W. Lawrence, *Shakespeare's Problem Comedies*, 1931.
[2] See *STC*, nos. 7269–73. For the currency of Christine de Pisan in England in the fifteenth and sixteenth
    centuries, see Enid McLeod, *The Order of the Rose: The Life and Ideas of Christine de Pizan*, 1976,
    pp. 162–7.
[3] Robert Speaight, *William Poel and the Elizabethan Revival*, 1954, p. 233.

the hatred of her churlish lord. So she leaves Rossillion and we next meet her in Florence.

For his heroine's itinerary, Shakespeare seems to be drawing on other old tales, besides that of Christine de Pisan. Helena's roundabout journey to Florence by way of the shrine of Saint Jacques, a famous place of pilgrimage in the north-west of Spain, has puzzled many. Florence, said Dr Johnson, 'was somewhat out of the road from Rousillon to Compostella'. Shakespeare may have been as ready to move the shrine to Italy as he was to provide Bohemia with a sea-coast. The memory of Compostella may be more than accidental, however.

Among the major medieval pilgrimages, that to the tomb of Saint James at Compostella ranked first. Helena makes her journey from Rossillion in southern France, but the name would recall to some of Shakespeare's audience that of the ninth-century Burgundian count, Girart of Rossillion, founder of the abbey of Vézelay. Girart or Gerardus, whose name chimes with that of Helena's father, Gerard de Narbonne, was another fabulous presence inherited from the Middle Ages in the popular stories of the sixteenth century. Like Bertram in the play, Girart in the epic named after him rebels against the king by declining to take a wife not of his liking. Since the king in question was Charlemagne, the old tale quickens our attention to Lafew's glance at Helena's power 'to araise King Pippen' and 'give great Charlemain a pen in's hand' (2.1.72–3). No rebel can prevail against such a sovereign, however, and the recalcitrant husband repents and builds, in piety and humility, the Church of the Madeleine at Vézelay. In this church he houses the relics of Mary Magdalene. Vézelay, graced with these relics, became an important place of pilgrimage at the start of one of the four routes that led pilgrims and merchants across France into Spain and thence to Santiago de Compostella. Mary Magdalene, herself the pilgrim heroine of many a medieval play and story, ended her days at Marseilles or 'Marcellus' (as the Folio calls it), to which Helena trails the King on his way to the court (4.4.9, 4.5.64). So we have a train of associations, linking Rossillion, Saint Jacques, Charlemagne and Marseilles. This associational train is problematic, like the nexus linking Helena and Christine de Pisan.

On the periphery of Girart's story, other stories accumulate, and their connection to Shakespeare's comedies, real or fancied, teases thought. Defeated by King Charles, Girart, like Orlando in *As You Like It*, flees to the Forest of Arden (Ardennes), where a pious hermit absolves him of his sins. He has a brother named Aymes or Aymon, the eponymous hero of the *Quatre fils Aymon* and familiar to Shakespeare as a romance, which appears to have been made into a play, called *The Four Sons of Aymon*.[1] These sons are rebels too, like their uncle and father, and having quarrelled with the king they also flee as outlaws to the Forest of Arden – where Shakespeare, with Charlemagne beating in his mind, imagines his Roland (Orlando) and his Oliver. Perhaps Shakespeare also recalls from the old story the twice-used name of Jaques and that of the wrestler Charles, who destroys an old man's hope in his sons and is himself destroyed by the prowess of a fourth contestant.

---

[1] An entry dated 1602 in Henslowe's Diary promises a stage version of the 'Four Sons'.

This network of associations and recollections reminds us that Shakespeare's knowledge of the many versions of popular stories told in his time is not likely to be confined to what he read; oral traditions are likely to be ólder and broader than literary ones, and a poet's 'sources' are not always to be traced in a library.

Shakespeare's immediate literary source is ascertainable, however. This is clearly Boccaccio's *Decameron*, the ninth novel of the third day, written 1348–58. Whether Shakespeare knew Italian and hence read Boccaccio in the original is uncertain. As it happens, he had nearer to hand an English version of his story in the *Palace of Pleasure*, a popular collection of *novelle* compiled and published by William Painter in 1566, and published again in 1569 and 1575. Painter in his thirty-eighth novel offers a close translation of Boccaccio's tale of the intrepid heroine Giglietta di Narbona, who contrives to make all things end well. Painter's edition of 1575 being closest in time to the composition of the play, scholars assume that it was this edition which Shakespeare consulted. A French translation of Boccaccio by Antoine le Maçon (1545) was also available. More than likely, however, Painter in English was his primary source, perhaps supplemented by le Maçon in French.

Painter's outline of the story (1575) runs as follows:

Giletta, a physician's daughter of Narbon, healed the French King of a fistula, for reward whereof she demanded Beltramo, Count of Rossiglione, to husband. The Count being married against his will, for despite fled to Florence and loved another. Giletta, his wife, by policy found means to lie with her husband, in place of his lover, and was begotten with child of two sons; which known to her husband, he received her again, and afterwards he lived in great honour and felicity.

On this, the bare form of *All's Well That Ends Well*, Shakespeare hung his drapery of purposes and effects. Painter is indulgent of time and detail; Shakespeare is in a hurry and characteristically economical. The bed-trick in the source is staled by repetition: Giletta after the first time comes to Beltramo in secret 'many other times'. For Shakespeare, once is enough, and one child does the business where the source requires 'two goodly sons'.

Painter's Giletta is rich and well-connected and, having her eye on Beltramo, refuses many husbands. Shakespeare's Helena has nothing but virtue's steely bones to commend her. Giletta, having achieved her marriage but forfeited her husband, goes first to Rossillion, where she plays a powerful role like that of Shakespeare's dowager Countess. 'Perceiving that through the Count's absence, all things were spoiled and out of order, she like a sage lady, with great diligence and care, disposed his things in order again, whereof the subjects rejoiced very much.' Meanwhile, time passes.

Having 'restored all the country', Giletta sets out on her pilgrimage, 'telling no man whither she went, and never rested till she came to Florence'. Shakespeare is more circumstantial. He complicates the pilgrimage, emphasising its function as an expiatory rite, and he complicates or aggrandises the character of his pilgrim. Helena on his reading is neither an immaculate heroine nor the scheming and aggressive heroine imagined by her detractors. Shakespeare's Helena is frail in that 'we are all frail', and it is this generic human frailty that dictates the pilgrimage to Saint Jacques.

Giletta's frailty in the source-story is more specific and more culpable. She falls in love with Beltramo 'more than meet for a maiden of her age', and she urges a marriage which the King 'was very loath to grant'. So the reluctant hero, 'knowing her not to be of a stock convenable to his nobility', is partly acquitted.

Shakespeare is adamant in declining to acquit his counterpart of Beltramo. The tissue of lies which Bertram elaborates and his meanness of behaviour are altogether Shakespeare's invention, and this is his most important divergence from the source. No Shakespearean hero is so degraded and so unsparingly presented. Other characters unknown to the source comment on his degradation: the Countess of Rossillion and her court fool Lavatch, the old courtier Lafew, the King of France (for whom Shakespeare creates a far more ponderable role than in the original), most of all the unsavoury Parolles. Critics who see Parolles as extenuating Bertram (as when they tell us that 'Bertram's fall is due to ill company') are presumably wrong. In the language of *Measure for Measure*, 'there went but a pair of shears between them'.

The play

All's Well That Ends Well is a great play whose time has come round. Not everyone thinks this. The older view of the play invokes Shakespeare the crowd-pleaser who 'seems not to have taken his story too seriously'.[1] *All's Well* on this view is 'just an "interlude", a means of passing away a couple of hours with a play that never demands too much emotion or thought'. Criticism in our own time will want to enter its circumstantial dissent.

How Shakespeare took his story is not for me to say. The play he made is, however, suffused with emotion, and the quickening of Helena, brought back from the dead, ranks high among his poignant scenes. This poignancy, begetting tears and laughter, is not contingent on Shakespeare's audience wringing the wet hankie, as perhaps it is in *King John* when Prince Arthur pleads for life, or in *Richard III* when we hear how the little princes are murdered. In the ending of *All's Well*, thought participates powerfully. Shakespeare wills us to consider how his vexed protagonists, completing the pilgrimage which is the business of the play, have found out salvation. Partly they achieve their salvation, and as that is so we rejoice. In disconcerting ways, however, salvation drops in their lap. The soiled hero is acquitted, but that is no thanks to him. In the course of justice he would hardly see salvation. So the rejoicing that belongs to comedy is qualified sharply, and the ending of the play compels us to take second thoughts.

Shakespeare is himself, as the ending is there in the beginning. Unlike those writers who reverse the beginning in the ending, he never surprises us. His characters may change for the better or worse, and things beginning at the worst may turn upwards in the course of the play. But no character puts off altogether what he was at first, and if the play begins in darkness, the darkness is never altogether dispelled. Characters in *All's Well* are left open to mortality, and in the world they inhabit the

---

[1] G. B. Harrison (ed.), *Complete Works*, 1948, p. 1019.

best is behind. This feeling, conveyed in the first scene of the play, is borne out in the ending. The King's decrepitude is notorious in the beginning, and the Epilogue resumes it. For a little while, he gets better. 'To be young again, if we could' (2.2.30), says the Countess, understanding how desire is mocked in the event. The tone or colour of the play is dark, though not dour, this being Shakespeare. Dubiety is epidemic. The last lines instruct us that 'All yet seems well.' 'Seems' is, however, the operative word.

In the opening lines, birth and death assert their connection, and this is Shakespearean too.

> The earth that's nature's mother is her tomb;
> What is her burying grave, that is her womb.

Friar Lawrence speaks these lines in *Romeo and Juliet* (2.3.9–10), when Shakespeare as a playwright was beginning his career. At the end of the career, in *Pericles*, for instance, we take their sense again, though the emphasis has shifted a little:

> Whereby I see that Time's the king of men,
> He's both their parent, and he is their grave,
> And gives them what he will, not what they crave.   (*Per.* 2.3.45–7)

Comedy is vindicated in the ending of *All's Well* partly as the time brings on summer (4.4.31), but the wheel of the seasons continues to run; summer goes down to fall, and winter is always in prospect, yet spring is in prospect too. Inevitably, Autolycus in *The Winter's Tale* makes us feel, 'the red blood reigns in the winter's pale' (4.3.4). This is like the constant turning of the wheel of Fortune, where nothing is at a stand and only change is constant. As that is so, the happy ending is necessarily provisional.

We recognise essential Shakespeare in this insistence on the community of beginnings and endings, and the peril in which we stand as we negotiate our progress between them. But the insistence is more or less marked from play to play, and put before us most emphatically in the world of the late romances. *All's Well That Ends Well* opens on this world. The Countess, 'delivering' her son on his way, buries a second husband. The son, addressing himself to a new life, weeps again for the death of his father. Helena also is bereaved and brought down to tears. Her tears are for the living, though, and there is a kind of propriety in that. The Countess, a surrogate for the rest of us, is very well, says the Clown, except for two things: 'One, that she's not in heaven, whither God send her quickly! the other, that she's in earth, from whence God send her quickly!' (2.4.8–9). This is typical Shakespeare fooling, tedious but to the point in its preoccupation with verbal latencies. Latent here is the sense of our fallen condition, which the first scene announces and the last scene engages with, but only by arbitrary fiat.

The King of France is like the Countess and presents another image of our 'inaidable estate' (2.1.115). The estate is inaidable in so far as we are human and will surely die. It is inaidable also, except as grace operates, because we are morally obtuse. In this sense, postlapsarian man is presented in the King. For the twin malady which afflicts him, no natural remedy offers itself. His heart will not confess this, however (2.1.8–10). The malady is real, but also emblematic, and evidently pervasive. 'The atmosphere at Rousillon', says Mark Van Doren in his *Shakespeare* (1939), 'is one of darkness, old age, disease, sadness and death.' But this atmosphere is not peculiar to Rossillion, and extends beyond the formal confines of the play. Bertram, transported to Florence, forgetting how Helena's eye is 'sick' for him (1.3.108), languishes in 'sick desires' there (4.2.35). Parolles, who is debauched with all the spots of the world, 'sickens' to speak a truth (5.3.204–5). The French gentry are also 'sick', and maybe or maybe not the wars will be good for what ails them. As the past is like the present, the play begins in the middle of things. Bertram's father lived long but age made him incapable, wore him 'out of act' (1.2.28–30). Helena's father might have lived forever, 'if knowledge could be set up against mortality' (1.1.23), but this contingency is evidently remote.

No doubt good health and new birth are in prospect for the future, and in the second half of the play, beginning in 3.3, the mathematical centre, we hear how the future is 'Great in our hope' (3.3.2). The auspicious imagery which carries this hope is summed up in the riddle which anticipates Helena's return: 'Dead though she be, she feels her young one kick' (5.3.292). So the play, beginning in darkness, emerges into light. But *chiaroscuro* is the mingled essence of the play and inevitably the aggrandising pattern or upward movement is accompanied by loss. The 'loss of men', says the Clown, essaying a bawdy quibble, is part and parcel of 'the getting of children' (3.2.35–6).

This sure sense of loss is corroborated in the fortunes of the older generation, condemned to live out the fag end of a life 'On the catastrophe and heel of pastime' (1.2.57). To be 'the snuff/Of younger spirits' (1.2.59–60) is their appointed role. The Countess remembers how Helena had a father. But the note of threnody is what we want to hear: 'O, that "had", how sad a passage 'tis' (1.1.13–14). This is like Shakespeare's voice in *The Two Noble Kinsmen*, presumably the last play in which he bore a part:

> O grief and time,
> Fearful consumers, you will all devour!   (1.1.69–70)

Reactionary Shakespeare often dwells on the past and it seems right to say that he prefers it to the present. For example, this from *As You Like It*:

> O good old man, how well in thee appears
> The constant service of the antique world,
> When service sweat for duty, not for meed!
> Thou art not for the fashion of these times.   (*AYLI* 2.3.56–9)

Shakespeare goes on like that. He and his characters frequently indulge backward-looking nostalgia, and this is true even of young Shakespeare. For instance, in the opening lines of *1 Henry VI*, probably his first play, the heavens are hung with black and comets signal an unhappy change as the past yields to the present. But that is not because the past is always better than the present. A great king has died and the present is uncertain. Our sense of declension is conditioned by a particular context. In *All's Well* the context is not political or particular, but more generally our human condition. The elegiac tone has its special decorum for a play in which the playwright is reflecting on what things we are. This tone suggests Shakespeare's increasing preoccupation with mortality; the great wheel of his *oeuvre* is coming full circle.

The diminishing of character under Shakespeare's eye and hand enforces this suggestion. In tragedy, his reading of character is formally 'Pelagian'. This early Christian heresy holds that we can achieve our salvation largely by ourselves and without the support of grace, or, let us say, without the sustaining presence of a *deus ex machina*. Conventional tragedy in the West, including Shakespearean tragedy, is often indebted, at least superficially, to this optimistic point of view, and perhaps tragedy demands it. We are made to feel that the hero or hero–villain stands or falls of his own volition. If he falls, that is because he is culpable. In *Antony and Cleopatra*, the hero is at fault, and inferentially he is destroyed, because he 'would make his will/ Lord of his reason' (3.13.2–4). That is a good rubric for Shakespearean tragedy on one side. There is another side, of course, more complicated and less hopeful, and on this other side Shakespeare lets us feel how his heroes are entoiled or beguiled, led by an air-borne dagger like Macbeth, or driven mad like Othello and Leontes. These are heroes who cannot control their fate, and the deeper one sees into Shakespeare, the more the reading of character as fettered and unfree appears to be emphasised.

So one can say that volition never gets high marks from Shakespeare. In the greater tragedies, however, Shakespeare's characters are aggrandised, and their uncommon stature sponsors the appearance of freedom. This means that for Shakespeare, two truths are told. They are contradictory but not mutually exclusive, and one can say, expressing the second truth, that Shakespeare in tragedy permits his heroes to walk with a larger tether. In *All's Well* this permission is withdrawn, and the limited freedom that belongs to characters in tragedy is radically abridged.

In this play the body governs, and 'the prince of the world' is sovereign. The path he marks out for us 'leads to the broad gate and the great fire' (4.5.39, 42–3). That is only a metaphor, though. More critically, the 'idle fire' (3.7.26) that consumes us is endemic. It is also 'too strong for reason's force' (5.3.7). The Clown, 'driven on by the flesh', is like the hero. 'He must needs go that the devil drives' (1.3.22–3). This apophthegm does duty for them both. 'Important' or importunate blood (3.7.21) in the hero throws him inevitably into 'the staggers and the careless lapse' (2.3.155) of his ignorant youth.

That is the process of 'all flesh and blood' (1.3.27–8) and feeling it will perhaps incline us to revise our reading of Bertram's behaviour. It speaks to Parolles in his reflections on virginity (1.1), and perhaps it supports him. It speaks to Helena, too. So we have an association of the hero and the villain and the heroine and the Clown. Smutty discourse denotes the Clown, where the heroine is all chaste odours. In either case, however, sexual passion is overmastering. The Victorians, who hated *All's Well That Ends Well*, understood at least what they were hating.

Everyone agrees that the hero is deplorable, perhaps a bad scion of a good stock, and Shakespeare in the first act implies a difference between this son and his father. But the difference is felt as superficial in last things. Oil and fire in the son fuel his 'natural rebellion' (5.3.5–6). Unexpectedly, this associates him with the good parent who would rather not live, after his flame lacks oil (1.2.58–9). The thorn of passion, says the Countess, 'Doth to our rose of youth rightly belong' (1.3.102). As it is with Helena, so it was with her. Lexical parallels underline the connection. Helena looks to the good time

> When briers shall have leaves as well as thorns,
> And be as sweet as sharp. (4.4.32–3)

To this context, the language assimilates Diana. Men serve us, says Diana, till women serve men:

> but when you have our roses,
> You barely leave our thorns to prick ourselves. (4.2.18–19)

Shakespeare, beginning with the plays of *Henry VI*, comments on the action through recurrences in language and the juxtaposing of complementary scenes. In the first of these plays, we are in France with York and his army (4.3). Their business is to rescue the English general Talbot, but private discord keeps them aloof. In the next scene, Somerset and his army, also in France, are committed to the same business and they also keep their distance. The common term that associates one scene to the next is 'the vulture of sedition' (4.3.47). As it feeds on these great commanders, the English cause is lost. A little later in the same play, two theatrical images that are superficially alike and crucially different are made to oppose each other in the same scene (5.3), and they 'say' the play between them. The first image presents the Duke of York and La Pucelle (Joan of Arc) 'fighting hand to hand'. Dialogue ensues and the perfidious Suffolk enters, with his paramour Margaret 'in his hand'. One of these Englishmen is doing his duty; the other betrays his duty. Comment is gratuitous, Shakespeare's point being clear enough without it. Complementarity and verbal recurrence are especially marked in *All's Well* but their purport is not obviously apparent. Italy and France are posed against each other, the court against the country, war against peace. These contrasts are more ostensible than real, or rather they complicate more than clarify. This difficult play instructs us that where hard questions are being canvassed, complication means clarification.

The Clown's fatiguing 'O Lord, sir!', reiterated in 2.2, meets Parolles's 'So I say' in the following scene. I don't think we call this parody, but neither is it simple replication. Lavatch has found an answer 'fit to all questions' (2.2.15). This answer prompts his litany; it also resumes the opening scene where Helena, we remember, extenuates Parolles because enduring evil sits 'so fit in him' (1.1.90). In the juxtaposing of 2.2 and 2.3, fitness is the common term.

Lafew in 2.3 'discovers' Parolles and calls him a 'knave': 'I have now found thee...Go to' (193–4, 237, 241). In the following scene, Parolles retorts this word 'knave' on Lavatch. 'Go to', he says, 'I have found thee' (2.4.25, 29). So 2.3 and 2.4 assert their connection, and the lexical parallels suggest that Lafew relates to Parolles as Parolles relates to the Clown.

'The court's a learning-place' (1.1.152) for Bertram and Lavatch, as each learns to desert a mistress there. Each therefore invites moral censure, but perhaps moral censure in this play gets its quietus. It seems to Parolles that virginity 'is not politic in the commonwealth of nature' (1.1.111–12), and that is Bertram's idea too (4.2.5–10). Virginity has no price current, where loss of virginity is rational increase, so perhaps we should 'answer the time of request' (1.1.109–39). But Parolles is a scoundrel who takes his cue from the market place, and Bertram has his ulterior reasons.

The good King, who bids his courtiers wed honour in the wars (2.1.15), anticipates the bad servant as Bertram leaves for the wars. Or Parolles recalls the King.

> He wears his honour in a box unseen,
> That hugs his kicky-wicky here at home.   (2.3.256–7)

These valedictory remarks take the wars for their context. The important term is honour, though, and honour has its different senses, depending on provenance. That at least is the convention, as illustrated, for example, in *1 Henry IV*. *All's Well* modifies the convention. It makes a nexus where we look for nice distinctions. Sexual activity plays into both passages, and in the second passage it cries out for notice, being both ribald and taking. 'Box' and 'kicky-wicky' make us blench and smile. The sexual current is persistent and turns up everywhere in *All's Well*. This suggests that we will want to read the play interstitially, between and under the lines, not only for the fable but for its intimations. Like much poetry written in the seventeenth century, *All's Well* is complex, thick and pestered, and needs and merits uncommon attention.

All's Well is like a piece of paper cut with scissors along the fold, which must be opened out to make the design visible, and how much of its cunning comes across in the theatre is a moot point. That is not to scant or underestimate its theatrecraft. This play's time has come precisely because it has proved live in the theatre of our time. It gives us enough to engage us powerfully as we look and listen. But much of what it gives us probably goes by unheeded in performance, and this is often true for Shakespeare's art of theatre. The Apothecary in *Romeo and Juliet* is a version of Friar Lawrence, Pyrrhus in *Hamlet* is a version of the Prince, and in *King Lear* the behaviour of Kent who has more man than wit about him (2.4.42) recapitulates and qualifies the behaviour of Cordelia in the first scene of the play. In all this there is conscious design, but to perceive it you must follow Lamb's advice and read and ponder Shakespeare in your closet. In *All's Well* and elsewhere, he is writing to please himself. Anyway, design is evident. The young in this play don't want for good advice, and a lot of good it does them. The Countess in 1.1 offers her few precepts, and the King in 2.1 his 'warlike principles', and, as the climax prepares, Helena decides to 'bestow some precepts' on Diana (3.5.91). 'Take heed', says the Duke, of those Italian girls (2.1.19), but no one is listening. Diana is wise as she determines to 'take heed' of Bertram (3.5.9). Potentially, Diana is like all those other unlucky girls, 'limed with the twigs' (3.5.19) prepared by her seducer. In the next scene, these twigs ensnare Parolles (3.6.85).

Bertram, potentially, 'sees the bottom of his success' (3.6.27–8). As *verso* follows *recto* or language and incident fold back on themselves, we hear the Widow say to Helena: 'I see the bottom of your purpose' (3.7.28–9). Bertram in the beginning repudiates Helena, in the end he repudiates Diana. A second chance is proffered him, the proffering is emphasised, and the second chance goes unused. Though Bertram is niggardly, the King is magnanimous, as when in 2.3 he empowers Helena to choose a husband. In 5.3 he confers this same power on Diana. 'One might think', says Anne Barton, the *Riverside* editor, 'that the misfortunes of Helena would make him wary of this particular matrimonial method.' He isn't made wary, however.

In Shakespeare, complementarities usually enforce discrimination. 'Minding true things by what their mockeries be' – the line from *Henry V* (4 Prologue 53) gives us our direction. The virtuous Richmond in his tent, dreaming auspicious dreams, makes a nice foil to the villainous Richard, whose dreams are troubled by the ghosts of his victims. In *All's Well*, however, discrimination is annulled. Powerful tides are working, defined as the show and seal of 'nature's truth' (1.3.104) and as their power is ungainsayable, substantial integrity in character is disallowed.

Morally, the sterling King and the counterfeit Parolles differ absolutely. Nonetheless, they take hands. Each fills a place (1.2.69, 4.3.286), and their similarity on this side is felt as more than moral difference. Nature abhors a vacuum, and nature gets precedence here. 'Our bloods,/Of colour, weight, and heat, poured all together,/Would quite confound distinction' (2.3.110–12). The complementarities with which *All's Well* abounds suggest the radical sameness of characters who differ superficially. Real difference isn't much – that is what the play is telling us – and the Psychomachia or war of good and evil is a casualty of this insight.

The Psychomachia, coming down from the Roman writer Prudentius in the early Christian centuries, furnishes a convenient pattern for Western drama from the beginning. *Angeli boni* and *angeli mali*, the good and bad angels, face each other on stage (as in *Dr Faustus*), and what they are contending for is the soul of the hero. Shakespeare internalises this spirit-war, as in *Macbeth*, where the hero weighs his promptings to good and evil and chooses the worser course. Making his choice, Macbeth is known for a wicked man. Banquo also is solicited, chooses the better course, and is a virtuous man. In *All's Well*, Helena (for example) is virtuous, where Parolles is wicked. He is like Bertram, as opposed to Bertram's father. But these moral distinctions are blurred, and we are made to feel that at bottom no one character is any more or less in need of 'grace' or 'salvation' than any other. No doubt the bottom is a long way down, and playgoers and readers will have to decide for themselves where the proper emphasis belongs in this play: on the obvious distinction that separates man and man or on the essential community between them.

Parolles deceives Bertram 'like a double-meaning prophesier' (4.3.83). But this similitude fits Helena, who 'riddle-like lives sweetly where she dies' (1.3.189). The sexual *entendre* is certainly not amiss. Both Helena and Parolles are full of sap, so although different they make a concinnity and go harmoniously together. Character for both is exhausted in vitality. His evils, like her intents, are 'fixed' (1.1.90, 200).

Hostile readers of the play understand this, however dimly, and bardolaters do their best to excuse it. 'Cruel, artful, and insolent', said Mrs Charlotte Lennox,[1] passing judgement on Helena in the Augustan Age. This judgement, which still echoes today, is excessively harsh but comprehends a piece of the truth. I agree with Muriel St Clare

---

[1] *Shakespeare Illustrated*, London, 1753, I, 189–95.

1 The unmasking of Parolles in Tyrone Guthrie's production of 1959 at the Shakespeare Memorial
Theatre: impression by Neil Harvey

Byrne that modern audiences not knowing the play would be puzzled, like Shakespeare's
audience, to be told that it is 'disgusting' and 'degrading'; forget about morals, she
says, and simply accept 'the myth or fairy-tale solution-by-stratagem of the
accomplishment of the impossible task'.[1] But though the task and stratagem are given,
they can still be scrutinised. Shakespeare isn't 'dead to all finer feeling' but alive to
the exigencies of convention. I think that is true for the love test in *King Lear*. *All's
Well* is substantially symbolic theatre, but realism gets a hearing and criticises the
convention. *Measure for Measure* is analogous and shows the same ambiguous mix.
Duke Vincentio is an emblematic figure, but he is also himself. On his emblematic
side, plying his music and practising upon people, he turns bad into good. But this
benign contriver is notably feline (perhaps like Shakespeare), not always successful
in his contrivance, and the too austere figure he presents in the beginning (scorning
the 'dribbling dart of love', 1.3.2) is reproved in the romantic ending. On this side,
the Duke is recognisably human and therefore equivocal. Helena is like this, as she

[1] 'The Shakespeare season at the Old Vic, 1958–9 and Stratford-upon-Avon, 1959', *SQ* 10 (1959), 556.

2 . Act 4, Scene 3. Clive Swift as Parolles, Patrick O'Connell as Morgan, Ian Richardson as Bertram and David Moynihan as Dumaine the Elder, in John Barton's production of 1967 at the Royal Shakespeare Theatre

performs her appointed role; the plot of the play commits her to it and she discharges it with a disregard for moral niceties that stage convention allows to a conspirator on behalf of the good. But the language she uses to describe the bed-trick, 'Where both not sin, and yet a sinful fact' (3.7.47), is vexed to the point of being casuistical, and she makes us feel that the expedient she hits on – like the remedy which presents itself to the Duke of dark corners – is a crooked expedient. It denotes the heroine whose intents are fixed and will not leave her.

'Simply the thing I am shall make me live' (4.3.280–1). The King glosses Parolles's spectacular saying – which is both vindicating and scary – and suggests the identity of villain and heroine, when he says how 'Good alone/Is good, without a name', adding in the same breath, 'vileness is so' (2.3.120–1). The ambiguity agrees with the mingled yarn of our life. One touch of nature makes the whole world kin, but the nature to which Shakespeare appeals in his play is aloof from moral or rational behaviour.

In so far as the body and its claims are imperious, characters in *All's Well* are necessarily hoodwinked. Their inability to see is not extrinsic – the stuff of comic farce, as when Parolles is blindfolded – but is a function of their 'muddy vesture of decay'. Scars won in the braving war constitute for Lafew the livery of honour. Captain Spurio, whose name denotes him, wears these scars (2.1.41–2), yet the patch of velvet that covers them might cover a syphilitic chancre, for all we know (4.5.75–81).

Shakespeare in *All's Well* is preoccupied with language, but not a language we can parse. 'The mere word's a slave' and 'debauched' on every tomb (2.3.129–30). The lying Parolles, whose name in this context signifies equivocation, is also 'debauched' (5.3.204), and fears to lose his life 'for want of language' (4.1.57). The riddle at the heart of the play, being repugnant to sense, is one version of this language; the 'choughs' language' (4.1.15) which confounds the villain is another. It occludes where it should clarify, so understanding is baffled. Shakespeare's phrase for this is 'linsey-woolsey' (4.1.9) – generically nonsense, specifically a coarse mixture of linen and wool. The mingled yarn which composes the web of our life (4.3.60) is like this doubtful mixture.

The comic centre of *All's Well* on a superficial reading is the melting down of Parolles, 'this counterfeit lump of ore' (3.6.28). But *All's Well* is not farce comedy, and the detecting of the villain is only incidental to its larger success. 'The soul of this man is his clothes' (2.5.38), so he forfeits the autonomy that goes with moral stature. Gloucester in *King Lear* and Lear himself, as they learn to see and feel, grow in moral stature and hence acquire autonomy. We recognise the autonomous man in that he is fully fledged, not 'callow'. Shakespeare in the tragedies has his eye on this man, and *King Lear* is inspiriting partly because it attests to his emergence. In the comedies he does not emerge. Comic Shakespeare is not so hopeful as Shakespeare the tragic playwright, and he seems not to credit the possibility of significant learning.

The language of the hunt that describes the 'embossing' or running down of the comic villain divests him of autonomy. But not of his humanity: it engrosses his humanity. The less capable and less 'sensible', the more human. That is the sceptical view of our condition which the play appears to endorse. Also this lack of capacity and sensibility in the comic villain keeps him out of harm's way. Like Demetrius and Lysander, if you prick him he doesn't bleed. Neither does he see, even if you unmuffle him. He is only a woodcock (4.1.77), and how should he see? But the harder truth will focus on Shakespeare's readiness to withhold powers of perception from characters of greater maturity.

Lack of autonomy in Parolles does not surprise us. This lack is generalised, however, and mocks our secure station as auditors of a play or 'interlude'. The Countess is one of Shakespeare's typically sagacious women, grown old, but having 'no skill in sense/To make distinction' (3.4.39–40). Bertram, who asks leave 'to use/The help of mine own eyes' (2.3.99–100), is 'mad in folly' (5.3.3) even as he asks. His choice and subsequent rejection of Lafew's daughter Maudlin before the play begins is assimilated to his rejection of Helena. In each case, the hero stumbles on error as he appeals to 'the impression of mine eye' (5.3.47).

Shakespeare's metaphor for this is the natural perspective (5.3.48) or distorting mirror, a familiar part of his battery of psychological terms at least from the time of *Richard II*. The objects commended to us by the eye of love or contempt are

Like pèrspectives, which rightly gazed upon
Show nothing but confusion; eyed awry
Distinguish form.   (*R2* 2.2.18–20)

The truth of things – what we call reality – is not open to our view but is occluded or deformed, like a distorted drawing or projection. If you view this confused image from a particular point, however, or by reflection from a suitable mirror, it will show as regular and properly proportioned. The trick is to find the right vantage point or mirror, but nobody has the knack of it here.

'As we are ourselves', says First Lord, 'what things are we!' (4.3.17–18). Characters in *All's Well* are not evil, or not especially so, but only human and hence their own traitors. They are themselves, or become themselves (4.3.20). They judge by appearances, square their guess by shows (2.1.146), so all of them are cozened. There are no exceptions. The picture Helena draws of Bertram in her heart's table is 'idolatrous fancy' (1.1.85) and comically remote from the fact. We think of Imogen in *Cymbeline*, mistaking the ignoble Cloten for her noble lord Posthumus, who perhaps is not so noble as she likes to suppose. So the heroine of *All's Well* is gulled, like the villain, and I think we are meant to feel this in the alacrity of her challenge to 'the fated sky' (1.1.188).

Analogy is always treacherous, and Shakespeare in each of his plays is always making a fresh start. This means that it is ticklish to compare one play with another. *Macbeth* and *Richard III* tell the same story of usurpation but are not at all the same play, and the great tragedies, though they agitate the same turbid material, are valuable first of all in that each has its peculiar and distinctive form. But Shakespeare has his poetics and his recurring points of view, and he seems not to alter in the scepticism, mounting sometimes to detestation, with which he views the emancipated man, such as Edmund in *King Lear*. Helena, however, presents the emancipated woman:

> Our remedies oft in ourselves do lie,
> Which we ascribe to heaven. The fated sky
> Gives us free scope; only doth backward pull
> Our slow designs when we ourselves are dull.   (1.1.187–90)

We are sufficient in ourselves to find out 'salvation', and we needn't appeal to grace or Fortune or heavenly interposing. Only we must exert ourselves. That is what Helena in her character of 'Pelagian' heretic is telling us. There is no intimation here that Fortune has nails for scratching and no man can pare them (remembering the exchange between Lafew and Parolles at 5.2.16–45), or that in a fallen world the right appeal is Parolles's appeal to 'bring me in some grace' (5.2.37). Helena, the forthcoming heroine who is herself alone, makes us think of Cassius's words to Brutus, Iago's to Roderigo, and Edmund's on his indifference to 'divine thrusting on'. Here are the relevant texts:

> The fault, dear Brutus, is not in our stars,
> But in ourselves, that we are underlings.   (*Julius Caesar* 1.2.140–1)

> Virtue? A fig! 'Tis in ourselves that we are thus or thus.   (*Othello* 1.3.319–20)

> This is the excellent foppery of the world, that when we are sick in fortune – often the surfeits of our own behaviour – we make guilty of our disasters the sun, the moon, and stars.
> (*King Lear* 1.2.118–21)

Cassius is instructed by the plot of the play that man does not hold the universe alone, and he begins to 'credit things that do presage' (5.1.78). What Iago learns is

3   Act 2, Scene 3. Helena (Harriet Walter) choosing Bertram (Philip Franks) in Trevor Nunn's production of 1982 at the Barbican Theatre. Set designed by John Gunter

mysterious, but the plot again is our warrant for supposing that the man who plumes himself on his own capacity is a gull or dolt. Gloucester in *Lear*, a superstitious man or 'sectary astronomical' (1.2.150–1), is proved in the event more enlightened than his bastard son. This son's power, like ours, is radically limited, where the gods 'make them honors/Of men's impossibilities' (4.6.73–4).

The emancipated man is the fettered man, that is what Shakespeare's work tells us, but Helena in *All's Well* does not know this. In her speech at the end of 1.1, she is very easy, and indeed 'emancipated' with respect to ends and means. In 2.1 and thereafter, she sings a different tune. Something happens in the interval between these two scenes, but Shakespeare keeps it to the wings or green room. I think he tells us subsequently that Helena who changes doesn't change altogether. Lafew in 4.5 wants to come before the King. He intermits the action, though, with questions of propriety (4.5.70–1). So does the Astringer in a parallel scene (5.3.129). Their little hesitations are unremarkable, perhaps inconsequent; nonetheless we are asked to remark them. Helena, by contrast, is 'goaded with most sharp occasions', so finds it convenient to dispense with 'nice manners' (5.1.14–15). In 5.1 she forwards a letter to the King by the hand of the Astringer. Parolles in 5.2 wants the Clown to bear a letter to Lafew. Never mind what the letters say. Form is more than content, and the formal structure – what Renaissance rhetoric calls *ratio* – tells us that Helena is to Parolles as Lafew is to the Gentle Astringer.

So Helena, in the King's words about Parolles, is an 'equivocal companion' and 'a knave and no knave' (5.3.244–5). As she takes her place in the repertory of Shakespeare's emancipated villains, she is reproved. She is also Shakespeare's heroine, and receives and merits our sympathy and suffrage. Only we are asked to make room, in a total estimate of this character, for the suggestion of equivocal behaviour. Her capaciousness allows of these differing responses. Helena is a woman, in Shakespeare's more comprehensive sense, playing in one person the parts of mother, mistress and friend, but also enemy (1.1.142–3). Diana the chaste goddess has her allegiance, but she flees from Diana's altar to imperial Love (2.3.68–9). Essentially, however, she mediates between the two, or enacts these two in one, as when she wishes that her Diana 'Was both herself and Love' (1.3.185). It can hardly be accidental that we have in this play a real Diana who 'lies' with Bertram (so he thinks), as Love or Venus does too. So the various roles Helena proposes to enact – 'a thousand loves', she calls them (1.1.141) – are fulfilled. For readers and auditors whose perception is unequivocal ('good' women being sexless, and so on), *All's Well* is hard going to the extent that it emphasises this amalgam of contradictory things.

In the crisis of the play, the King supposes the intervention of an exorcist or spirit-raiser who has beguiled 'the truer office' of his eyes (5.3.294–5). This perhaps is not an idle supposition. Helena, revived, is 'the shadow of a wife.../The name and not the thing' (5.3.297–8). That, at any rate, is what she says. Evidently Shakespeare's Second Lord is wise in that he forbears to venture his opinion,

> since I have found
> Myself in my incertain grounds to fail
> As often as I guessed.   (3.1.14–16)

This failure, as it ramifies, supports a definition of Shakespeare's later comedy, not new for his work, but now more at the front of our minds. Aggressive choice will figure in the definition, and the posturing, too, of self-reliant men and women. Characters who believe that their remedies lie in themselves are apt to 'fail' upon the 'incertain grounds' of human perception, judgement, choice and purpose. As often as not, they mistake their purpose, and in the tragedies – *Hamlet*, for example – the mistaking is fatal. It isn't fatal in the comedies because the beneficent playwright has his hands on all the ropes. But in comedy and tragedy alike, it is clear that our remedies do not lie in ourselves. 'Thou wrong'st thyself', says the King, 'if thou shouldst strive to choose' (2.3.138). The point is made to Bertram, but it encompasses the spectrum of character in *All's Well*.

In Shakespeare's time and a little later, an optimistic psychology, embodied in the 'new science' or 'new philosophy', carried everything before it and had an answer for everything. Lafew addresses this psychology in one of the central passages in the play.

They say miracles are past, and we have our philosophical persons, to make modern and familiar, things supernatural and causeless. Hence it is that we make trifles of terrors, ensconcing ourselves into seeming knowledge, when we should submit ourselves to an unknown fear.

(2.3.1–5)

Seeming knowledge confronts our incapacity to know, and in the jar between them lies the meaning (but not the moral) of this ambiguous play. Comic characters say how all's well. Tragic characters are doubtful, understanding that we 'float upon a wild and violent sea'. The quotation is from *Macbeth* (4.2.21), a play which instructs us that 'in this earthly world' (4.2.75) it rains on the just and the unjust. Shakespeare, enacting the tragic point of view, makes it sovereign for comedy. His characters are helpless, and with respect to their success, grace or the lack of grace is decisive.

Measure for Measure, which has its points for comparison, is at least in one particular the more inspiriting play, in that Shakespeare allows to the hero the manage of great power. Duke Vincentio is the unseen good old man behind the arras, and moves the play to its happy conclusion. The King in *All's Well* is, however, a beggar, 'now the play is done' (Epilogue 1). But this destitute condition, beggared of hope, describes him from the beginning, and almost until the end he is wrapped in dismal thinking (5.3.128). The play being comedy, all's well in the event, but that is only as the greatest Grace lends grace (2.1.156).

Philosophical persons meet their match in Shakespeare's 'poor unlearnèd virgin' (1.3.212). That isn't because she is poor, ignorant or virginal. Shakespeare, though not an 'intellectual', is not a sentimentalist either. Helena is lucky in so far as she has the backing of the luckiest stars (1.3.218). In herself, she is insistently the weakest minister (2.1.133). Heaven, which might turn a deaf ear to her prayers, delights to hear them (3.4.27). The magic potion she inherits and bestows on the King is the stuff of romance. It is also emblematic, like the sickness it cures, and suggests that our salvation is gratuitous, not less than our success in material ways.

This possibly dispiriting truth is Shakespeare's possession from the beginning, for instance in *Love's Labour's Lost* (1.1.151–2), where we hear how 'every man with his affects is born/Not by might mastered, but by special grace'. In the late plays, however, emphasis goes to our weakness and debility, as in the exchange between Lafew and Parolles (2.3.30–1). Affects or natural disposition are conceived as overbearing (5.3.6–8), and what we can do of ourselves gets short shrift. Tiresome characters never weary of telling us how the power and corrigible authority of everything lies in our wills. The myopic man or villain sees the business and undertakes to resolve it. He is the master of his fate. We learn, however, from *Cymbeline* (4.3.46) that 'Fortune brings in some boats that are not steered.' Fortune, endlessly the butt of a more purposive psychology, is discovered in the context of *All's Well* to be 'a good lady' (5.2.24–5). So let us trust to Fortune, or Opportunity or Occasion, and 'take the instant by the forward top' (5.3.39). That, in part, is the conclusion to which *All's Well* conducts.

It is not an inspiriting conclusion and it argues a sceptical view of flesh and blood. Shakespeare's 'wise fool', as often, speaks for this view. To meditated choice, he opposes a lottery (1.3.70). 'Marriage comes by destiny' (1.3.48), whatever the natural philosophers say. 'One good woman in ten' is a prodigious overestimate (1.3.64), but there is no harm in that. A 'bad' woman is no better than she should be. For papists and puritans, however they differ in what it pleases them to call their convictions, 'their heads are both one: they may jowl horns together like any deer i'th'herd' (1.3.42–3). No harm in that either: the cuckoo sings by nature (1.3.49). Only let men 'be contented to be what they are' (1.3.39–40). These are the accepted sayings, and Shakespeare entertains them equably. They incline him to a certain cursoriness, though.

4 Set for the Countess's drawing-room, designed by John Gunter for Trevor Nunn's production at Stratford-upon-Avon, 1981

Helena (so they think) is hardly cold in her grave, and already Lafew is devising a new match for Bertram. How does the Countess like this? 'With very much content' (4.5.62). Sound Helena's knell, says the King, 'and now forget her' (5.3.67). That sorts with the brusque psychology *All's Well* develops. 'Moderate lamentation is the right of the dead; excessive grief the enemy to the living' (1.1.43–4). We are only flesh and blood, and who should be mindful of us?

Brusque is the word for Shakespeare's disposing or dismissing of his hero. Bertram is the hero in his basic condition – again, the radical case; that is, he presents us all; and I call him Shakespeare's ultimate and most audacious essay in the hero. 'He's guilty, and he is not guilty' (5.3.279). This hero wants autonomy, and, as the King says, every feather starts him (5.3.230). The Countess tells us that her son has been corrupted by Parolles, 'A very tainted fellow, and full of wickedness' (3.2.79), and Lafew shares her opinion. Bertram, he thinks, has been 'misled with a snipped-taffeta fellow' (4.5.1). But the play itself does not corroborate this opinion. No doubt Bertram, like all of us, is seduced or deceived simply as he is human, hence flawed in the grain. 'Who cannot be crushed with a plot?' (4.3.272). This native incapacity is generic, however. What is peculiar to the equivocal hero is his meditated baseness. We are not made to feel that he has been enticed by the devil. We feel rather that Parolles is an extension of Bertram; in Helena's words: 'One that goes with him'

5 Set for the Countess's drawing-room, designed by Tanya Moiseiwitsch for Tyrone Guthrie's
production, 1959

(1.1.87). Prospero's relation with Caliban is analogous: 'this thing of darkness
I/Acknowledge mine' (*Temp.* 5.1.275–6). The thing of darkness is a necessary part
of the hero in his mingled condition. As Prospero says of Caliban: we cannot 'miss'
or do without him (1.2.311). Bertram in *All's Well* does not acknowledge a connection
between himself and Parolles, and it is left for the audience to recognise that the
'finding' of Parolles in the course of the play is very like the 'finding' or finding-out
of Bertram.

This hero cannot thrive unless reprieved by heaven (3.4.26–9). 'At the end', says
Irving Ribner (in Kittredge, 1968), he 'is a man who has been tested and matured
by experience'. On the contrary. Bertram, who never changes, never repents. In 4.3
he gets a letter that is said to sting his nature. But the promptings of remorse, like
the testing and maturing, are not open to inspection. That is just as well.

For repentance in this context is neither here nor there. 'Is't enough I am sorry?'
asks the hero in *Cymbeline* (5.4.11), and the wretched question answers itself. 'Do
not repent these things', says Paulina to Leontes in *The Winter's Tale* (3.2.208),
understanding how what's done can hardly be amended. There isn't any redress for
what Bertram has done, and expiation must always come too short.

But forgiveness, an arbitrary or gratuitous gesture, remains available to the
playwright as to his dramatis personae, and that is why the ending, which has outraged
so many critics, must be as it is. Redress and expiation are impossibilities; however,

it is open to Shakespeare's characters and to the playwright himself to extend to the undeserving a forgiveness that is both unearned and unexpected. 'Pardon's the word to all' (*Cym.* 5.5.422). In the ending of *All's Well*, Shakespeare resumes his *Two Gentlemen of Verona*. Bertram is Proteus all over again, not tested and matured but confirmed. Dr Johnson, in his note on the play's Epilogue, describes this ending very fairly. Like most of us who hanker after just deserts, he cannot reconcile his heart to Bertram –

a man noble without generosity, and young without truth; who marries Helena as a coward and leaves her as a profligate; when she is dead by his unkindness, sneaks home to a second marriage, is accused by a woman whom he has wronged, defends himself by falsehood, and is dismissed to happiness.

'Dismissed to happiness' is just right, and the best we can look for.

But the ending of *All's Well* is affectively happy, not simply by decree. It touches our feelings and teaches the triumph of our unregenerate flesh. As often in Shakespeare's comedies, the auditors of the play learn more than the actors in it, and the triumph to which the play conducts is celebrated with more awareness on the other side of the footlights than up there on stage. At the end we see Parolles accepting his fallen condition and seeking grace, like Caliban. But whether either will find it is not within the control of either. Bertram at the end is subdued to his fallen condition, but it is too much to say and perhaps too much to hope that the scales have dropped from his eyes. Lafew and Helena are rewarded, perhaps in so far as they are frail or fallen, and the conclusion shows them carrying off their unregenerate prizes. Lafew is a static character whose goodness is evident from the beginning, and we leave him where we found him. Helena in the beginning is purblind or partially blind, a benighted heroine whom the plot of the play must set to school, and at the end of the play she looks less like an unschooled figure at Fortune's disposal than like Fortuna herself. You can say that in the interval between the first and last scenes, she has learned humility, hence grown in stature. But what she learns is not so much dramatised or verified by the play as it is given by the playwright. Perhaps on Shakespeare's 'comic' view, all learning is problematic, and the resources of the theatre are not sufficient to present it.

The maturing of Helena, whether real or merely stipulated, is signified by an access of humility; paradoxically also, since she goes 'to the world' (1.3.14), her experience, like the Clown's, is spiritual and carnal too. This is the metaphorical sense of her pilgrimage, and associates *All's Well* with the late romances. All of them dramatise a voyage of discovery. For all of them, however, the discovery is not earned but inspired (2.1.144).

In the opening scene, we are told how Helena inherits her 'dispositions', and also her 'honesty'. She achieves her goodness, though (1.1.30–5). Evidently, natural disposition makes an antithesis to goodness. The papist and the puritan come down hard on this antithesis, but their psychology is disabling and they fail to grasp what it means. Goodness involves a return on the talents which a provident man puts out at interest, and Parolles calls this return a 'rational increase' (1.1.112).

6 'A Gentle Astringer' (see 5.1.6 SD). From George Turberville's *Booke of Faulconrie or Hawking* (London, 1575), part 2, p. 75

Bertram also has his legacy and will likely inherit his father's moral parts (1.2.21–2). Achievement isn't in question for him, and we feel how these moral parts are not just the same as goodness. His mother hopes for the contention of blood and virtue in this son (1.1.50–1). The key terms are equivocal, and Shakespeare is partly asking us to see this. 'Blood' means 'noble breeding', and 'virtue' means 'goodness'. So far, the two terms go together. But 'blood' is also 'flesh and blood', and all the old connotations of an unruly passion that ought to be coerced come into play here. 'Virtue' is 'manliness', where Latin *vir* is 'man', and often this word will emphasise the radical sense of manly integrity, hence moral excellence, particularly sexual purity. So we have an opposition between 'blood' and 'virtue'. But 'virtue' (or *vertu* or *virtus*) is also a quality that inheres in us, it is simply there, not earned, and we cannot help performing the actions that flow from this inborn quality. As that is so, the contention of blood and virtue is partly subverted, and these two opposed qualities will be felt to come together. The ascetic psychology proposes an absolute contention between them, and wants to settle the contention, blood being understood as inimical to virtue. *All's Well* controverts this myopic or simplistic psychology. Not in so many words. Shakespeare is in character in being mute. The plot of the play speaks for him,

7 'Occasion on her wheel' (see 5.1.14, 5.3.39). From Geoffrey Whitney's *A Choice of Emblems* (Leyden, 1586), Sig. z3ʳ, p. 181

however, and promotes a quarrel between blood and virtue that differs in important ways from the unambiguous quarrel between bad and good. The issue of this quarrel is goodness, but not goodness judged by our success in whipping out the offending Adam, much less in expiating what gloomy conscience calls 'ambitious love' (1.1.78, 3.4.5). Our disposition isn't to evil, nor is the goodness we achieve defined exclusively in mortifying the flesh. We achieve our goodness in so far as the simple thing we are by nature is adulterated or mixed. 'Best men are moulded out of faults', Mariana tells us in *Measure for Measure* (5.1.439–41), and 'become much more the better,/For being a little bad'. That, in the Countess's phrase, is as adoption strives with nature (1.3.117).

This swapping back and forth of goodness and badness, faults and virtues, thorns and leaves – disparate things on any conventional reading – affords the central insight of *All's Well That Ends Well*. This insight is refracted into many images and effects, lest we fail to take its sense. The 'catastrophe and heel of pastime' (1.2.57) is one compendious illustration, and complete in itself as 'catastrophe' makes a portmanteau term. It signifies 'disaster', as well as the final event, which need not be disastrous. 'Joy after woe', says Chaucer in *The Knight's Tale*, and the other way round is true, too. Sweet and sharp have their fellowship (4.4.33). The Countess embodies it, as 'joy and grief' contend in her (3.2.42). The King embodies it too, and in him we see at once 'a sunshine and a hail' (5.3.33).

A 'day of season' is a seasonable day, suitable to the time of year that brought it to birth. It designates also a flourishing or fructifying time, and in this sense a 'day of season' is a day to rejoice in. But *All's Well* is a crucible for meanings and invites the conclusion that the fruition in which we rejoice comes with seasoning. This means something different. Helena approximates what it means. Though she declares for happiness, tears 'season' praise in her (1.1.37). Bertram is 'unseasoned' (1.1.59) in that the sense of this decorous mingling eludes him. Shakespeare, who never speaks *in propria persona*, perhaps comes close to it in the homely figure he gives to First Lord:

> The web of our life is of a mingled yarn, good and ill together: our virtues would be proud, if our faults whipped them not, and our crimes would despair, if they were not cherished by our virtues.   (4.3.60–3)

Helena is our heroine just as the 'goodly clew' (1.3.154) she winds is like this mingled yarn. The amalgamation in the heroine of things immiscible to ordinary sense is the index of goodness achieved. This achievement is contingent, however. 'My instruction', says the villain, 'shall serve to naturalise thee' (1.1.180–1), and he is right. Like Lucio in *Measure for Measure*, 'the first knave that e'er mad'st a duke' (5.1.356), Parolles has a decisive part in the happy ending; Diana, who is reluctant to invoke 'So bad an instrument' (5.3.200), evidently has no option.

This villain is a kind of burr, and characteristically a survivor. But what he is is not merely enduring but efficient, and his quality, however 'bad', isn't negative but plays an active role. The play drives us towards this reading. Like the relics of Bertram's bad behaviour, the badness of the villain is 'incensing' (5.3.25). This means that it infuriates but also that it perfumes. The hard heroine in *Measure for Measure* (3.1.137) who wants to know 'Wilt thou be made a man out of my vice?' is answered affirmatively here.

Parolles fills a place, but not concessively. His fixed evils 'take place' – I think they get precedence – 'when virtue's steely bones/Looks bleak i'th'cold wind' (1.1.91–2). Virtue isn't fleshed, it has no weight, and virtue's bones are steely. The wind that plays over them, like wisdom, is cold. What does this say to 'superfluous folly' (1.1.93)? In Parolles, vice and virtue jostle for place, and his virtues are traitors too (1.1.31–3). The 'composition' they make is 'a virtue of a good wing' (1.1.177–8), however. He is the rare bird who has 'out-villained villainy so far, that the rarity redeems him' (4.3.230–1).

In the event, a plot brings him low. His fall is fortunate, however, and not only for himself. Bertram's fall is like this. Meditating adultery, he is potentially guilty of a sinful act. But the heroine who brings him low, and who is both his enemy and his good angel, sees a 'lawful meaning' where his meaning is 'wicked', and in the event the act is lawful too (3.7.45–7). But neither the hero nor the villain is schooled. Grace is crucial for our schooling, and none of us, apparently, has much skill in grace

(4.5.16–17). This lack emphasises the peril in which we stand, and is lucky, like the fortunate fall.

Stage history

In the seventeenth century, Jonsonian comedy was in, Shakespearean comedy was out, and *All's Well That Ends Well* failed to get a hearing. 'No man', said Charles Gildon, 'can allow any of Shakespear's comedies, except the Merry Wifes of Windsor.'[1] Subsequent auditors have been less severe, but *All's Well* has remained an unpopular play in the theatre.

In the eighteenth century, it received only 51 performances in the London theatre, as against 274 performances for *As You Like It* and 133 for *Measure for Measure*. Such success as it enjoyed turned mostly on its supposed character of rudimentary farce. In the nineteenth century, five revivals are recorded but only 17 performances. All five revivals made a hash of the text. The twentieth century has done better but not a lot better until quite recently. It took thirty-five years for the new Shakespeare Theatre at Stratford-upon-Avon to get around to *All's Well* (leaving only *Titus Andronicus* still to be played at that time). As late as 1929, Harold Child, in the New Shakespeare, could find 'no record of its ever having been staged in the United States of America'.[2]

The early English theatre shows the same dismal blank. There is no record of a production of *All's Well* in Shakespeare's time and no record in the century that followed his death. We cannot be certain, however, that there were no performances, and we are free to speculate about possibilities (see illustrations 8, 9 and 10). When the play came to be performed, in the eighteenth century and later, it was generally trivialised almost beyond recognition. This isn't surprising. *All's Well*, said M. C. Bradbrook, 'is a play which is of its age rather than for all time'.[3] Over the centuries, that has been the accepted view, and stage directors have no doubt appealed to this view to justify their maladroit reading of the play. 'If *All's Well* must be played', said Joseph Price satirically in his account of the stage history, 'then play it as removed as possible from the original.'[4] By and large, that is how it has been played.

The first recorded performance of *All's Well* took place on 28 September 1741 at Henry Giffard's theatre in Goodman's Fields. Where Giffard was more or less satisfied with Shakespeare's text, his successors received it as a blank page and filled the page as they pleased. The eighteenth century saw *All's Well* as a comic vehicle for 'Monsieur Parolles', and Theophilus Cibber and Charles Macklin contended for this part in the Drury Lane production of 1742. 'Young Cibber's exhibition' – Macklin having had to settle for the role of Lavatch – elicited from the poet Shenstone 'as

[1] *The Life of Betterton*, London, 1710, p. 173.
[2] Harold Child (who supplied the stage history), in *All's Well That Ends Well*, 1929, p. 189. The first American production of *All's Well* occurred 8 March 1799 at the Federal Street Theatre, Boston.
[3] *Shakespeare and Elizabethan Poetry*, 1951, p. 162.
[4] *The Unfortunate Comedy: A Study of 'All's Well that Ends Well' and Its Critics*, 1968, p. 54. Price, supplemented by George C. D. Odell, *Shakespeare from Betterton to Irving*, 2 vols., 1921, is my authority for most of the factual matter digested here.

3.
Alarum
within

1. "I would I had any
drum of the enemy's,
I would swear I recovered it."

2. "You shall hear
one anon."

Parolles

C.W.H.

8 Parolles in ambush (Act 4, Scene 1); reconstruction of an early performance, by C. Walter Hodges

sincere a laugh as I can ever recollect'.[1] Peg Woffington, 'the most captivating comedienne of her time',[2] played Helena. But in the eighteenth century the part of the heroine attracted little attention, the part of Bertram still less, and no leading actor ventured to perform it between Giffard in 1741 and John Philip Kemble a half century later.

During the first five years following the 1741 performance, *All's Well* was played 22 times in four different theatres. Then for ten years it fell from the stage.[3] David Garrick engineered a second major revival on 24 February 1756. For this performance at Drury Lane, Garrick prepared an acting version which held the stage for eighteen years. In his reductionist view, *All's Well* was exhausted in the comedy of Parolles, and the comedy itself was pure and simple. 'One of the greatest on the English stage', said the London *Chronicle* (1 December 1757) of the character of Parolles as

[1] Marjorie Williams (ed.), *The Letters of William Shenstone*, 1939, p. 42.
[2] Odell, *Betterton to Irving*, I, 336.
[3] It continued to be played in the provinces, as at Norwich between 1750 and 1758.

personated by Harry Woodward, who made the part his own for the next generation. Woodward played Parolles at the Crow Street Theatre in Dublin on 24 October 1760, and again at Covent Garden in 1762. Abruptly the play was popular, and Garrick, Woodward's erstwhile employer, mounted a rival production at Drury Lane with Thomas King as the cowardly soldier.

The popularity of *All's Well* depended substantially on eviscerating the play. Frederick Pilon's adaptation of 1785 for the comedian John Bannister suggests how this was so. The adaptation was played at the Haymarket, a house of farce, and the smoking of Parolles was the centrepiece of the play. To heighten this business, Pilon cut the first three acts almost in their entirety.

A new reading of *All's Well* is evident in its third stage incarnation. For this, responsibility belongs to John Philip Kemble. In 1793, Kemble published his adapted version in which the focus shifts to Helena and her selfless love. Kemble's *All's Well*, produced at the new Theatre Royal in Drury Lane on 12 December 1794, is a sentimental comedy. In the early years of the nineteenth century, the literary essayist Nathan Drake filled out the portrait which Kemble had sketched in outline:

Helen, the romantic, the love-dejected Helen, must excite in every feeling bosom a high degree of sympathy; patient suffering in the female sex, especially when resulting from ill-acquitted attachment, and united with modesty and beauty, cannot but be an object of interest and commiseration.

Musing on Helena's flight from Rossillion, this writer concludes: 'how does she, becoming thus an unprotected wanderer, a pilgrim *barefoot plodding the cold ground* for him who has contemned her, rise to the tone of exalted truth and heroism!'[1]

Though Kemble took the part of Bertram (where his predecessors would have chosen Parolles), *All's Well* failed to please and closed after a single performance. The damage to Shakespeare's text proved more enduring, however. Seventeen years later, Charles Kemble, the manager of Covent Garden, revived his older brother's lachrymose adaptation. Performances were scheduled on 24 May 1811 and again on 22 June. Then Covent Garden dropped the play, and a revival at Bath ten years later did nothing to persuade the public that *All's Well* was worth serious attention.

As the taste of the Regency was displaced by that of the Victorians, it was not the sentimentality of Kemble's version that gave rise to objection but its carnality. 'The plot', said *The Theatrical Observer* in 1832, 'is in itself so objectionable to modern refinement, that it has long been acknowledged not to be fit for representation.' In this year the dramatist Frederic Reynolds did his best to make amends for Shakespeare's plot. He created an operatic version at Covent Garden (11 October 1832), admitting nothing offensive and nothing farcical either. A sweetly suffering Helena was acted, and also sung, by Miss Inverarity. 'I am Saint Jaques' Pilgrim', this Helena sang. Material from other plays was grafted to this stock. *A Midsummer Night's Dream* provided a chorus of fairies. Songs were set from verses in *Othello*, *Love's Labour's Lost* and *The Two Gentlemen of Verona*, to music by Rophino Lacy. Taking his cue from *Romeo and Juliet*, Bertram sang how 'Love is a smoke.' The entire

---

[1] *Shakespeare and His Times*, London, 1817, II, 423–4.

9   'Here, take her hand,
      Proud scornful boy, unworthy this good gift...'
A possible Elizabethan staging of Act 2, Scene 3, drawn by C. Walter Hodges

chorus, accompanied by Helena, Diana, the Gentle Astringer and assorted Falconers, rendered the lines from *Twelfth Night*: 'If music be the food of love'.

Still the critics declined to be mollified. 'The revival at all, at this time of day', said the *Court Journal* (20 October 1832), 'of the *only* play of Shakespeare that is really exceptionable in its moral tone and tendency, is a sufficient blunder.' The blunder was compounded by uniting *All's Well* 'in a forced marriage with the most touchingly pure, innocent, and pastoral, and at the same time most exquisitely and exclusively poetical, and most divinely human and beautiful, of all the same author's plays'. This was *A Midsummer Night's Dream*.

Two decades later, Samuel Phelps tried again. For the production of *All's Well* in 1852 at his theatre, Sadler's Wells, Phelps relied on J. P. Kemble's adaptation. He left nothing to chance, though, further expurgating the text and further refining the character of Helena (no reflections on 'my virginity'). He eliminated the bed-trick. But the critics found him out or they found Shakespeare out. Alter the play as you will, said *John Bull* (4 September 1852), it cannot 'be made presentable to an audience of which decent females form a portion'.

For almost half a century, that was the last of *All's Well*. In 1895, for only the fourth time on the London stage in the nineteenth century, the Irving Dramatic Club put on a performance. This prompted a review by Bernard Shaw, who thought the play had been 'vivisected' – an intolerable fault to the anti-vivisectionist – and the fragments mutilated in the interest of accessories 'which were in every particular silly and ridiculous'. When the Florentine army passed beneath the walls of the city, 'a few of the band gave a precarious selection from the orchestral parts of Berlioz's version of the Rackoczy March'. The dresses of the ladies 'were the usual fancy ball odds and ends, Helena especially distinguishing herself by playing the first scene partly in the costume of Hamlet and partly in that of a waitress in an Aerated Bread market'.[1]

Later Shaw wrote that in Shakespeare there were parts – 'like that of Helena in All's Well for instance – which are still too genuine and beautiful and modern for the public'.[2] That of the Countess was among them, he said, 'the most beautiful old woman's part ever written'. *All's Well* stood out artistically by virtue of the sovereign charm of the young woman and the old woman, 'and intellectually by the experiment, repeated nearly three hundred years later in *A Doll's House*, of making the hero a perfectly ordinary young man, whose unimaginative prejudices and selfish conventionality make him cut a very mean figure in the atmosphere created by the nobler nature of his wife'.[3]

The nobler nature commended itself to the actor-manager Frank Benson in his production for the Shakespeare Memorial Theatre at Stratford-upon-Avon in the spring of 1916. Benson's ignoble Bertram was redeemed by Lady Benson in the role of Helena. For William Poel, the celebrated revivalist of Elizabethan plays, Helena's wooing of Bertram manifested a love, 'religious in impulse, which no convention could repress'. In Poel's production on 20 May 1920 at the Ethical Church in Bayswater, the play acquired 'an ethical significance which gave it a place in the history of woman's emancipation'.[4]

There was more comedy than social history in the Old Vic performance of 28 November 1921, directed by Robert Atkins, and in the Bridges-Adams revival at Stratford in 1922. Interest in Parolles was on the upswing again and brought with it renewed attention to the long-neglected role of the Clown. This role got special mention in a revival at the Maddermarket, a new theatre in Norwich, in September 1924. Three years later, a production in modern dress at the Birmingham Repertory Theatre featured young Laurence Olivier as Parolles; 'an amiable, too smart young man, a sommelier's scourge', said Bernard Shaw.[5] None of these productions was especially convincing to the critics, however, and when Robert Atkins repeated his version at the Arts Theatre Club in 1932, they went away, said one of them, 'with no idea in head except that it was Shakespeare botching and bungling at his worst'.[6]

The idea persisted. 'Dull' was the judgement passed on the Stratford 'birthday' production in 1935, presided over by B. Iden Payne.[7] When Atkins offered a third

---

[1] *Saturday Review*, 2 February 1895.
[2] Letter to Janet Achurch, 23 April 1895, in *Shaw on Theatre*, ed. E. J. West, 1958, p. 56.
[3] John F. Matthews (ed.), *Shaw's Dramatic Criticism (1895–98)*, 1959, pp. 12–18.
[4] Speaight, *Elizabethan Revival*, pp. 233–4.
[5] J. C. Trewin, *The Birmingham Repertory Theatre: 1913–63*, 1963, p. 90.
[6] James Agate, *Brief Chronicles: A Survey of the Plays of Shakespeare and the Elizabethans in Actual Performances*, 1943.
[7] Gordon Crosse, *Shakespearean Playgoing: 1890–1952*, 1953, p. 81.

revival in the fall of 1940, the ugly duckling had another chance to prove itself 'a true cygnet of Avon'.[1] It failed this chance. The play was 'too grim, unwitty and disconcerting to be called comedy at all', and 'anybody heard defending its poetry should be asked point-blank to quote two consecutive lines'.[2]

Tyrone Guthrie made a notable defender, though not of the poetry and not of the play as Shakespeare conceived it, and he chose *All's Well* (and *Richard III*) to inaugurate the Shakespeare Festival at Stratford, Ontario, in 1953. Alec Guinness in a wheel-chair presented the King of France, and the play went off to stormy applause. Six years later, at Stratford-upon-Avon, Guthrie broadened the farce and repeated his initial success (see illustrations 1 and 5). The costumes and settings were Edwardian except for the war scenes, which Guthrie located in the North African desert. There was a lot of suppositious, spurious fun in the desert. Diana, whom Bertram found chaste to a fault, was played 'as a wartime factory tart who sits on the doorstep in nightgown and housecoat, with a turban on her head and a lollipop in her mouth, giggling the lines in coffee-bar cockney'.[3] For one scholar-critic with a turn for understatement, this 1959 production 'revealed in every aspect the strong hand of the director'.[4]

The director who brooks no interference from the playwright was fully realised by Michael Benthall in the Old Vic production at Edinburgh on 15 September 1953. This comic rendition, distinguished by 'drastic cutting, transposing, the masking of awkward speeches with music or outrageous buffoonery', struck Richard David in his review for *Shakespeare Survey* (1955) with the force of revelation. 'King and Countess as Disney dwarfs, the hero and heroine reduced to decorative pasteboard, Parolles taking over ... as a sort of amateurish Mephistopheles' – this, David thought, made a play. No doubt, said another reviewer, some of the finer moments were diminished, 'but in the lightness of the production we gain a sort of surface plausibility, and laughter is the kindest anaesthetic against the increasing outrage of the plot'.[5]

The pendulum swung back in Noel Willman's production at Stratford-upon-Avon in 1955, in which Helena, far from acquiescing in the role of a pasteboard heroine, demonstrated 'a pertinacity worthy of the Royal Northwest Mounted Police'.[6] It moved backward still further, perhaps in the general direction of Shakespeare, in John Houseman's tragi-comic reading of 1959 for the American Shakespeare Festival at Stratford, Connecticut. Houseman was humble, and also eccentric; he took the text as Shakespeare wrote it. This revolutionary gesture of acceptance inspired and animated the great production at Stratford, Ontario, in 1977, directed by David Jones. William Hutt defined the King and Margaret Tyzack the Countess, and the result was among those incandescent evenings when all the myopic conceit of reviewers and

[1] Ivor Brown, rev. in *Punch*, 16 October 1940, p. 388.
[2] Alan Dent, *Preludes and Studies*, 1942, pp. 121–2.
[3] Alan Brien, 'All's Well that Ends Well', *The Spectator*, 24 April 1959, pp. 578–9.
[4] Price, *Unfortunate Comedy*, p. 59.
[5] Eric Keown, 'All's Well that Ends Well', *Punch*, 30 September 1953, p. 416.
[6] Peter Fleming, 'All's Well that Ends Well', *The Spectator*, 6 May 1955, p. 586.

the bumptiousness of poor players and the bustle of vulgar directors falls away, and we participate in that communal experience which is the drama at its highest pitch.[1]

In the last generation, directors have been willing to let the play be seen without cosmetics, and the reward for their scrupulousness – or say their humility – has been the emergence of a great play. That the greatness of *All's Well* has rarely been evident to previous generations of theatregoers is owed to the fact that we see only so far as our cultural conditioning allows. Brander Matthews, a distinguished Shakespearean, estimating Helena's conversation with Parolles, found it 'reeking with vulgarity and quite impossible to a modest-minded girl'.[2] Essentially, he is asking: How can we find the concord of this discord where tears mingle with laughter? How could Helena, a chaste woman, engage in smutty discourse, or give her love to a cad? How can Parolles, knowing what he is, be what he is? The governing psychology from the mid seventeenth century to the second half of the twentieth century has precluded answers to these questions. It seems presumptuous to conclude that only in our time has Shakespeare recovered the audience once available to him. But the history of *All's Well* in the theatre appears to support this conclusion.

Recent years

In 1967 John Barton for the Royal Shakespeare Company set out, as he put it, to 'trust the play', and the result, it was said, 'was a blessedly direct production'.[3] It was achieved at the cost of some five hundred lines, including the whole of Act 3, Scene 4, and a number of telescopings and transpositions. The gain in economy and clarity of narrative line did not wholly atone for the loss of some emotional subtleties and tensions, but in one reviewer's judgement the play was 'raised to the head of the corner' of Shakespearean comedy.[4] Lavatch, omitted from the play by Tyrone Guthrie, was admitted in a much reduced role by Barton, and played by Ian Hogg as if his devotion to the Countess were dangerously simple-minded. A certain responsiveness to the mood of the 1960s ('Crabbed age and youth cannot live together') was offset by graces of style and by costumes that recalled the early seventeenth century. The set, by Timothy O'Brien, evoked a neo-classic stage-upon-a-stage, 'patterned like French marquetry', it was said, and 'elegant and functional as a huge musical instrument'.[5] The only staging extravagance was a 'red flamed romp' at the start of the Florentine campaign, with soldiers 'wheeling and marching in time to the muffled barks and howls of a gargantuan drill major'.[6] War became a gentlemen's game played with toy combatants, and more was made of the elegant, humorous ironies of the play than of its moral astringency and weight. Brewster

---

[1] Memory impels me to single forth Hutt and Tyzack, but I am sure that Nicholas Pennell as Bertram and Martha Henry as Helena were their customarily excellent selves.
[2] *Shakespeare as a Playwright*, 1913, pp. 222–6.
[3] *Illustrated London News*, 10 June 1967 (unsigned review).
[4] Harold Hobson, *Sunday Times*, 21 January 1968.
[5] Ronald Bryden, *The Observer*, 4 June 1967.
[6] Peter Ansorge, *Plays and Players*, August 1967.

Mason's Lafew, for example, was described as 'master of the graceful insult, the thrust and lazy flick',[1] and he was clearly a better swordsman than Parolles. Helena persuaded the King to yield to therapy with a mesmeric tenderness that kept a tactful distance from sexual enticement. The unmasking of Parolles (see illustration 2) was cruelly executed (with drum rolls and a falling axe at the moment of revelation) while that of Bertram was more generously hilarious. Helena's entry was a moving event to which Bertram responded with a passionate cry on the words, 'Both, both. Oh pardon!'; his 'ability to collapse', in R. L. Smallwood's phrase, was 'his salvation'.[2]

Trevor Nunn's 1981 production for the RSC opened with a waltzing couple in silhouette, recalling the music of Vienna and the art of John Singer Sargent. It was the prelude to an English Edwardian and Imperial European rendering of the play which was comprehensively retentive of the text and attentive to its significances. Fewer than a hundred lines were cut and, as in 1967, Act 4, Scene 3 was recast to bring Parolles's discovery to a climax in the reading of the letter to Diana. The transmutations of time and place did more to sharpen than to diminish the play's social and historical impact. The Countess (Peggy Ashcroft) and Lafew (Robert Eddison) were enlightened and cultivated survivors of a Victorian dispensation, looking critically but solicitously upon their heirs. But the play's tensions were not naïvely expressed as a conflict between generations. Lavatch's cryptic, reductive wit was consistent with deep devotion to his mistress; the Dumaine brothers (the First and Second Lords) sustained traditions that Bertram flouted; and Helena's daring, new-style deceptions were endorsed by the Countess and served at once a divine and human comic purpose. The itinerant form of the play, scattering events and colloquies all over Italy and France, was served by a beautifully articulated glass and wrought-iron set (by John Gunter; see illustrations 3 and 4) which made a conservatory, a gymnasium, a railway station (for the Florence battle scenes) and a wartime canteen. The war was reminiscent of the Crimea and prescient of 1914, with Helena's speech about 'tender limbs' and 'smoky muskets' spoken with great conviction. The deaths were actual enough, and Bertram owed his promotion to 'general of our horse' to a manifestly high casualty rate. But the drums and colours on parade were an engaging show, the soldiery (Parolles in the rear) in its element, under the searching gaze of the pilgrim Helena. War-delight and woman-delight kept festive company in a scene (insinuated before 4.2) in which Diana's seductive vivacity was expressed in song and Bertram looked like its easy prey. As in *Measure for Measure*, however, his passion was the more excited by her resisting virtue, much to the disgust of his fellow officers; the words 'he fleshes his will in the spoil of her honour' were spoken with vehement contempt. The production allowed the audience to reflect, however, that it is in this 'ruttish', 'dangerous' and 'lascivious' state that he goes unaware to consummate his marriage. Bertram, like Parolles, was clearly 'crushed with a plot', but he was not allowed the same resilient power of recovery. No attempt was made to charge his last words with great feeling and very little of the man was left for Helena to take by the hand and lead away. The golden

---

[1] Hilary Spurling, *The Spectator*, 9 June 1967.
[2] R. L. Smallwood, 'The design of *All's Well that Ends Well*', *S. Sur.* 25 (1972), 45–61 (p. 60).

10 'Drum and Colours. Enter Bertram, Parolles and the whole army.' A reconstruction with Elizabethan costumes for Act 3, Scene 5, by C. Walter Hodges

harmonies prefigured at the start were restored as the waltz resumed, but they had been bought by 'expense of spirit in a waste of shame' – by 'lust in action'.

Between the two RSC versions there appeared Jonathan Miller's BBC production in 1980, directed by Elijah Moshinsky. It used the constraints of the medium to remarkable effect, revealing through close-up much of the emotional intensity latent in the play. The creative, generative energies of sexuality were fully expressed in word and symbol, as in the firelight that literally plays upon Helena's face as she speaks for her 'flame of liking', and in her cure of the King we saw 'grace lending grace' with something of 'a strumpet's boldness'. The play's resolution was accomplished with great confidence in the romance tradition – Bertram, said Moshinsky, 'has achieved a potential for change'. It may be coincidence that when the television cameras in recent years have given us an *All's Well* that does indeed end well, the theatre has left us a touch more sceptical – 'All yet seems well.'

NOTE ON THE TEXT

The Folio is the only authoritative text of the play and all later texts derive from it. It is probable that the text was first set from Shakespeare's manuscript, with a number of confusions and anomalies owed to authorial slips or changes of mind. Stage directions have been clarified (but rarely amplified or supplemented) and speech headings made consistent. Spellings have been modernised in accordance with the conventions of the series, old forms being retained only when they are judged to have an expressive significance. The collation records only those variants and emendations which seem likely to correct or illuminate the Folio text. The authority for the reading in the text follows immediately upon the square bracket after the lemma; other readings, if any, follow in chronological order. Where the authority is in a form differing from that of the text, the old form is quoted first in the gloss (e.g. vilest] vildest F). Readings that differ substantially are divided by a semi-colon (;), those that differ only formally, by a comma (e.g. lose] F4, loose F). Where syllables require an emphasis not usual in modern speech they are marked with a *grave* accent (`). Significant additions to the Folio stage directions, and occasionally to the text, are enclosed in square brackets. An asterisk in the lemma of a note in the Commentary is used to call attention to a word or phrase that has been emended in the text. References and abbreviations are listed under Abbreviations and Conventions (pp. x–xiii above), and a fuller account of the text is given in the Textual Analysis (pp. 149–52 below).

All's Well That Ends Well

LIST OF CHARACTERS

KING OF FRANCE
DUKE OF FLORENCE
BERTRAM, *Count of Rossillion*
LAFEW, *an old lord*
PAROLLES, *a follower of Bertram*
The brothers DUMAINE, *two French lords in the Florentine service*
RINALDO, *steward of the Countess*
LAVATCH, *a Clown, servant of the Countess*
A PAGE
A MESSENGER
COUNTESS OF ROSSILLION, *mother of Bertram*
HELENA, *a gentlewoman protected by the Countess*
WIDOW CAPILET *of Florence*
DIANA, *her daughter*
VIOLENTA ⎫ *neighbours and friends of the Widow*
MARIANA ⎭
A GENTLE ASTRINGER
French and Florentine LORDS, ATTENDANTS, SOLDIERS, CITIZENS

SCENE: *Rossillion, Paris, Florence, Marseilles*

Notes

The list of characters was first supplied by Rowe; not in F.

brothers DUMAINE The Lords Dumaine are named for the first and last times in Act 4, Scene 3 (176–283), where Parolles is tormented by his captors. Otherwise they appear in stage directions as *Lords, French Lords, French Gentlemen, Frenchmen, Gentleman*, and *French Captaines*. The Folio speech headings include the use of letters G and E, apparently to distinguish the FIRST and SECOND LORDS (*Lord. G.*, 1.*Lo.G.*, *L.G.*, 2.*Lo.E.*, *Cap.E.*, etc.). The present text usually interprets G as FIRST LORD and E as SECOND LORD, but a few emendations are necessary (see notes on SHS 3.6.2, 87, 89; 4.1.1) to maintain consistency. It is often assumed for production purposes that one brother is the elder, and some editors have emended in an attempt to give the initiatives to the FIRST LORD; there is no reason for supposing them twins, but it seems likely that Shakespeare gave little thought to precedence.

RINALDO So named for the first time at 3.4.19. In Folio stage directions he is *Steward* and in speech headings *Stew.* or *Ste.*

LAVATCH So named for the first and only time by Parolles in 5.2.1. Otherwise he appears as *Clown* throughout the Folio.

HELENA So named and spelt in the Folio at 1.1.0 SD and at 1.1.52; but Parolles calls her 'Little Hellen' (1.1.188 F) and in 1.3 the forms Helen and Hellen are used exclusively. The present text retains the forms 'Helen' and 'Helena' in the dialogue but regularises all stage directions as HELENA, without collation.

GENTLE ASTRINGER Noble falconer. See 5.1.6 SD n. and 5.3.127 SD n.

SOLDIERS Including an important role for the INTERPRETER in 4.1 and 4.3 – perhaps the 'Morgan' named at 4.3.91.

ALL'S WELL THAT ENDS WELL

1.1 *Enter young* BERTRAM, *Count of Rossillion, his Mother* [*the* COUNTESS], *and* HELENA, *Lord* LAFEW, *all in black*

COUNTESS In delivering my son from me, I bury a second husband.

BERTRAM And I in going, madam, weep o'er my father's death anew; but I must attend his majesty's command, to whom I am now in ward, evermore in subjection.

LAFEW You shall find of the king a husband, madam; you, sir, a father. 5
He that so generally is at all times good must of necessity hold his virtue to you, whose worthiness would stir it up where it wanted, rather than lack it where there is such abundance.

COUNTESS What hope is there of his majesty's amendment?

LAFEW He hath abandoned his physicians, madam, under whose 10
practices he hath persecuted time with hope, and finds no other advantage in the process but only the losing of hope by time.

COUNTESS This young gentlewoman had a father – O, that 'had', how sad a passage 'tis – whose skill was almost as great as his honesty; had it stretched so far, would have made nature immortal, and death 15

Act 1, Scene 1 1.1] *Actus primus. Scaena Prima.* F   0 SD *Enter*] *Eneer* F   1 SH COUNTESS] *Rowe; Mother* F *(Mo./hereafter through scene)*   2 SH BERTRAM] *Rowe; Ros.* F *(through scene)*

Act 1, Scene 1

1.1 F marks act and scene here, and act divisions hereafter. Editors, following Theobald or Capell, locate the scene in the Count's palace at Rossillion.

0 SD *Rossillion* The English form of French 'Rousillon', an ancient province separated from Spain by the Pyrenees.

1 **delivering** sending away. With a residual sense of 'childbirth', opposing or complementing the death of Bertram's father; and hence opening immediately one of the principal themes of the play, the intimate connection between birth and death.

3 **attend** obey.

3–4 **in ward** This fatherless heir is still a minor and hence under the protection of the King, who acts as trustee for the estate.

5 **of** in.

6 **generally** Probably 'to all people'; also 'usually'.

6–7 **hold his virtue** continue his virtuous behaviour.

7–8 **whose...abundance** worthiness in you would stir up his virtue towards you, even were he lacking in virtue, rather than fail to stir it where it is so abundant.

8 **lack** Theobald's 'slack' is often preferred but requires that the King be understood as subject of this clause.

9 **amendment** recovery.

11 **practices** medical treatment. Some editors (e.g. Thiselton) detect a legal metaphor in the conjunction of 'practices', 'persecuted' and 'process' (11–12).

14 **passage** (1) occurrence (with the sense of time passing away), (2) word.

14 **honesty** integrity, honour.

15 **had...far** had his skill been equal to his absolute integrity.

should have play for lack of work. Would for the king's sake he were
living! I think it would be the death of the king's disease.

LAFEW How called you the man you speak of, madam?

COUNTESS He was famous, sir, in his profession, and it was his great
right to be so – Gerard de Narbon. 20

LAFEW He was excellent indeed, madam. The king very lately spoke
of him admiringly and mourningly. He was skilful enough to have
lived still, if knowledge could be set up against mortality.

BERTRAM What is it, my good lord, the king languishes of?

LAFEW A fistula, my lord. 25

BERTRAM I heard not of it before.

LAFEW I would it were not notorious. Was this gentlewoman the
daughter of Gerard de Narbon?

COUNTESS His sole child, my lord, and bequeathed to my overlooking.
I have those hopes of her good that her education promises. Her 30
dispositions she inherits, which makes fair gifts fairer; for where
an unclean mind carries virtuous qualities, their commendations go
with pity – they are virtues and traitors too. In her they are the
better for their simpleness. She derives her honesty and achieves
her goodness. 35

LAFEW Your commendations, madam, get from her tears.

COUNTESS 'Tis the best brine a maiden can season her praise in. The
remembrance of her father never approaches her heart but the
tyranny of her sorrows takes all livelihood from her cheek. No more
of this, Helena. Go to, no more, lest it be rather thought you affect 40
a sorrow than to have.

30 promises. Her] *Rowe (subst.)*; promises her F; promises her; *Theobald*   41 than to have.] *Var. 73*; then to haue – F;
than have it. *Capell*

16 **should have** would have had.

22 **admiringly and mourningly** with wonder
for his skill and with sorrow for his death.

23 **still** forever.

25 **fistula** Strictly, a long, flute-shaped abscess,
but the word is used by Painter in the source-story
to describe a painful swelling on the King's breast.

27 **notorious** known to everyone.

29 **overlooking** supervision.

30 **education** upbringing.

31 **dispositions** natural tendencies.

31 **gifts** i.e. those conferred by her upbringing.

32 **unclean mind** bad nature.

32–3 **their...pity** praises of them are mingled
with regret.

33 **traitors** i.e. to their bad nature as they
misrepresent that nature by the virtue that denotes
them. Warburton glosses: 'the advantages of

education enable an ill mind to go further than it
would have done without them'.

34 **simpleness** singleness, not mixed with evil.

34 **derives** inherits.

34 **achieves** acquires by her own efforts.

36 **get** beget; as at 113.

37 **season** preserve (as in brine). The word
suggests the recurrent theme of seasoning, i.e.
preserving or improving with experience.

39 **tyranny...cheek** i.e. her sorrows, as they
tyrannically exact their tribute of blood, turn her
cheek pale.

39 **livelihood** animation.

40 **Go to** Interjection in mild reproof.

40 **affect** (1) assume the character of, (2) love.

41 **have** have it. F's reading, 'have –', suggests
that the compositor failed to recognise that the sense
was complete.

HELENA I do affect a sorrow indeed, but I have it too.

LAFEW Moderate lamentation is the right of the dead; excessive grief
the enemy to the living.

COUNTESS If the living be enemy to the grief, the excess makes it soon   45
mortal.

BERTRAM Madam, I desire your holy wishes.

LAFEW How understand we that?

COUNTESS Be thou blest, Bertram, and succeed thy father
    In manners as in shape. Thy blood and virtue   50
    Contend for empire in thee, and thy goodness
    Share with thy birthright. Love all, trust a few,
    Do wrong to none. Be able for thine enemy
    Rather in power than use, and keep thy friend
    Under thy own life's key. Be checked for silence,   55
    But never taxed for speech. What heaven more will,
    That thee may furnish, and my prayers pluck down,
    Fall on thy head. – Farewell, my lord.
    'Tis an unseasoned courtier; good my lord,
    Advise him.

LAFEW   He cannot want the best   60
    That shall attend his love.

COUNTESS   Heaven bless him!
    Farewell, Bertram.   [*Exit*]

61–6 Heaven...father.] *As verse, Cam.; as prose,* F   62 SD] F2; *not in* F

42 As we learn in her next soliloquy, Helena's
sorrow is occasioned by her love for Bertram. The
line may be spoken as an aside.

43–4 **Moderate...living** Richmond Noble
(*Shakespeare's Biblical Knowledge*, 1935) compares
Ecclus. 38.17 and 20–2. Hunter, citing Seneca and
Plutarch, points to the classical *topos* behind the
passage.

45 **be enemy to** resist.

45–6 **excess...mortal** grief dies quickly of its
own excess.

47–8 **Madam...that?** Theobald, who transposes these two lines, is frequently followed by later
editors.

48 **How...that?** Lafew's question, which has
puzzled editors, refers presumably to 'wishes' and
is answered in the speech that follows.

50 **manners** moral behaviour.

50 **Thy...virtue** (May) your inherited and
acquired qualities.

51 **Contend for empire** Strive for sovereignty.

52 **Share...birthright** Divide the sovereignty
with your nobility of birth.

52 **Love** Behave kindly to; as again at 87.

53 **able for** capable of dealing with.

54 **in power** potentially.

54–5 **keep...key** guard your friend's life as you
would your own.

55 **checked** reproved.

56 **taxed for speech** censured for talking too
much.

57 **furnish** endow.

57 **pluck** draw.

59 **unseasoned** inexperienced; with a reminiscence of 'brine' and 'season' at 37. (The Countess
turns to Lafew.)

60–1 **He...love** A cryptic thought; it may mean
that Bertram cannot lack the best rewards in return
for devoted service to the court. But 'best' could
signify either moral or material benefits, and 'love'
could mean amiable or well-disposed behaviour, as
in 52 and 87.

BERTRAM   The best wishes that can
                 Be forgèd in your thoughts be servants to you.
                 [*To Helena*] Be comfortable to my mother, your mistress,
                 And make much of her.
LAFEW   Farewell, pretty lady.   65
                 You must hold the credit of your father.
                                 [*Exeunt Bertram and Lafew*]
HELENA O, were that all! I think not on my father,
                 And these great tears grace his remembrance more
                 Than those I shed for him. What was he like?
                 I have forgot him. My imagination   70
                 Carries no favour in't but Bertram's.
                 I am undone! There is no living, none,
                 If Bertram be away. 'Twere all one
                 That I should love a bright particular star
                 And think to wed it, he is so above me.   75
                 In his bright radiance and collateral light
                 Must I be comforted, not in his sphere.
                 Th'ambition in my love thus plagues itself.
                 The hind that would be mated by the lion
                 Must die for love. 'Twas pretty, though a plague,   80
                 To see him every hour; to sit and draw
                 His archèd brows, his hawking eye, his curls,
                 In our heart's table – heart too capable
                 Of every line and trick of his sweet favour.
                 But now he's gone, and my idolatrous fancy   85
                 Must sanctify his relics. Who comes here?

66 SD] *Rowe; not in* F   75 me.] *After Rowe* (me:); me F   81 hour;] *Theobald;* houre F

63 forgèd shaped. Compare *H5* 1 Chorus 25: 'In the quick forge and working-house of thought'.
64 comfortable comforting, helpful.
65 make much of attend sedulously on.
66 hold the credit keep up the reputation.
68–9 his...him Helena thinks at once of Bertram ('his') and of her father ('him'); compare the shift of pronouns in 87.
71 favour (1) face (as generally, e.g. 84 below), (2) love-token.
73–4 'Twere...That It would be the same thing if.
76 collateral reflected, as from a different sphere. In the geocentric (Ptolemaic) scheme, the motion of the spheres was parallel or collateral. Hence the heavenly bodies were visible to one another but never made physical contact.

78 ambition i.e. which aims beyond my sphere.
79 hind female deer.
80 pretty pleasing to the fancy.
82 hawking piercing.
83 table Usually taken to be 'the board or flat surface on which a picture is painted' (Onions). But since Helena has been drawing surreptitiously, it may be a table-book, meant for private notes (see *OED* Table *sb* 2b).
83 capable (1) susceptible, (2) easily drawn upon.
84 trick characteristic expression.
85 fancy (1) love, (2) imagination.
86 sanctify his relics worship his remains (as they exist in her imagination).

Enter PAROLLES

One that goes with him. I love him for his sake;
And yet I know him a notorious liar,
Think him a great way fool, solely a coward.
Yet these fixed evils sit so fit in him   90
That they take place when virtue's steely bones
Looks bleak i'th'cold wind. Withal, full oft we see
Cold wisdom waiting on superfluous folly.

PAROLLES 'Save you, fair queen!

HELENA And you, monarch!   95

PAROLLES No.

HELENA And no.

PAROLLES Are you meditating on virginity?

HELENA Ay. You have some stain of soldier in you: let me ask you a
question. Man is enemy to virginity; how may we barricado it   100
against him?

PAROLLES Keep him out.

HELENA But he assails, and our virginity, though valiant, in the defence
yet is weak. Unfold to us some warlike resistance.

PAROLLES There is none. Man, setting down before you, will undermine   105
you and blow you up.

HELENA Bless our poor virginity from underminers and blowers-up! Is
there no military policy how virgins might blow up men?

PAROLLES Virginity being blown down, man will quicklier be blown
up. Marry, in blowing him down again, with the breach yourselves   110
made, you lose your city. It is not politic in the commonwealth of

---

100 barricado] *Rowe;* barracado F   103 valiant,...defence] F; valiant...defence, *Var. 73*   105 setting] F; sitting *Johnson*

---

86 SD PAROLLES From French *paroles*, meaning
'words'.

89 a great way mostly a.

90 fixed evils strongly seated vices.

90 sit...him fit him so well (i.e. denote him
naturally).

91–2 take place...wind i.e. take precedence in
society, while virtue is left out in the cold.

91 steely bones The hard and bare quality of
virtue, making an unattractive antithesis to the
becoming or natural vice of Parolles.

92 Looks Abbott (333) notes Shakespeare's
common use of a singular verb with a plural subject.

92 Withal With this.

93 Cold Naked, unprovided.

93 superfluous (1) excessively provided, (2)
overclothed.

94 'Save God save.

94 queen With a quibble on 'quean' = hussy.

96–7 No. And no I am no monarch. And I am
no queen.

99 stain trace.

105 setting down before laying siege to.

106 blow you up explode you; make you
pregnant.

107 Bless God preserve.

108 policy stratagem.

108 how to indicate how.

108 blow up With a pun here and what follows
on tumescence.

110 Marry A mild interjection: 'By the Virgin
Mary' (as at 130).

111 city i.e. virginity.

111 politic expedient.

nature to preserve virginity. Loss of virginity is rational increase, and there was never virgin got till virginity was first lost. That you were made of, is metal to make virgins. Virginity by being once lost may be ten times found; by being ever kept it is ever lost. 'Tis too 115 cold a companion. Away with't!

HELENA I will stand for't a little, though therefore I die a virgin.

PAROLLES There's little can be said in't; 'tis against the rule of nature. To speak on the part of virginity is to accuse your mothers, which is most infallible disobedience. He that hangs himself is a virgin: 120 virginity murders itself, and should be buried in highways out of all sanctified limit, as a desperate offendress against nature. Virginity breeds mites, much like a cheese; consumes itself to the very paring, and so dies with feeding his own stomach. Besides, virginity is peevish, proud, idle, made of self-love, which is the most inhibited 125 sin in the canon. Keep it not; you cannot choose but lose by't. Out with't! Within ten year it will make itself two, which is a goodly increase, and the principal itself not much the worse. Away with't!

HELENA How might one do, sir, to lose it to her own liking?

PAROLLES Let me see. Marry, ill, to like him that ne'er it likes. 'Tis 130

---

113 got] F2; goe F   123 paring] *Rowe*, payring F   127 ten] F; the *Harrison*; t'one *Evans*   127 two] F; ten *Hanmer*

---

112 **rational increase** reasonable increase; increase of reasonable beings.

113 **That** That which.

114 **metal** mettle. The words are indistinguishable in Elizabethan usage, and hence the ideas of 'substance' and more specifically 'coin' are both present here. The same double sense recurs at 2.1.40.

115 **ten times found** i.e. by creating ten new virgins.

117 **stand for't** defend it; with a quibble on tumescence.

117 **die** With the common secondary sense of sexual intercourse. See, for example, *Sonnets* 151.

118 **in't** in its defence.

119 **on the part** in defence.

120 **infallible** certain.

120 **He...virgin** Since virgins, by declining to propagate, are suicides..

121 **buried in highways** i.e. at the crossroads, where Elizabethan suicides were buried.

121–2 **out...limit** away from consecrated ground.

123 **mites** These tiny spiders carry disease and are therefore inimical to the host. (As mites are also paltry coins, this residual sense continues the monetary image begun at 112.)

123 **paring** last particle (with residual sense of 'pairing' or 'coupling', as in *WT* 4.2.154). Parolles's comparison of virginity to 'withered pears' (137) is anticipated.

124 **his** its (as generally in Shakespeare).

124 **stomach** With residual sense of 'pride'.

125 **idle** worthless.

125 **inhibited** prohibited.

126 **canon** Generically 'law' or 'rule', in particular, 'Church law'. Noble compares Deut. 6.4–5, Lev. 19.18 and Mark 12.29–33.

126–7 **Out with't!** (1) away with it! (as at 128), (2) put it out at interest!

127 **ten...two** If we admit the first reading above (126–7) this line is comprehensible only if meant sardonically; if we admit the second, the line explains itself. Ten per cent per year, the allowed rate of interest, would double the capital in ten years. Editors who are disinclined to see this as a 'goodly increase' frequently emend 'ten' to 'the' or 'two' to 'ten'. Reading 'the' for 'ten' could mean 'get a second virgin', which would emphasise the 'goodly increase' of virgins, as distinct from return on capital.

129 **How** What.

130 **ill...likes** i.e. to do ill by preferring a man who does not like virginity.

a commodity will lose the gloss with lying; the longer kept, the less
worth. Off with't while 'tis vendible. Answer the time of request.
Virginity, like an old courtier, wears her cap out of fashion; richly
suited, but unsuitable: just like the brooch and the toothpick, which
wear not now. Your date is better in your pie and your porridge   135
than in your cheek; and your virginity, your old virginity, is like
one of our French withered pears: it looks ill, it eats drily. Marry,
'tis a withered pear; it was formerly better; marry, yet 'tis a
withered pear! Will you anything with it?

HELENA Not my virginity yet: 140
        There shall your master have a thousand loves,
        A mother, and a mistress, and a friend,
        A phoenix, captain, and an enemy,
        A guide, a goddess, and a sovereign,
        A counsellor, a traitress, and a dear;   145

135 wear] *Capell;* were F   140 virginity yet:] F; virginity; yet…*Hunter*   145 traitress] F2, Traitoresse F

131 **will** that will.
131 **gloss** appearance of newness.
131 **lying** remaining unused.
132 **Off with't** Get rid of it.
132 **Answer…request** Sell it while it is
marketable.
133–4 **richly…unsuitable** dressed richly but
unfashionably.
134 **brooch…toothpick** Each worn in the hat,
the latter denoting a travelled man, and evidently
no longer in fashion ('wear not now', as at 178)
when the play was written. Perhaps an obscene
quibble is intended, remembering 'breach' at 110.
135–6 **Your…your** An impersonal use of the
possessive to indicate people or things of a certain
type. Thus 'your pie' is equivalent to 'a pie', and
'your virginity' to 'this virginity we are talking
about'. The idiom was common in Shakespeare's
time. See Abbott 221 and *OED* Your 5b.
135 **date** (1) fruit, (2) age. The Elizabethans often
used dates rather than sugar for sweetening.
137 **ill** unappetising.
137 **eats drily** tastes dry.
139 **Will you** Will you do.
140 **Not…yet:** Presumably 'my' is emphasised,
as against the aspersions of Parolles. Editors
conjecture that something has dropped out here, but
a moment of meditative silence is often found
appropriate in performance.
141 **There** This adverb is supposed by most
editors to refer to the court (152). In grammatical
propriety it could refer also to 'my virginity', and

that is the reading proposed here. For a corroborative
view, see G. Wilson Knight, 'The third eye', in *The
Sovereign Flower*, 1958, p. 137.
141–50 **There…gossips** Editors generally suppose that Helena is recapitulating the stock business
of Elizabethan love poetry, and that it is this
business which will engross Bertram at court. Her
paradoxes and oxymorons seem, however, to be
descriptive of herself, and to anticipate the riddle
on which the resolution of the play depends. Like
Rosalind (in *AYLI* 3.2.141–8), she includes all
women in herself, not only Lucrece but Helen of
Troy, Cleopatra and Atalanta.
142 **A…friend** i.e. every kind of love,
enumerated in the four lines that follow. Editors
have been troubled by the bizarre-seeming collocation of 'mother' and 'mistress' and have tried to get
round it by making 'mother' mean something else,
e.g. 'mauther', dialect for 'maiden'. It is quite
possible, however, to hold that the collocation is
deliberate and emphatic: Helena presents a range of
possible emotional relationships.
142–5 **mother…dear** Helena lists, in the
language of courtly love, the titles of the lady that
Parolles's 'master' will serve.
143 **phoenix** one of a kind, the unique thing.
143 **enemy** By convention, the lady was foe as
well as friend.
145 **traitress** Like 'enemy' (143) 'traitress' perhaps anticipates Helena's frustration of Bertram's
later determination to put her away.

—

His humble ambition, proud humility,
His jarring, concord, and his discord, dulcet,
His faith, his sweet disaster; with a world
Of pretty, fond, adoptious christendoms
That blinking Cupid gossips. Now shall he –   150
I know not what he shall. God send him well!
The court's a learning-place, and he is one –

PAROLLES What one, i'faith?

HELENA That I wish well. 'Tis pity –

PAROLLES What's pity?   155

HELENA That wishing well had not a body in't
Which might be felt; that we, the poorer born,
Whose baser stars do shut us up in wishes,
Might with effects of them follow our friends
And show what we alone must think, which never   160
Returns us thanks.

Enter PAGE

PAGE Monsieur Parolles, my lord calls for you.   *[Exit]*

PAROLLES Little Helen, farewell. If I can remember thee, I will think
of thee at court.

HELENA Monsieur Parolles, you were born under a charitable star.   165

PAROLLES Under Mars I.

HELENA I especially think, under Mars.

PAROLLES Why under Mars?

HELENA The wars hath so kept you under that you must needs be born
under Mars.   170

---

147 jarring, concord…discord, dulcet] F, jarring concord…discord dulcet F4   152 one –] *Rowe;* one. F   162 SD]
Theobald; not in F   166 Under Mars I] F; Under Mars, ay *conj. Hunter*

---

146 humble…humility These ostensible disjunctions define the foolishly ambitious hero who craves only the 'help of mine own eyes' (2.3.100), but cannot estimate the riches that are his for the taking.

147 jarring A substantive, and making an unexpected complement with 'concord'.

147 dulcet soothing (of sounds).

148 disaster calamity (literally 'an unfavourable aspect of a star or planet'). And compare 5.3.112.

149 fond foolish.

149–50 adoptious…gossips christenings of adopted children for which blind ('blinking') Cupid stands godfather. Here 'gossips' is a verb. 'Christendoms' means Christians or Christian

countries, and also nicknames or Christian names which will continue the litany of 142–8.

151 send him well! give him good fortune!

152 learning-place school.

157 felt apprehended by the senses.

157 poorer of lowly station.

158 baser stars lowly fortunes.

158 shut…wishes confine us to mere wishing.

159 effects of them our actualised wishes.

160 show…think manifest what we can only think about or purpose.

161 Returns us thanks Brings us gratitude.

169 hath The singular verb following a plural subject is common Elizabethan usage.

169 under down.

PAROLLES When he was predominant.

HELENA When he was retrograde, I think rather.

PAROLLES Why think you so?

HELENA You go so much backward when you fight.

PAROLLES That's for advantage.   175

HELENA So is running away when fear proposes the safety. But the
composition that your valour and fear makes in you is a virtue of
a good wing, and I like the wear well.

PAROLLES I am so full of businesses I cannot answer thee acutely. I
will return perfect courtier, in the which my instruction shall serve   180
to naturalise thee, so thou wilt be capable of a courtier's counsel
and understand what advice shall thrust upon thee; else thou diest
in thine unthankfulness, and thine ignorance makes thee away.
Farewell. When thou hast leisure, say thy prayers; when thou hast
none, remember thy friends. Get thee a good husband, and use him   185
as he uses thee. So, farewell.   [*Exit*]

HELENA Our remedies oft in ourselves do lie,
Which we ascribe to heaven. The fated sky
Gives us free scope; only doth backward pull
Our slow designs when we ourselves are dull.   190
What power is it which mounts my love so high?
That makes me see, and cannot feed mine eye?
The mightiest space in fortune nature brings
To join like likes, and kiss like native things.

---

186 SD] F2; *not in* F   194 like likes] F4; like, likes F

171 **predominant** in the ascendant, and therefore most influential.

172 **retrograde** moving backwards from east to west, and therefore in an unfavourable direction and exerting a malignant influence.

175 **advantage** strategic reasons.

177 **composition** make-up of your character (with a quibble on 'truce').

177–8 **virtue...wing** i.e. the ability to fly, to run away rapidly; with a quibble on the ostentatious flaps or wings which presumably – as the next line suggests – distinguish Parolles's costume. 'Virtue' means characteristic excellence or property.

178 **wear** fashion (of your clothes).

180 **perfect** complete.

180 **which** i.e. which role.

181 **naturalise** familiarise.

181 **so** if.

181 **capable of** receptive to. 'Capable' also means 'sexually capable' and begins a train of obscene quibbles continuing with 'understand',

'thrust' and 'diest', all of which gloss a 'courtier's counsel'.

183 **makes thee away** destroys you.

184 **leisure** opportunity.

184–5 **when...friends** i.e. don't remember them (there being no opportunity).

185 **use** treat.

187–200 The transition to rhyme suggests the intervention of miraculous power.

188 **fated** fateful, determining our destiny.

190 **dull** inactive.

191 **mounts...high** makes my love aspire so far beyond itself.

192 **see** i.e. my love's object (which occupies a higher sphere, as at 77.

192 **feed** satisfy the longing of.

193–4 **The...things** Persons separated by the greatest disparity in worldly fortune are united by the agency of nature as if they were alike in fortune and inherently alike.

Impossible be strange attempts to those   195
That weigh their pains in sense, and do suppose
What hath been cannot be. Who ever strove
To show her merit that did miss her love?
The king's disease – my project may deceive me,
But my intents are fixed and will not leave me.   *Exit*   200

[1.2] *Flourish cornets. Enter the* KING OF FRANCE *with letters,* [*the* FIRST
and SECOND LORDS DUMAINE] *and divers* ATTENDANTS

KING The Florentines and Senoys are by th'ears,
       Have fought with equal fortune, and continue
       A braving war.
FIRST LORD   So 'tis reported, sir.
KING Nay, 'tis most credible. We here receive it
       A certainty, vouched from our cousin Austria,   5
       With caution, that the Florentine will move us
       For speedy aid; wherein our dearest friend
       Prejudicates the business, and would seem
       To have us make denial.
FIRST LORD   His love and wisdom,
       Approved so to your majesty, may plead   10
       For amplest credence.
KING   He hath armed our answer,

199 The king's disease –] *Rowe;* (The King's disease) F   Act 1, Scene 2   1.2] *Capell; not in* F   3, 9 SH FIRST LORD]
Rowe (subst.); 1. Lo.G. F   4–5 it A] *Capell;* it, A F

195 strange extraordinary.

196 That…sense Who estimate rationally the arduous nature of the undertaking.

196–7 do…be think those feats impossible which have been accomplished before.

198 miss fail to win.

200 fixed This play is notable for suggesting unlikely associations through the recurrence of words and phrases. Helena's 'fixed intents' recall the 'fixed evils' (90) that sit so becomingly on Parolles.

Act 1, Scene 2

1.2 Editors, following Capell, locate the scene in the King's palace in Paris.

0 SD *Flourish cornets* Sound a fanfare of horns. In modern productions the King often enters on a litter or in a wheel-chair.

1 Senoys People of Siena.

1 by th'ears quarrelling.

3 braving full of mutual defiance.

3 SH FIRST LORD The speech heading in F reads: 1. Lo.G., leading to the conjecture (e.g. by Evans) that 'G' is perhaps an actor's initial, as also 'E' at 15.

4 We The royal plural.

5 from by.

5 our cousin Austria my fellow sovereign the Duke of Austria.

6 Florentine The Duke of Florence, or possibly the Florentines of 1.

6 move importune.

7 our dearest friend Presumably (but for no apparent reason) the Duke of Austria.

8 Prejudicates Prejudges.

10 Approved Fully attested.

11 credence belief.

11 armed armoured; i.e. the King will be obdurate in his denial of Florence.

And Florence is denied before he comes.
Yet for our gentlemen that mean to see
The Tuscan service, freely have they leave
To stand on either part.

SECOND LORD   It well may serve   15
A nursery to our gentry, who are sick
For breathing and exploit.

KING   What's he comes here?

Enter BERTRAM, LAFEW, *and* PAROLLES

FIRST LORD It is the Count Rossillion, my good lord,
Young Bertram.

KING   Youth, thou bear'st thy father's face;
Frank nature, rather curious than in haste,   20
Hath well composed thee. Thy father's moral parts
Mayst thou inherit too! Welcome to Paris.

BERTRAM My thanks and duty are your majesty's.

KING I would I had that corporal soundness now
As when thy father and myself in friendship   25
First tried our soldiership! He did look far
Into the service of the time, and was
Discipled of the bravest. He lasted long,
But on us both did haggish age steal on,
And wore us out of act. It much repairs me   30
To talk of your good father. In his youth
He had the wit which I can well observe
Today in our young lords; but they may jest
Till their own scorn return to them unnoted

---

15 SH SECOND LORD] *Rowe (subst.)*; 2 *Lo.E.* F   18 SH FIRST LORD] *Rowe (subst.)*; 1. *Lor.G.* F   18 Rossillion] F2
(Rosillion); *Rosignoll* F

13 **for** with respect to.
13 **see** participate in.
15 **stand...part** Remarkably, the King is inviting his nobles to fight on either side.
15–16 **serve A nursery** do duty as a training school.
16–17 **sick For** desirous of.
17 **breathing** military exercise.
18 **Rossillion** The F reading 'Rosignoll' recalls French *rossignol*, variously a nightingale or a picklock – or, in the compound *rossignol d'Arcadie*, a braying jackass.
20 **Frank** Liberal, bountiful.
20 **curious** (1) fastidious, (2) working carefully.

21 **parts** qualities.
25 **As** That I had.
26 **look far** see deeply.
27 **service** military service.
27–8 **was Discipled of** (1) had as his pupils, or possibly (2) was apprenticed to.
29 **haggish** repulsive (as of a hag); that makes one haggard.
30 **act** fitness for action.
30 **repairs** restores.
34 **scorn...unnoted** Perhaps 'scornful taunts or jests are made so habitual by repetition as to be unremarked even by themselves'. Scornful and disdainful manners were the less attractive aspects

Ere they can hide their levity in honour. 35
So like a courtier, contempt nor bitterness
Were in his pride or sharpness; if they were,
His equal had awaked them, and his honour,
Clock to itself, knew the true minute when
Exception bid him speak, and at this time 40
His tongue obeyed his hand. Who were below him
He used as creatures of another place,
And bowed his eminent top to their low ranks,
Making them proud of his humility,
In their poor praise he humbled. Such a man 45
Might be a copy to these younger times;
Which followed well, would demonstrate them now
But goers backward.

BERTRAM His good remembrance, sir,
Lies richer in your thoughts than on his tomb.
So in approof lives not his epitaph 50
As in your royal speech.

KING Would I were with him. He would always say –
Methinks I hear him now; his plausive words
He scattered not in ears, but grafted them,
To grow there and to bear – 'Let me not live' – 55
This his good melancholy oft began,
On the catastrophe and heel of pastime,
When it was out – 'Let me not live', quoth he,

of *sprezzatura*, the courtly self-possession much cultivated in Renaissance Italy and imitated elsewhere in Europe.

35 hide…honour mark their ignoble jesting by honourable activity.

36 courtier The epitome of courtesy, as illustrated, for example, in Castiglione's *Courtier* or in Spenser's *Faerie Queene*, VI.

36 contempt neither contempt.

36 bitterness asperity.

37 sharpness i.e. of wit.

38 equal i.e. in rank.

39 Clock to itself i.e. requiring no prompter but itself to tell him when to respond.

39 true minute exact moment.

40 Exception Taking exception.

41 obeyed his hand said no more than his hand was willing to answer for.

41 Who Those who.

41 below him i.e. in rank.

42 of another place i.e. as if they were from another country rather than of another social rank.

43 top head.

45 In…humbled Perhaps 'before whose poor praises he humbled himself'. Otherwise the words may repeat the effect of the previous line: 'he humbled himself to praise the poor'.

46 copy example.

47 Which Can refer to 'copy' or 'times'. The former seems preferable.

48 goers backward If 'Which' refers to 'copy' and 'them' to 'times' (i.e. men of these 'younger times'), this will mean 'followers of the past'.

50 So…epitaph The truth of his epitaph is nowhere so fully confirmed.

53 plausive pleasing.

54 ears With a quibble on the spike or head of corn.

54 grafted planted deeply.

55 bear bear fruit.

57 catastrophe latter end.

58 out (1) finished, but also (2) out at heel. The word refers proleptically to the snuffed candle in 59.

'After my flame lacks oil, to be the snuff
Of younger spirits, whose apprehensive senses   60
All but new things disdain; whose judgements are
Mere fathers of their garments; whose constancies
Expire before their fashions.' This he wished.
I, after him, do after him wish too,
Since I nor wax nor honey can bring home,   65
I quickly were dissolvèd from my hive,
To give some labourers room.
SECOND LORD   You're loved, sir;
They that least lend it you shall lack you first.
KING I fill a place, I know't. How long is't, count,
Since the physician at your father's died?   70
He was much famed.
BERTRAM   Some six months since, my lord.
KING If he were living, I would try him yet –
Lend me an arm – the rest have worn me out
With several applications. Nature and sickness
Debate it at their leisure. Welcome, count,   75
My son's no dearer.
BERTRAM   Thank your majesty.
                        [Exeunt] Flourish

[**1.3**] *Enter* COUNTESS, [RINALDO, *the*] *Steward, and* [LAVATCH, *the*]
Clown

COUNTESS I will now hear. What say you of this gentlewoman?
RINALDO Madam, the care I have had to even your content, I wish

---

67 SH SECOND LORD] *Rowe (subst.); L.2.E.* F   76 SD *Exeunt*] *Rowe; Exit* F   Act 1, Scene 3   1.3] *Capell; not in* F

59 snuff The burnt-out part of the wick which, if not trimmed off, prevents the lower part of the wick (analogically 'younger spirits') from burning properly.

60 apprehensive quick perceiving. Here pejorative: 'too quick perceiving' and therefore inconstant.

62 Mere...garments i.e. productive of nothing but new fashions.

63 before their fashions even before the fashions change.

64 after...him following him (in time), and agreeing with his views.

66 dissolvèd separated.

67 labourers i.e. as opposed to drones.

68 it The reference is ambiguous. It may mean 'room' (67), anticipating 'place' (69); or it may mean 'love', from 'loved' (67).

68 lack feel the want of.

73 rest i.e. of the physicians.

74 several applications separate treatments (peculiar to each physician).

75 it i.e. the question of his survival.

Act 1, Scene 3

1.3 Editors, following Capell, locate the scene in the Count's palace at Rossillion.

2 even make even, satisfy.

might be found in the calendar of my past endeavours, for then we
wound our modesty, and make foul the clearness of our deservings,
when of ourselves we publish them.   5

COUNTESS What does this knave here? Get you gone, sirrah. The
complaints I have heard of you I do not all believe; 'tis my slowness
that I do not, for I know you lack not folly to commit them, and
have ability enough to make such knaveries yours.

LAVATCH 'Tis not unknown to you, madam, I am a poor fellow.   10

COUNTESS Well, sir.

LAVATCH No, madam, 'tis not so well that I am poor, though many
of the rich are damned, but if I may have your ladyship's good will
to go to the world, Isbel the woman and I will do as we may.

COUNTESS Wilt thou needs be a beggar?   15

LAVATCH I do beg your good will in this case.

COUNTESS In what case?

LAVATCH In Isbel's case and mine own. Service is no heritage, and I
think I shall never have the blessing of God till I have issue a'my
body; for they say barnes are blessings.   20

COUNTESS Tell me thy reason why thou wilt marry.

LAVATCH My poor body, madam, requires it. I am driven on by the
flesh, and he must needs go that the devil drives.

COUNTESS Is this all your worship's reason?

LAVATCH Faith, madam, I have other holy reasons, such as they are.   25

COUNTESS May the world know them?

LAVATCH I have been, madam, a wicked creature, as you and all flesh
and blood are, and indeed I do marry that I may repent.

COUNTESS Thy marriage, sooner than thy wickedness.

---

12 'tis...many] *As prose, Capell; as verse, F*   14 I] F2; *w* F

---

3 **calendar** record.

4 **make...clearness** sully the lustre.

6 **sirrah** Form of address used to an inferior.

7 **all** altogether.

14 **go...world** i.e. accept the ways of the world
and the flesh, by marrying. Compare *Ado*
2.1.218–19.

14 **woman** servingwoman.

14 **do...may** do as well as we can; with an
obscene quibble on 'do' = 'have sexual intercourse'.

16 **case** With a quibble on 'vagina'.

18 **Service...heritage** i.e. because servants
do not inherit estate. The expression is proverbial
(see Tilley S253).

19 **issue** children.

19 **a'** of (as again at 30).

20 **they say** i.e. the expression being proverbial.

20 **barnes** bairns, children.

23 **he...drives** More proverbial wisdom.
See Tilley D278.

25 **other holy reasons** 'other' because procreation is commended in the marriage-service; but
'other' also because Lavatch puns obscenely on
'holy' and 'reasons' = 'raisings' (these two words
being nearly identical in Shakespeare's pronunciation).

28 **marry...repent** Alluding to the proverb
'Marry in haste and repent at leisure', as the
Countess's rejoinder makes clear.

LAVATCH I am out a'friends, madam, and I hope to have friends for my   30
    wife's sake.
COUNTESS Such friends are thine enemies, knave.
LAVATCH Y'are shallow, madam, in great friends, for the knaves come
    to do that for me which I am a-weary of. He that ears my land spares
    my team, and gives me leave to in the crop. If I be his cuckold,   35
    he's my drudge. He that comforts my wife is the cherisher of my
    flesh and blood; he that cherishes my flesh and blood loves my flesh
    and blood; he that loves my flesh and blood is my friend: *ergo*, he
    that kisses my wife is my friend. If men could be contented to be
    what they are, there were no fear in marriage, for young Charbon   40
    the puritan and old Poysam the papist, howsome'er their hearts are
    severed in religion, their heads are both one: they may jowl horns
    together like any deer i'th'herd.
COUNTESS Wilt thou ever be a foul-mouthed and calumnious knave?
LAVATCH A prophet I, madam, and I speak the truth the next way: 45
        For I the ballad will repeat,
           Which men full true shall find:
        Your marriage comes by destiny,
           Your cuckoo sings by kind.
COUNTESS Get you gone, sir, I'll talk with you more anon.   50
RINALDO May it please you, madam, that he bid Helen come to you.
    Of her I am to speak.
COUNTESS Sirrah, tell my gentlewoman I would speak with her – Helen,
    I mean.
LAVATCH   'Was this fair face the cause', quoth she,   55

---

31 wife's] wives F   33 madam,] F3; Madam F   33 in] F; e'en *Hanmer*   46–9] *As verse, Rowe³ (subst.); as prose,* F

33 shallow superficial (i.e. your understanding of real friendship is slight).

34 ears ploughs (resuming the King's image from husbandry in the preceding scene, 54–5).

35 in harvest, bring in.

35–6 If...drudge Another proverb.

38 *ergo* therefore, Lavatch uses the Latin word to conclude his comic version of a *Sorites*, a device in logic by which a series of linked propositions is used (often with an ingenious trick) to lead to a conclusion which refers back to the original proposition.

40 what they are i.e. cuckolds.

40 Charbon Good flesh (*chair bonne*).

41 Poysam Fish (French, *poisson*). Appropriate to the papist or Catholic who practised fasting as opposed to the puritan who contemned it.

41 howsome'er howsoever.

42 both one i.e. in bearing horns, the mark of the cuckold. Hunter sees this as a comic inversion of the proverb 'Hearts may agree though heads differ' (Tilley H341).

42 jowl knock.

44 ever always.

45 next nearest, most direct (the prophet being divinely inspired).

48 Your...destiny i.e. the married man is a cuckold by destiny.

49 kind nature.

55 this fair face i.e. Helen of Troy's, suggested to Lavatch by the Countess's summoning of Helena at 53.

55 she Perhaps Helen is the speaker, perhaps Hecuba, wife of King Priam of Troy and the mother of Paris.

> 'Why the Grecians sackèd Troy?
>
> Fond done, done fond,
>
> Was this King Priam's joy?'
>
> With that she sighèd as she stood,
>
> With that she sighèd as she stood, 60
>
> And gave this sentence then:
>
> 'Among nine bad if one be good,
>
> Among nine bad if one be good,
>
> There's yet one good in ten.'

COUNTESS What, one good in ten? You corrupt the song, sirrah. 65

LAVATCH One good woman in ten, madam, which is a purifying a'th'song. Would God would serve the world so all the year! we'd find no fault with the tithe-woman if I were the parson. One in ten, quoth'a? And we might have a good woman born but ore every blazing star or at an earthquake, 'twould mend the lottery well; a 70 man may draw his heart out ere 'a pluck one.

COUNTESS You'll be gone, sir knave, and do as I command you?

LAVATCH That man should be at woman's command, and yet no hurt done! Though honesty be no puritan, yet it will do no hurt; it will wear the surplice of humility over the black gown of a big heart. 75 I am going, forsooth. The business is for Helen to come hither.

Exit

COUNTESS Well, now.

---

57 done fond] *Rowe;* done, fond F   59 stood,] *Var. 73;* stood, *bis* F   60] *After Var. 73; not in* F   61–4] *As verse, Rowe; as prose,* F   69 ore] F; o'er *Rowe;* or *Capell;* for *Craig*   72 be gone] F2; begone F

---

57 **Fond** Foolishly.

58 **this** Helen, or possibly the rape of Helen by Paris which assured the destruction of Troy.

60 **With...stood** The Folio omits this line and follows the preceding line with *bis* (Latin, 'twice'), indicating that the verses were set to music.

61 **sentence** judgement.

65 **corrupt the song** Possibly by inverting the optimistic sense of the original ballad which editors suppose to lie behind these lines. In the original they may have read: 'Among nine good if one be bad...There's yet nine good in ten', where the ten refers to the sons of Priam and the one to Paris.

66 **One...purifying** i.e. since the original song, which makes no mention of women, has now been amended to include one good woman.

67–8 **we'd...parson** i.e. if the proportion of good women were as high as a tithe or one in ten, the parson (who was entitled to the tenth part of farm produce) would be as satisfied as with his tithe-pig.

69 **quoth'a** did he say.

69 **And** If.

69 **ore** ere (i.e. in conjunction with).

70 **blazing star** comet or nova (the type of a prodigious event, like 'earthquake').

70 **mend the lottery** improve the odds (of finding a good woman).

71 **pluck one** draw a good woman.

73 **at woman's command** As opposed to the Pauline notion that the man is head of the woman.

74–5 **Though...heart** i.e. no matter that I am not over-strict in moral matters; I will conceal my pride under the appearance of humility. Analogically, the puritan minister hides his unlawful black Genevan gown, the garb of the Calvinist, beneath the canonical surplice or loose-fitting white gown of the Church of England. Perhaps a bawdy quibble is intended, 'honesty' meaning 'chastity', 'hurt' the loss of chastity, and 'no puritan' suggesting the Catholic espousal of celibacy, which the puritans condemned.

RINALDO I know, madam, you love your gentlewoman entirely.

COUNTESS Faith, I do. Her father bequeathed her to me, and she
herself, without other advantage, may lawfully make title to as much   80
love as she finds. There is more owing her than is paid, and more
shall be paid her than she'll demand.

RINALDO Madam, I was very late more near her than I think she wished
me. Alone she was, and did communicate to herself her own words
to her own ears; she thought, I dare vow for her, they touched not   85
any stranger sense. Her matter was, she loved your son. Fortune,
she said, was no goddess, that had put such difference betwixt their
two estates; Love no god, that would not extend his might only
where qualities were level; [Diana no] queen of virgins, that would
suffer her poor knight surprised without rescue in the first assault   90
or ransom afterward. This she delivered in the most bitter touch
of sorrow that e'er I heard virgin exclaim in, which I held my duty
speedily to acquaint you withal, sithence in the loss that may
happen, it concerns you something to know it.

COUNTESS You have discharged this honestly, keep it to yourself. Many   95
likelihoods informed me of this before, which hung so tottering in
the balance that I could neither believe nor misdoubt. Pray you
leave me. Stall this in your bosom, and I thank you for your honest
care. I will speak with you further anon.

Exit [Rinaldo, the] Steward

Enter HELENA

Even so it was with me when I was young.   100

---

89 level; Diana no queen] *Theobald;* leuell, Queene F   99 SD *Exit Steward*] *Placed as* F; *following 108, Singer*
100 Even] *Singer; Old Cou.* Even F

80 **herself** in herself.
80 **advantage** interest (as on money, and
pursuing the figure begun with 'bequeathed' (79)).
80 **make title** to claim.
82 **demand** ask; not peremptorily as in the
modern sense of 'demand' (used again at 2.1.21).
83 **late** lately.
86 **any stranger sense** anyone else's ears.
86 **matter** subject.
87 **no goddess** i.e. because the difference in
social station between Helena and Bertram is not
divinely ordained but turns on chance. For
reflections on Fortune, see pp. 18–21 above.
88 **extend his might** employ his power.
88 **only** except.
89 **qualities were level** the social positions
were the same.

89 **Diana no** This interpolation is Theobald's
and clarifies the F reading, which otherwise makes
no sense. Hunter compares *Ado* 5.3.12–13.
90 **suffer** allow.
90 **knight** i.e. servant of the goddess of chastity.
90 **surprised** i.e. surprised to be taken captive.
91 **touch** note (as in music).
92 **exclaim** complain.
92 **which** which thing.
93 **withal** with.
93 **sithence** since.
94 **something** to some extent.
96 **tottering** waveringly.
97 **misdoubt** doubt.
98 **Stall** Enclose.
100 **Even so** The Countess is observing Helena's
melancholy entrance.

If ever we are nature's, these are ours. This thorn
Doth to our rose of youth rightly belong;
Our blood to us, this to our blood is born.
It is the show and seal of nature's truth,
Where love's strong passion is impressed in youth.   105
By our remembrances of days foregone,
Such were our faults, or then we thought them none.
Her eye is sick on't; I observe her now.

HELENA What is your pleasure, madam?

COUNTESS   You know, Helen,
I am a mother to you.   110

HELENA Mine honourable mistress.

COUNTESS   Nay, a mother,
Why not a mother? When I said 'a mother',
Methought you saw a serpent. What's in 'mother',
That you start at it? I say I am your mother,
And put you in the catalogue of those   115
That were enwombèd mine. 'Tis often seen
Adoption strives with nature, and choice breeds
A native slip to us from foreign seeds.
You ne'er oppressed me with a mother's groan,
Yet I express to you a mother's care.   120
God's mercy, maiden! does it curd thy blood
To say I am thy mother? What's the matter,
That this distempered messenger of wet,
The many-coloured Iris, rounds thine eye?
– Why, that you are my daughter?

102 rightly] *Rowe;* righlie F   102 belong;] *Theobald;* belong F   105 youth.] *After Rowe;* youth, F   109, 111, 126, 132, 139 SH COUNTESS] *Old.Cou.* F   109–10 You...you] *As Capell; as one line* F   111–12 Nay...'a mother'] *After Pope; as one line* F

101 A hexameter line.
101 these i.e. tokens of love.
103 blood i.e. as we are born with blood a passionate disposition is born in our blood. There may be a pun on 'borne' = carried in.
104 show sign.
105 impressed As by a seal.
107 then...none at the time we did not consider them faults.
108 on't with it.
108 observe see through.
116 enwombèd mine born as my children.
117 strives competes.

117–18 choice...seeds we choose a scion or slip grown from someone else's seeds and graft it to our own stock, where our affectionate choice makes it appear to have grown there naturally.
119 a mother's groan i.e. childbirth.
123 distempered sick, afflicted (as when the weather is bad or the eyes tearstained). Compare *Lucrece* 1586–7.
123 messenger of wet tear.
124 Iris (1) rainbow, (2) Iris, goddess of the rainbow.
124 rounds encircles. Helena has tearful rings about her eyes through crying.

HELENA   That I am not.   125

COUNTESS I say I am your mother.

HELENA   Pardon, madam;
     The Count Rossillion cannot be my brother;
     I am from humble, he from honoured name;
     No note upon my parents, his all noble.
     My master, my dear lord he is, and I   130
     His servant live, and will his vassal die.
     He must not be my brother.

COUNTESS   Nor I your mother?

HELENA You are my mother, madam; would you were –
     So that my lord your son were not my brother –
     Indeed my mother! Or were you both our mothers,   135
     I care no more for than I do for heaven,
     So I were not his sister. Can 't no other,
     But, I your daughter, he must be my brother?

COUNTESS Yes, Helen, you might be my daughter-in-law.
     God shield you mean it not! 'Daughter' and 'mother'   140
     So strive upon your pulse. What, pale again?
     My fear hath catched your fondness! Now I see
     The mystery of your loneliness, and find
     Your salt tears' head. Now to all sense 'tis gross:
     You love my son. Invention is ashamed,   145
     Against the proclamation of thy passion,
     To say thou dost not: therefore tell me true,
     But tell me then 'tis so; for look, thy cheeks
     Confess it, t'one to th'other, and thine eyes

---

133 mother, madam; would you were –] *Rowe³ (subst.)*; mother Madam, would you were F   143 loneliness] *Theobald;* louelinesse F   149 t'one to th'other] F2; 'ton tooth to th'other F

125 That…not Meaning both 'That I am not your daughter' and (since the terms were interchangeable in Elizabethan usage) 'That I am not your daughter-in-law'.

129 note distinguishing mark.

129 parents antecedents.

135 both our mothers mother of us both.

136 An understated way of saying how very much Helena would wish to be daughter to the Countess – but with the reservation expressed in the next line.

137 Can 't no other Can it not be otherwise.

138 But, I But that I being.

140 shield forbid. (The Countess is playing with Helena.)

141 So strive upon Equally agitate.

142 fear…fondness suspicion has found out your foolishness and your love ('fondness' had both meanings).

143 *loneliness keeping apart. The Folio reading 'louelinesse' is no doubt occasioned by the transposing of 'n' and 'u' – i.e. 'v' – one of the commonest errors.

144 head source.

144 sense perception.

144 gross obvious (as at 150).

145 Invention The ability to fabricate lies.

146 Against In the face of.

148 then in such case (i.e. if you are going to speak the truth).

149 t'one the one. F2 corrects a manifest slip in F.

See it so grossly shown in thy behaviours   150
That in their kind they speak it. Only sin
And hellish obstinacy tie thy tongue,
That truth should be suspected. Speak, is't so?
If it be so, you have wound a goodly clew;
If it be not, forswear't; howe'er, I charge thee,   155
As heaven shall work in me for thine avail,
To tell me truly.

HELENA   Good madam, pardon me!

COUNTESS Do you love my son?

HELENA   Your pardon, noble mistress!

COUNTESS Love you my son?

HELENA   Do not you love him, madam?

COUNTESS Go not about; my love hath in't a bond   160
Whereof the world takes note. Come, come, disclose
The state of your affection, for your passions
Have to the full appeached.

HELENA   Then I confess
Here on my knee, before high heaven and you,
That before you, and next unto high heaven,   165
I love your son.
My friends were poor but honest, so's my love.
Be not offended, for it hurts not him
That he is loved of me; I follow him not
By any token of presumptuous suit,   170
Nor would I have him till I do deserve him,
Yet never know how that desert should be.
I know I love in vain, strive against hope;

---

155 forswear't; howe'er, I] *Theobald;* forsweare't how ere I F; forswear't: how ere I F3   161 disclose] F3; disclose: F

---

151 **in their kind** according to their nature (i.e. by weeping).

151–3 **Only...That** i.e. the only reason...is that.

153 **suspected** (1) confounded, (2) called in question.

154 **goodly clew** fine ball of twine (i.e. you have made a mess of things). Proverbial, and anticipating the 'mingled yarn' of 4.3.60.

155 **forswear't** deny it.

155 **howe'er** but whatever you do.

156 **thine avail** your benefit.

160 **Go not about** Don't quibble (by talking evasively).

160 **bond** maternal bond.

161 **Whereof...note** Which society recognises.

162 **affection** feeling.

163 **appeached** informed (against you).

165 **before you** more than you.

167 **friends** relatives.

167 **honest** honourable.

169 **follow him not** i.e. as by sending letters after him – or, alternatively, by pursuing him before he left Rossillion.

170 **By** With.

172 **never know** i.e. never can know.

Yet in this captious and intenible sieve
I still pour in the waters of my love   175
And lack not to lose still. Thus Indian-like,
Religious in mine error, I adore
The sun, that looks upon his worshipper,
But knows of him no more. My dearest madam,
Let not your hate encounter with my love   180
For loving where you do; but if yourself,
Whose agèd honour cites a virtuous youth,
Did ever in so true a flame of liking
Wish chastely, and love dearly, that your Dian
Was both herself and Love, O then give pity   185
To her whose state is such that cannot choose
But lend and give where she is sure to lose;
That seeks not to find that her search implies,
But riddle-like lives sweetly where she dies.

COUNTESS Had you not lately an intent – speak truly –   190
        To go to Paris?
HELENA   Madam, I had.
COUNTESS   Wherefore? tell true.
HELENA I will tell truth, by grace itself I swear.
        You know my father left me some prescriptions
        Of rare and proved effects, such as his reading

---

174 intenible] F2; intemible F   174 sieve] F3, Siue F, Sive F2   176 lose] F4, loose F   187 lose] F4, loose F

174 captious Shakespeare apparently plays upon the usual sense 'deceitful' and 'capacious'. *OED* gives only this instance of 'captious' = capacious.

174 *intenible F2's reading, meaning 'unretentive, not holding'. F's reading 'intemible' is sometimes retained and taken to mean 'incapable of being poured out'.

175 still continually.

176 lack...still (1) fail not to continue losing (as the sieve is unretentive), (2) lack not reserves to continue squandering love.

176 Indian-like Like the American Indians; generically, 'heathenish'.

179 no more i.e. than to look on him.

180 encounter with oppose in combat.

182 agèd honour honourable old age.

182 cites gives evidence of.

183 liking love. Compare *Ado* 1.1.298–300.

184 Wish...dearly Desire to be both sexually passionate and chaste (faithful) at the same time. A recurring to the oxymorons of 1.1.141–8.

184–5 your...Love i.e. the Diana you worshipped was both the goddess of chastity and the goddess of love. ('Love' is without a capital in F.)

186 state Helena may refer both to her state as lover and to her status in society.

186 that as.

186–7 cannot...lose has no choice but to render her affections with no hope of return.

188–9 i.e. Helena has no prospect of finding the object of her search (Bertram's love), but will live in the sweetness of disappointed expectation. There may be a suggestion of the Phoenix riddle of love's dying into life – Helena finds solace even in the death of her aspirations. Later in the play Helena's renewed quest takes a different riddling form (3.2.50–3).

188 that what.

192 grace the grace of God.

And manifest experience had collected   195
For general sovereignty; and that he willed me
In heedfull'st reservation to bestow them,
As notes whose faculties inclusive were
More than they were in note. Amongst the rest,
There is a remedy, approved, set down,   200
To cure the desperate languishings whereof
The king is rendered lost.

COUNTESS   This was your motive
For Paris, was it? Speak.

HELENA My lord your son made me to think of this;
Else Paris, and the medicine, and the king,   205
Had from the conversation of my thoughts
Haply been absent then.

COUNTESS   But think you, Helen,
If you should tender your supposèd aid,
He would receive it? He and his physicians
Are of a mind; he, that they cannot help him,   210
They, that they cannot help. How shall they credit
A poor unlearnèd virgin, when the schools,
Embowelled of their doctrine, have left off
The danger to itself?

HELENA   There's something in't
More than my father's skill, which was the great'st   215
Of his profession, that his good receipt
Shall for my legacy be sanctified
By th'luckiest stars in heaven, and would your honour
But give me leave to try success, I'd venture

202–3 This...Speak] *As Capell; as one line,* F   **203** it? Speak.] *Var. 73;* it, speake? F   **207** Haply] Happily F

---

195 manifest (1) open to the eye, (2) empirical (i.e. deriving from a knowledge of manifestations or symptoms, and contrasting with 'reading').

196 general sovereignty universal panaceas, remedies for every disease.

196 willed desired.

197 Most carefully to reserve them for use.

198 notes prescriptions.

198 faculties inclusive comprehensive powers.

199 in note recognised to be.

200 approved tested.

202 rendered lost said to be dying.

203 For i.e. for going to.

206 conversation back-and-forth movement.

208 tender offer.

208 supposèd supposedly efficacious.

210 of a mind agreed.

211 credit believe.

213 Embowelled Disembowelled, emptied.

213 left off abandoned.

214 danger to itself disease to its own course.

216 that so that (i.e. by virtue of the 'something in't').

216 receipt prescription.

217 sanctified blessed.

218 luckiest beneficent (i.e. those conferring luck).

219 try success test the outcome.

The well-lost life of mine on his grace's cure   220
By such a day, an hour.

COUNTESS   Dost thou believe't?

HELENA Ay, madam, knowingly.

COUNTESS Why, Helen, thou shalt have my leave and love,
Means and attendants, and my loving greetings
To those of mine in court. I'll stay at home   225
And pray God's blessing into thy attempt.
Be gone tomorrow, and be sure of this,
What I can help thee to thou shalt not miss.

Exeunt

2.[1] *Enter the* KING *with divers young* LORDS *[with the* FIRST *and*
SECOND LORDS DUMAINE] *taking leave for the Florentine war;*
*[*BERTRAM*] Count Rossillion, and* PAROLLES. *Flourish cornets*

KING Farewell, young lords, these warlike principles
Do not throw from you; and you, my lords, farewell.
Share the advice betwixt you; if both gain all,
The gift doth stretch itself as 'tis received,
And is enough for both.

FIRST LORD   'Tis our hope, sir,   5
After well-entered soldiers, to return
And find your grace in health.

KING No, no, it cannot be; and yet my heart
Will not confess he owes the malady
That doth my life besiege. Farewell, young lords,   10
Whether I live or die, be you the sons

221 an] F; and F2   227 Be gone] F3; Begon F   Act 2, Scene 1   2.1] *Rowe; Actus Secundus.* F   3 you;] *Rowe;* you, F
3 gain all,] *Johnson;* gaine, all F   5 SH FIRST LORD] *After Rowe; Lord.G.* F

220 **well-lost** i.e. worth losing in such a cause.
221 **such a** a specified.
222 **knowingly** knowing what I am doing.
225 **those of mine** my friends (or relations).
226 **into** upon.
228 **miss** lack.

Act 2, Scene 1
2.1 Editors, following Capell, locate the scene in
the King's palace in Paris.
0 SD The King takes leave of two parties, who
may leave by different stage-doors.

1 **warlike principles** military maxims.
2 **and you** The King turns from the first group
of lords, bound perhaps for Florence, to a second
group, bound for Siena.
3 **gain all** profit fully from (my advice).
4 **gift…received** advice will expand to the
degree that it is accepted.
6 **well-entered** having become experienced as.
Abbott (418) cites as a foreign (Latin) idiom.
9 **owes** possesses.

Of worthy Frenchmen. Let higher Italy
(Those bated that inherit but the fall
Of the last monarchy) see that you come
Not to woo honour, but to wed it, when   15
The bravest questant shrinks. Find what you seek,
That fame may cry you loud. I say farewell.
FIRST LORD Health, at your bidding, serve your majesty!
KING Those girls of Italy, take heed of them.
They say our French lack language to deny   20
If they demand. Beware of being captives
Before you serve.
BOTH LORDS   Our hearts receive your warnings.
KING Farewell. – Come hither to me.
FIRST LORD O my sweet lord, that you will stay behind us!
PAROLLES 'Tis not his fault, the spark.
SECOND LORD   O, 'tis brave wars!   25
PAROLLES Most admirable! I have seen those wars.
BERTRAM I am commanded here, and kept a coil with,
'Too young' and 'the next year' and ''tis too early'.
PAROLLES And thy mind stand to't, boy, steal away bravely.

---

13 bated] F; bastards *Hanmer*   15 it, when] F; it; when *Pope*   18 SH FIRST LORD] *Rowe; L.G.* F; *Second Lord / Rowe*[3]
22 SH BOTH LORDS] *After Capell; Bo.* F   23] *As* E; SD *Exit / Pope;* SD *To Attendants / Theobald;* SD *retires to a couch
/ Capell*   24, 34, 37 SH FIRST LORD] *Rowe; Lo.G.* F.   25, 35, 38 SH SECOND LORD] *Rowe; 2.Lo.E.* F

---

12 **worthy** i.e. be you worthy sons.
12 **higher** Referring either to social class (as perhaps in *Lear* 3.6.111: 'high noises') or geographical location – mountainous Tuscany where both Florence and Siena are located.
13–14 **Those...monarchy** This often-discussed passage turns partly on the sense of 'bated'. (1) Those dejected ones ('bated' being understood as a substantive) who possess only the poor remains of (?) the Holy Roman Empire (the last of the canonical four monarchies or empires familiar to Shakespeare's time from Dan. 2.40). (2) Those of higher Italy 'excepted' who inherit only (but do not earn) their places. The second reading has the merit of enforcing the antithesis, familiar from the opening scene, of acquired and inherited virtue. See e.g. 1.1.34–5. However, line 13 is partly autonomous when spoken, and suggests the reproving of those who inherit only our fallen condition.
15 **woo** flirt with.
15 **wed it** make it your own.
16 **questant** seeker after honour.
16 **shrinks** With a pun on detumescence. Here, as often, achieving is commended, and the sexual

suggestion associates the King with Parolles, 2.3.256–60.
17 **cry you loud** proclaim you loudly.
19 **girls of Italy** Proverbial for their importunate charms.
21 **captives** slaves to love.
22 **Before you serve** i.e. before you are 'well-entered' (6). The King mingles the language of war and the language of love.
23 **Come hither** The King presumably retires to a corner of the stage with some of the lords, leaving others to converse with Bertram and Parolles.
24 **sweet** dear. Used impartially of either sex – as again at 38.
25 **spark** gay blade. As again at 39.
25 **brave** splendid.
26 **seen** experienced.
27 **commanded** ordered to remain.
27 **kept...with** made a fuss about.
29 **And** If.
29 **stand to't** be resolute.
29 **bravely** becomingly. But perhaps with play upon 'courageously' and 'showily'.

BERTRAM I shall stay here the forehorse to a smock,   30
    Creaking my shoes on the plain masonry,
    Till honour be bought up, and no sword worn
    But one to dance with! By heaven, I'll steal away.
FIRST LORD There's honour in the theft.
PAROLLES   Commit it, count.
SECOND LORD I am your accessory, and so farewell.   35
BERTRAM I grow to you, and our parting is a tortured body.
FIRST LORD Farewell, captain.
SECOND LORD Sweet Monsieur Parolles!
PAROLLES Noble heroes! my sword and yours are kin. Good sparks and
    lustrous, a word, good metals: you shall find in the regiment of the   40
    Spinii one Captain Spurio, with his cicatrice, an emblem of war,
    here on his sinister cheek; it was this very sword entrenched it. Say
    to him I live, and observe his reports for me.
FIRST LORD We shall, noble captain.
PAROLLES Mars dote on you for his novices!   45

                                      [Exeunt Lords]
    What will ye do?
BERTRAM Stay: the king.
PAROLLES Use a more spacious ceremony to the noble lords; you have
    restrained yourself within the list of too cold an adieu. Be more

---

41 with his cicatrice, an] *Theobald;* his sicatrice, with an F   44 SH FIRST LORD] *Rowe; Lo.G.* F   45 SD] *Theobald (after*
49); Capell (after 47); not in F   47 Stay:] F2; Stay F

30 forehorse...smock leading horse of a team
driven by a woman.
31 plain masonry i.e. the smooth, paved floors
of the court, as opposed to the field of battle.
32 bought up (1) sold out, (2) engrossed by
others.
33 to dance with for fashion only. Hunter
compares *Ant.* 3.11.35–6, where Octavius is said to
have worn his sword 'e'en like a dancer'.
34 theft Picking up Bertram's 'steal' (33) and
anticipating 'Commit' and 'accessory' (34–5).
35 accessory Trisyllabic, with accent on first
syllable.
36 I...body I am becoming so attached to you
that separation is like being torn apart on the rack.
39, 42 sword It is likely that Parolles flourishes
his sword at these points.
40 metals (1) swordsmen, (2) mettlesome
fellows.
41 Spurio Italian for 'counterfeit'.
41 cicatrice scar.
42 sinister left.

43 reports for me (1) replies for me, (2) reports
of me.
45 novices youthful followers.
47 Stay Stop talking; i.e. the King is within
earshot. This reading depends on F2, where the
colon following 'Stay' makes the verb an imperative.
F omits punctuation and might be glossed: '(I will)
Attend the King'. This reading, however, contradicts
Bertram's expressed intention to 'steal away' (33).
'Business' is sometimes interpolated here, as if
Bertram is vacillating – with a shrug of the
shoulders he decides to stay because the King
requires him to.
48 spacious ceremony ample courtesy.
49 list In the primary sense of 'boundary' or
'limit'. The literal meaning of 'list' as the selvage
of cloth continues to function residually, even
subliminally, as it points to 'wear themselves in the
cap of the time' (50). Walter Whiter, *A Specimen
of a Commentary on Shakespeare* (1794), ed. Alan
Overand and Mary Bell, London, 1967, shows how
this 'associative' habit of mind forms clusters of

expressive to them, for they wear themselves in the cap of the time,   50
there do muster true gait; eat, speak, and move under the influence
of the most received star, and though the devil lead the measure,
such are to be followed. After them, and take a more dilated
farewell.

BERTRAM And I will do so.   55

PAROLLES Worthy fellows, and like to prove most sinewy swordmen.

Exeunt

Enter LAFEW. [*The* KING *comes forward*]

LAFEW [*Kneeling*] Pardon, my lord, for me and for my tidings.

KING I'll see thee to stand up.

LAFEW Then here's a man stands that has brought his pardon.
        I would you had kneeled, my lord, to ask me mercy,   60
        And that at my bidding you could so stand up.

KING I would I had, so I had broke thy pate,
        And asked thee mercy for't.

LAFEW   Good faith, across!
        But, my good lord, 'tis thus: you will be cured
        Of your infirmity?

KING   No.

LAFEW   O, will you eat   65
        No grapes, my royal fox? Yes, but you will
        My noble grapes, and if my royal fox
        Could reach them. I have seen a medicine

---

56 SD *The...forward*] *Collier MS.; not in* F   57 SD] *After Johnson; not in* F   58 see] F; fee *Theobald;* sue *conj. Staunton*
63–8] *Divided as Capell;* And...for't. / Goodfaith...thus, / Will...infirmitie? / No. / O...foxe? / Yes...if /
My...medicine F   66 will] *Knight;* will, F

---

related imagery in Shakespeare's verse. Helena's
tears are 'the best brine a maiden can season her
praise in' (1.1.37). Twenty lines or so later, the
Countess, bidding Bertram goodbye, calls him 'an
unseasoned courtier'. See 4.5.59 n.

50 wear...time are leaders in the fashionable
world. (This recalls the brooch worn in the hat,
1.1.134–5.)

51 there...gait i.e. in the world of fashion
they manifest the approved courtly behaviour.

51–2 influence...star Parolles plays upon the
idea of following the latest fashion and coming
under the astrological influence (flowing-in) from
a dominant planet.

52 measure dance.

53 dilated (1) expansive, (2) circumstantial.

56 like likely.

56 SD *comes forward* In a number of productions

it has been found appropriate to have the King enter
in a wheel-chair; this gives added point to Lafew's
kneeling and to the King's apparent incapacity to
stand (61).

58 Let me see you rise.

59 his pardon i.e. Helena, and the prospect of
his cure.

62 pate head.

63 across i.e. clumsily, and so without doing
harm (as when in tilting a clumsily handled lance
strikes its object athwart rather than with the point).

65–6 eat No grapes Like the fox in Aesop's fable
who rejected the grapes as sour because they were
out of reach.

66 you will i.e. you will eat.

67 and if if.

68 medicine physician (as well as physic).

That's able to breathe life into a stone,
Quicken a rock, and make you dance canary   70
With spritely fire and motion, whose simple touch
Is powerful to araise King Pippen, nay,
To give great Charlemain a pen in's hand
And write to her a love-line.
KING   What her is this?
LAFEW Why, Doctor She! My lord, there's one arrived,   75
If you will see her. Now by my faith and honour,
If seriously I may convey my thoughts
In this my light deliverance, I have spoke
With one, that in her sex, her years, profession,
Wisdom, and constancy, hath amazed me more   80
Than I dare blame my weakness. Will you see her –
For that is her demand – and know her business?
That done, laugh well at me.
KING   Now, good Lafew,
Bring in the admiration, that we with thee
May spend our wonder too, or take off thine   85
By wondering how thou took'st it.
LAFEW   Nay, I'll fit you,
And not be all day neither.
                    [*Goes to the door*]
KING Thus he his special nothing ever prologues.
LAFEW Nay, come your ways.

                    Enter HELENA

KING   This haste hath wings indeed.
LAFEW Nay, come your ways;   90

75 Doctor She] *White;* doctor she F   87 SD] *Sisson; not in* F

---

70 **Quicken** Give life to.
70 **canary** A lively Spanish dance.
71 **simple** mere; with the residual sense of 'simples' or medicinal herbs.
72 **araise** raise from the dead.
72 **Pippen** The Frankish king Pepin, father of Charlemagne, died in 768.
78 **light deliverance** joking manner of speaking.
79 **profession** i.e. what she professes herself able to do.
81 **dare...weakness** would venture to attribute to the susceptibility of an old man.
84 **admiration** object of wonder.

85 **spend** expend.
85–6 **take...took'st it** take the edge off your wonder by wondering how you came to be so mistaken.
86 **fit** satisfy.
87 SD It would appear from the dialogue that Lafew has Helena waiting at the door, perhaps for his signal.
88 **special nothing** particular trifles.
88 **prologues** introduces.
89 **come your ways** come along (spoken to Helena).

This is his majesty, say your mind to him.
A traitor you do look like, but such traitors
His majesty seldom fears. I am Cressid's uncle,
That dare leave two together; fare you well.   *Exit*

KING Now, fair one, does your business follow us?   95
HELENA Ay, my good lord.
      Gerard de Narbon was my father,
      In what he did profess, well found.
KING   I knew him.
HELENA The rather will I spare my praises towards him,
      Knowing him is enough. On's bed of death   100
      Many receipts he gave me; chiefly one,
      Which as the dearest issue of his practice,
      And of his old experience th'only darling,
      He bade me store up, as a triple eye,
      Safer than mine own two, more dear. I have so,   105
      And hearing your high majesty is touched
      With that malignant cause wherein the honour
      Of my dear father's gift stands chief in power,
      I come to tender it, and my appliance,
      With all bound humbleness.
KING   We thank you, maiden,   110
      But may not be so credulous of cure,
      When our most learnèd doctors leave us, and
      The congregated college have concluded

105 two, more dear] *Var. 78;* two: more deare F

92 **traitor…like** Alluding perhaps to Helena's apprehensive appearance.

93 **Cressid's uncle** Pandarus, the type of the go-between.

95 **follow** concern.

98 **well found** found to be good.

100 **On's** On his.

101 **receipts** medical prescriptions.

102 **dearest issue** (1) favourite child, (2) most valuable product.

103 **old experience** many years' experience.

103 **only** chief.

104 **triple eye** i.e. third eye. The odd notion of a third eye probably comes to Shakespeare from Chaucer, who represents Prudence with three eyes in *Troilus and Criseyde*, v, 744–9. F. N. Robinson in his edition of Chaucer (*Works*, 1933) derives the underlying idea, that Prudence regards past,

present and future, from Dante, *Purgatorio*, XX, 130–2. See also C. S. Singleton's note on Dante's lines in his Commentary on the *Purgatorio* (1973), p. 723.

105 **Safer** i.e. in safer keeping.

106 **touched** afflicted.

107 **cause** disease.

107 **wherein** i.e. for the cure of which.

107 **honour** Essentially, 'medicinal quality'.

108 **chief** particularly.

109 **appliance** skill (in treatment).

110 **bound** dutiful.

111 **credulous of** willing to believe in the possibility of.

112 **leave** abandon hope for.

113 **congregated college** assembled society of physicians, like the Royal College of Physicians in Shakespeare's London.

That labouring art can never ransom nature
From her inaidable estate; I say we must not   115
So stain our judgement, or corrupt our hope,
To prostitute our past-cure malady
To èmpirics, or to dissever so
Our great self and our credit, to esteem
A senseless help when help past sense we deem.   120

HELENA My duty then shall pay me for my pains.
I will no more enforce mine office on you,
Humbly entreating from your royal thoughts
A modest one, to bear me back again.

KING I cannot give thee less, to be called grateful.   125
Thou thought'st to help me, and such thanks I give
As one near death to those that wish him live.
But what at full I know, thou know'st no part,
I knowing all my peril, thou no art.

HELENA What I can do can do no hurt to try,   130
Since you set up your rest 'gainst remedy.
He that of greatest works is finisher
Oft does them by the weakest minister:
So holy writ in babes hath judgement shown,
When judges have been babes; great floods have flown   135
From simple sources; and great seas have dried

---

115 inaidable] inaidible F

114 **labouring art** the endeavours of medical skill.
115 **inaidable estate** incurable condition.
116 **stain** sully.
116 **corrupt our hope** i.e. by willing it to expect the impossible.
117–18 **prostitute...èmpirics** basely give over our incurable disease to the ministrations of quacks.
118 **dissever** separate.
119 **credit** integrity.
119–20 **esteem...deem** think worthwhile a remedy which has no support in reason when we judge any remedy beyond reason. (The adverbial phrase is not simply tautologous but suggests implicitly that only what is beyond reason can effect a cure.)
121 **duty** discharging of my duty as a subject.
122 **enforce mine office** press my services.
124 **modest one** (1) slight thought, (2) thought recognising the maidenly modesty with which I have acted (Helena supposing that her forward behaviour has called this modesty in question).

124 **to...again** to take back with me.
126–206 The shift to rhyming couplets suggests the intervention of divine power, as at 1.1.187–200.
127 **live** to live.
128 **no part** not at all.
131 **set...rest** stake everything. A metaphor derived from the card game of primero. Compare *Rom.* 5.3.109–10.
134–5 **So...babes** Recalling e.g. Matt. 11.25: 'thou has hid these things from the wise and men of understanding, and has opened them unto babes'; and 1 Cor. 1.27: 'God hath chosen the weak things of the world, to confound the things which are mighty.' Perhaps there is also a reminiscence here of the judgement of Daniel in the Apocryphal story of Susannah and the Elders.
135–6 **great...sources** Shakespeare is perhaps remembering Moses' striking water from the rock in Horeb, Exod. 17.6.
136 **great...dried** Like the Red Sea when the Israelites escaped from Egypt, Exod. 14.21.

When miracles have by the great'st been denied.
Oft expectation fails, and most oft there
Where most it promises; and oft it hits
Where hope is coldest, and despair most shifts.   140
KING I must not hear thee; fare thee well, kind maid,
Thy pains not used must by thyself be paid.
Proffers not took reap thanks for their reward.
HELENA Inspired merit so by breath is barred.
It is not so with Him that all things knows   145
As 'tis with us that square our guess by shows;
But most it is presumption in us when
The help of heaven we count the act of men.
Dear sir, to my endeavours give consent,
Of heaven, not me, make an experiment.   150
I am not an impostor that proclaim
Myself against the level of mine aim,
But know I think, and think I know most sure,
My art is not past power, nor you past cure.
KING Art thou so confident? Within what space   155
Hop'st thou my cure?
HELENA   The greatest grace lending grace,
Ere twice the horses of the sun shall bring
Their fiery torcher his diurnal ring,
Ere twice in murk and occidental damp
Moist Hesperus hath quenched her sleepy lamp,   160

---

140 shifts] F; sits *Pope*; fits *Evans, conj. Theobald*   151 impostor] F3; Impostrue F; imposture *Capell*

---

137 **the great'st** Presumably Pharaoh.

138 **fails** is disappointed.

139 **hits** is gratified.

140 **shifts** (1) blows hot and cold, (2) contrives (i.e. governs). Some editors read 'fits' or 'sits', to rhyme with 'hits', but as Johnson points out, 'there' (138) is also unrhymed.

142 Your troubles, taken to no purpose, must be their own reward.

143 **Proffers not took** Offers not accepted.

144 **Inspired** Divinely inspired, breathed in from God.

144 **breath** i.e. words, breathed out by man.

146 **square...shows** adjust or shape our conjectures by outward appearance.

148 **count** account.

150 **an experiment** trial.

151–2 **that...aim** who promises more than she can pay.

153 Helena's certainty is expressed with philosophic ambiguity.

154 **My...power** What I profess is not beyond my power to perform.

155 **space** period of time.

156 **greatest grace** God.

157–8 **horses...torcher** Horses were supposed to draw the fiery chariot of the sun-god. This is the only use of 'torcher', meaning torch-bearer, recorded in *OED*. Hunter's reading 'coacher' is, however, a needless improvement.

158 **diurnal ring** daily circuit.

159 **murk...damp** The gloom and fog that accompanies the setting of the sun in the west.

160 **Hesperus** The evening star, referred to as 'her' because Hesperus is also the planet Venus.

Or four and twenty times the pilot's glass
Hath told the thievish minutes how they pass,
What is infirm from your sound parts shall fly,
Health shall live free, and sickness freely die.
KING Upon thy certainty and confidence   165
    What dar'st thou venter?
HELENA   Tax of impudence,
    A strumpet's boldness, a divulgèd shame,
    Traduced by odious ballads; my maiden's name
    Seared otherwise; ne worse of worst – extended
    With vilest torture, let my life be ended.   170
KING Methinks in thee some blessed spirit doth speak
    His powerful sound within an organ weak;
    And what impossibility would slay
    In common sense, sense saves another way.
    Thy life is dear, for all that life can rate   175
    Worth name of life in thee hath estimate:
    Youth, beauty, wisdom, courage, all
    That happiness and prime can happy call.
    Thou this to hazard needs must intimate
    Skill infinite, or monstrous desperate.   180
    Sweet practiser, thy physic I will try,
    That ministers thine own death if I die.
HELENA If I break time, or flinch in property
    Of what I spoke, unpitied let me die,
    And well deserved. Not helping, death's my fee,   185
    But if I help, what do you promise me?

167 shame,] *Capell;* shame F   169 otherwise; ne] *Singer;* otherwise, ne F; otherwise, no F2; otherwise; nay *Singer²*
169 worst –] *Alexander;* worst F   170 vilest] vildest F

161 **glass** hour glass.
164 **freely** of its own accord.
166 **venter** venture.
166 **Tax of impudence** Accusation of shamelessness.
167 **divulgèd** laid open.
169 **Seared otherwise** Branded in other ways.
169 **ne...worst** Perhaps 'nay, the worst of all possible evils'.
169 **extended** stretched out (upon the rack).
172 **organ** (1) voice, (2) instrument.
173–4 **what...way** that which common sense calls impossible, some other kind of sense declares possible.
175–6 **rate...life** value with the name of life.

176 **in thee...estimate** is to be found and esteemed in you.
178 **prime** youth.
179 **hazard** venture.
179 **intimate** argue.
180 **monstrous desperate** (that you are) monstrously reckless.
181 **practiser** practitioner (with the residual and opposed sense of 'cozener', 'impostor').
181 **physic** medicine.
182 **ministers** administers.
183 **break time** fail to keep the time limit assigned.
183 **flinch in property** come short in respect.
185 **Not helping** If I fail to help (cure you).

KING Make thy demand.

HELENA   But will you make it even?

KING Ay, by my sceptre and my hopes of help.

HELENA Then shalt thou give me with thy kingly hand
   What husband in thy power I will command.   190
   Exempted be from me the arrogance
   To choose from forth the royal blood of France,
   My low and humble name to propagate
   With any branch or image of thy state;
   But such a one thy vassal, whom I know   195
   Is free for me to ask, thee to bestow.

KING Here is my hand, the premises observed,
   Thy will by my performance shall be served.
   So make the choice of thy own time, for I,
   Thy resolved patient, on thee still rely.   200
   More should I question thee, and more I must –
   Though more to know could not be more to trust –
   From whence thou cam'st, how tended on, but rest
   Unquestioned welcome and undoubted blest. –
   Give me some help here ho! – If thou proceed   205
   As high as word, my deed shall match thy deed.

                                  Flourish. Exeunt

[2.2] *Enter* COUNTESS *and* [LAVATCH, *the*] *Clown*

COUNTESS Come on, sir, I shall now put you to the height of your
   breeding.

188 help] F; heaven *Theobald, conj. Thirlby*   206 SD *Exeunt*] F2; *Exit.* F   Act 2 Scene 2   2.2] *Capell; not in* F
1 SH COUNTESS] Rowe; *Lady* F *(and subst. through scene)*

187 **make it even** fulfil it.

188 **help** Theobald and most subsequent editors
avoid a break in the rhyme scheme here by
emending to 'heaven'. But the break from rhyme
makes the King's word expressive of his need for
help rather than his prospects of heaven.

190 **in thy power** i.e. whom you have power to
dispose of.

191 **Exempted** Far removed.

194 **branch or image** As in a genealogical tree,
from whose branches hung likenesses of members
of the family.

197 **premises observed** conditions of the
agreement fulfilled.

200 **resolved** determined in mind.

200 **still** ever.

203 **tended on** attended (as with a retinue or
train).

204 **Unquestioned** (1) before being questioned,
(2) without question.

206 **high as word** amply as you have promised.

Act 2, Scene 2

2.2 Editors, following Capell, locate the scene in
Rossillion, the Count's palace.

1 **put you to the height** make a thorough test.

2 **breeding** upbringing (as at 2.3.106).

LAVATCH I will show myself highly fed and lowly taught. I know my
business is but to the court.

COUNTESS To the court! Why, what place make you special, when you   5
put off that with such contempt? But to the court!

LAVATCH Truly, madam, if God have lent a man any manners, he may
easily put it off at court. He that cannot make a leg, put off's cap,
kiss his hand, and say nothing, has neither leg, hands, lip, nor cap;
and indeed such a fellow, to say precisely, were not for the court;   10
but for me, I have an answer will serve all men.

COUNTESS Marry, that's a bountiful answer that fits all questions.

LAVATCH It is like a barber's chair that fits all buttocks: the pin-buttock,
the quatch-buttock, the brawn-buttock, or any buttock.

COUNTESS Will your answer serve fit to all questions?   15

LAVATCH As fit as ten groats is for the hand of an attorney, as your
French crown for your taffety punk, as Tib's rush for Tom's
forefinger, as a pancake for Shrove Tuesday, a morris for May-day,
as the nail to his hole, the cuckold to his horn, as a scolding quean
to a wrangling knave, as the nun's lip to the friar's mouth, nay, as   20
the pudding to his skin.

COUNTESS Have you, I say, an answer of such fitness for all questions?

10 court;] *Rowe;* Court, F

3 **highly...taught** over-fed and inadequately
educated (like the children of the rich). Hunter cites
as proverbial: 'Better fed than taught', and sees in
this interchange a comic version of the distinction
between birth and breeding on which the play
insists.

4 **but to the court** i.e. where gentle nurture is
disvalued. The negligent tone begets the Countess's
surprise and is justified in the rejoinder at 7–8.

5 **make you** do you consider.

6 **put off** dismiss.

7 **lent...manners** i.e. as superficial accoutre-
ment.

8 **put it off** carry it off, make a success. Lavatch
seems to mean that any fool can pass himself off
as a courtier, whose manners are exhausted in mere
bowing and scraping.

8 **make a leg** bend his knee in obeisance.

8 **put off's** take off his.

11 **for me** as for me.

13 **like...chair** Proverbial comparison for what
is endlessly accommodating.

13 **pin** narrow.

14 **quatch** Probably 'squat' (otherwise unre-
corded).

14 **brawn** fleshy.

16 **ten groats** ten fourpenny pieces. The usual
fee for an attorney.

17 **French crown** Syphilis, the so-called 'French
disease', induced baldness. A crown = (1) top of the
head, (2) five shillings. Thus the French crown is
both 'the punk's fee and the punk's disease'
(Hunter).

17 **taffety punk** whore dressed showily in taffeta.

17 **Tib's rush** Country girls (for whom 'Tib' is
generic) made rings of reed for love tokens to be
used in rural mock-weddings. Perhaps here and
subsequently Lavatch is glancing obscenely at the
conventional phallic–vulval similitude.

18 **pancake** Eaten traditionally on Shrove
Tuesday, the feasting day before the beginning of
Lent.

18 **morris** Traditional dance for May festivals

19, 21 **his** its.

19 **quean** hussy.

20 **nun's...mouth** A bawdy version of the
proverb 'as fit as a pudding for a friar's mouth'
(Tilley P620).

21 **pudding** sausage.

LAVATCH From below your duke to beneath your constable, it will fit
    any question.

COUNTESS It must be an answer of most monstrous size that must fit 25
    all demands.

LAVATCH But a trifle neither, in good faith, if the learned should speak
    truth of it. Here it is, and all that belongs to't. Ask me if I am a
    courtier: it shall do you no harm to learn.

COUNTESS To be young again, if we could! I will be a fool in question, 30
    hoping to be the wiser by your answer. I pray you, sir, are you a
    courtier?

LAVATCH O Lord, sir! – There's a simple putting off. More, more, a
    hundred of them.

COUNTESS Sir, I am a poor friend of yours that loves you. 35

LAVATCH O Lord, sir! – Thick, thick, spare not me.

COUNTESS I think, sir, you can eat none of this homely meat.

LAVATCH O Lord, sir! – Nay, put me to't, I warrant you.

COUNTESS You were lately whipped, sir, as I think.

LAVATCH O Lord, sir! – Spare not me. 40

COUNTESS Do you cry, 'O Lord, sir!' at your whipping, and 'Spare
    not me'? Indeed your 'O Lord, sir!' is very sequent to your
    whipping; you would answer very well to a whipping, if you were
    but bound to't.

LAVATCH I ne'er had worse luck in my life in my 'O Lord, sir!' I see 45
    things may serve long, but not serve ever.

COUNTESS I play the noble housewife with the time,
    To entertain it so merrily with a fool.

LAVATCH O Lord, sir! – Why, there't serves well again.

COUNTESS An end, sir; to your business: give Helen this, 50
    And urge her to a present answer back.
    Commend me to my kinsmen and my son.
    This is not much.

31 I pray] F3; *La.* I pray F   47–8] *As verse, Knight; as prose,* F   50 An end, sir; to] *Rowe³;* And end sir to F; And
end; sir to F3

23 **below...constable** With a sexual in-
nuendo, as perhaps in the Countess's rejoinder.

27 **neither** on the contrary (intensifying
Lavatch's negative answer).

30 **be...question** ask questions like a fool.

33 **O Lord, sir** A fashionable expletive used to
evade an awkward question. Compare Parolles at
4.3.259.

33 **putting off** evasion.

36 **Thick** Quickly.

37 **homely meat** plain food.

42 **is very sequent to** follows logically on
(because it constitutes a plea for mercy).

43 **answer...to** (1) have a good reply to, (2) be
a suitable subject for.

44 **bound to't** (1) compelled by oath to answer,
(2) tied to the whipping-post.

51 **present** immediate.

52 **Commend me** My greetings.

LAVATCH Not much commendation to them.

COUNTESS Not much employment for you. You understand me?   55

LAVATCH Most fruitfully. I am there before my legs.

COUNTESS Haste you again.

Exeunt

[2.3] *Enter* COUNT [BERTRAM], LAFEW, *and* PAROLLES

LAFEW They say miracles are past, and we have our philosophical
   persons, to make modern and familiar, things supernatural and
   causeless. Hence is it that we make trifles of terrors, ensconcing
   ourselves into seeming knowledge, when we should submit ourselves
   to an unknown fear.   5

PAROLLES Why, 'tis the rarest argument of wonder that hath shot out
   in our latter times.

BERTRAM And so 'tis.

LAFEW To be relinquished of the artists –

PAROLLES So I say, both of Galen and Paracelsus.   10

LAFEW Of all the learned and authentic fellows –

PAROLLES Right, so I say.

LAFEW That gave him out incurable –

PAROLLES Why, there 'tis, so say I too.

LAFEW Not to be helped –   15

---

55 me?] *Capell;* me. F   56 legs] F3; legegs F; legges F2   **Act 2, Scene 3**   2.3] *Capell; not in* F   1 SH LAFEW] *Rowe;*
Ol. Laf. F *(and subst. through scene)*   2 familiar,] *Theobald;* familiar F   8 SH BERTRAM] *Rowe; Ros.* F   10 say,] *Rowe;*
say F

55 understand Lavatch in what follows picks
this up in the sense of 'stand' = erect penis, and so
introduces a bawdy quibble on 'fruitfully' meaning
'abundantly' but also 'sexually fruitful'.

56 there i.e. in understanding. Also 'in Paris',
to which he has been commended.

57 again back home again.

Act 2, Scene 3

2.3 Editors, following Capell, locate the scene in
the King's palace, Paris.

2 modern commonplace.

3 causeless inexplicable.

3–4 ensconcing ourselves into fortifying ourselves with.

5 an unknown fear fear of the unknown, i.e.
of the inexplicable things and 'terrors' of 2–3.

6 rarest argument most extraordinary subject.

6 shot out i.e. like a nova or blazing star.

7 latter recent.

8 And so 'tis Bertram is given enough words to
draw attention to his passivity and silence, distinguishing it from the parasitic volubility of Parolles.

9 relinquished...artists abandoned by the
scholars (i.e. physicians).

10 Galen and Paracelsus The ancient and
modern schools of medicine. Galen, the Greek
physician of the second century A.D., was the
principal medical authority of Shakespeare's time.
Paracelsus (Theophrastus Bombastus von Hohen-
heim), a Swiss alchemist and physician of the early
sixteenth century, propounded new theories of
treating disease.

11 authentic fellows qualified members of the
medical profession. Possibly alluding to 'Fellows'
of the Royal College of Physicians.

13 gave him out proclaimed him.

15 helped cured.

PAROLLES Right, as 'twere a man assured of a –

LAFEW Uncertain life, and sure death.

PAROLLES Just, you say well; so would I have said.

LAFEW I may truly say it is a novelty to the world.

PAROLLES It is indeed; if you will have it in showing, you will read   20
it in what-do-ye-call there.

LAFEW [*Reading*] 'A showing of a heavenly effect in an earthly actor'.

PAROLLES That's it I would have said, the very same.

LAFEW Why, your dolphin is not lustier. 'Fore me, I speak in respect –

PAROLLES Nay, 'tis strange, 'tis very strange, that is the brief and the   25
tedious of it, and he's of a most facinerious spirit that will not
acknowledge it to be the –

LAFEW Very hand of heaven.

PAROLLES Ay, so I say.

LAFEW In a most weak –   30

PAROLLES And debile minister, great power, great transcendence,
which should indeed give us a further use to be made than alone
the recovery of the king, as to be –

LAFEW Generally thankful.

Enter KING, HELENA, *and* ATTENDANTS

PAROLLES I would have said it; you say well. Here comes the king.   35

LAFEW *Lustique*, as the Dutchman says; I'll like a maid the better whilst
I have a tooth in my head. Why, he's able to lead her a coranto.

PAROLLES *Mor du vinager*! is not this Helen?

LAFEW 'Fore God, I think so.

20 indeed;] *Hanmer*; indeede F   21 what-do-ye-call] *Case, conj. Glover*; what do ye call F   22 SD] *Alexander*; *not in* F   23 it] *Var. 78*; it, F   24 'Fore] *Capell*; fore F   36 *Lustique*] Lustique F, Lustick F3   38 *Mor du vinager*] F (*vinager*,); *Mort du Vinaigre* / *Rowe*³

18 **Just** Exactly.

20 **in showing** visible (by being printed).

21 **what...there** Parolles presumably indicates a ballad Lafew is holding, and the title of which he proceeds to read.

24 **dolphin** Emblematic of lustiness (and perhaps punning on the French Dauphin, regularly anglicised by the Elizabethans as 'Dolphin', the form in the Folio).

24 **'Fore** Before. A mild oath, like 'Upon my soul' or ''Fore God' (39).

25–6 **brief...tedious** short and long. (Parolles lapses, as often, into affected speech.)

26 **facinerious** Form of 'facinorous' ('most wicked'); the word was commoner then, but still highfalutin.

31 **debile minister** weak agent.

34 **Generally** Universally.

36 **Lustique** Frolicsome.

37 **tooth** sweet tooth (for girls).

37 **coranto** spirited dance.

38 **Mor du vinager**! Pseudo-French. Editors who translate this mock oath (e.g. as 'death of the vinegar') and refer it to the Crucifixion are being over-literal.

39 **'Fore...so** Lafew ignores Parolles (whose eye is on the lady) and continues to marvel at the King's fitness. Some productions have found occasion in Lafew's 'coranto' (37) to have the King and Helena enter dancing.

KING Go call before me all the lords in court.   40
       Sit, my preserver, by thy patient's side,
       And with this healthful hand, whose banished sense
       Thou hast repealed, a second time receive
       The confirmation of my promised gift,
       Which but attends thy naming.   45

Enter three or four LORDS

       Fair maid, send forth thine eye. This youthful parcel
       Of noble bachelors stand at my bestowing,
       O'er whom both sovereign power and father's voice
       I have to use. Thy frank election make;
       Thou hast power to choose, and they none to forsake.   50
HELENA To each of you one fair and virtuous mistress
       Fall, when Love please! Marry, to each but one!
LAFEW I'd give bay curtal and his furniture,
       My mouth no more were broken than these boys',
       And writ as little beard.
KING   Peruse them well.   55
       Not one of those but had a noble father.
HELENA *(She addresses her to a Lord)* Gentlemen,
       Heaven hath through me restored the king to health.
ALL We understand it, and thank heaven for you.
HELENA I am a simple maid, and therein wealthiest   60
       That I protest I simply am a maid.

---

51 mistress] *Rowe;* Mistris; F   53 curtal] F; Curtal *Evans*   54 boys'] *Capell;* boyes F   57 SD] *Placed as* F; *following stream (70) NS*   57–8 Gentlemen…health] *As verse, Capell; as prose,* F

42 **healthful** healthy.
42 **banished sense** lost power of feeling.
43 **repealed** called back (from banishment).
45 **attends** waits on.
45 SD The permissive form of F's SD suggests tentative first thoughts. Productions usually require at least half a dozen lords to form the 'youthful parcel'. The FIRST and SECOND LORD at 71 and 77 may or may not be the Lords Dumaine; they are not marked *G* and *E* in the Folio.
46 **parcel** small group.
47 **stand…bestowing** are in my power to give in marriage. The bachelors being wards of the King, he could marry them as he pleased so long as he did not give them to a commoner. Shakespeare deliberately ignores this proviso.
49 **frank election** free choice.
50 A hexameter line.

50 **forsake** refuse.
52 **to…one** (1) only one to each, (2) excepting one of you (whom I choose).
53 Lafew here, and in his speeches down to 93, speaks aside – to himself or to the audience.
53 **bay…furniture** my bay horse with the docked tail and his trappings.
54 **My…than** If I were still as sexually vigorous as. Literally, Lafew is saying: 'If I still had all my teeth' (compare 37 above). Residually, he is remembering his bay curtal: a 'broken' horse because its mouth is furnished with a bit.
55 **writ** (1) proclaimed, (2) showed.
57 SD *She…Lord* 'She squares up to the first candidate while speaking to them all' (Hunter, justifying the singular 'Lord' of the Folio SD).
61 **protest** avow.

Please it your majesty, I have done already.
The blushes in my cheeks thus whisper me,
'We blush that thou shouldst choose; but be refused,
Let the white death sit on thy cheek for ever,   65
We'll never come there again.'
KING   Make choice and see,
Who shuns thy love shuns all his love in me.
HELENA Now, Dian, from thy altar do I fly,
And to imperial Love, that god most high,
Do my sighs stream. [*To a first Lord*] Sir, will you hear my
      suit?   70
FIRST LORD And grant it.
HELENA   Thanks, sir; all the rest is mute.
LAFEW I had rather be in this choice than throw ames-ace for my life.
HELENA [*To a second Lord*] The honour, sir, that flames in your fair
      eyes,
Before I speak, too threat'ningly replies.
Love make your fortunes twenty times above   75
Her that so wishes, and her humble love!
SECOND LORD No better, if you please.
HELENA   My wish receive,
Which great love grant, and so I take my leave.
LAFEW Do all they deny her? And they were sons of mine, I'd have
      them whipped, or I would send them to th'Turk to make eunuchs 80
      of.
HELENA [*To a third Lord*] Be not afraid that I your hand should take,
I'll never do you wrong for your own sake.

---

64 choose; but be refused,] *After Rann;* choose, but be refused; F   69 imperial Love] *Pope;* imperiall loue F;
imperiall Ioue F2; impartiall Jove F3   70 SD] *Capel; not in* F   72] *As prose, Pope; as verse,* F   73 SD] *Capell; not in* F
79 And] F; An *Capell*   82 SD] *Capell; not in* F

---

63 whisper whisper to.
64 be if you are.
68–96 Stage-productions have often turned the
parade of nobles from which Helena makes choice
into a dance or musical game. For dialogue and
dance compare *Ado* 2.1.85–154.
68 Dian...fly I desert the goddess of chastity.
71 all...mute I have no more to say.
72 throw...life stake my life on throwing two
aces at dice ('ames-ace', or 'ambs-ace', is a term for
a pair of aces). Lafew says ironically that he would
rather take his chance with the bachelors than play
at Russian roulette.

73 honour (1) high station, (2) willingness to do
me the honour of marrying me. If the first reading
is right, 'threat'ningly' (74) signifies disdain on the
part of the second Lord, and this is Lafew's
understanding (79 ff.). But 'threat'ningly' can also
mean that Helena feels herself in danger of being
accepted by the wrong suitor, as in fact she is (77).
76 so thus.
77 No better i.e. than you.
77 receive accept.
78 great love As distinct from Helena's 'humble
love' (76). Some read 'Love', supposing Helena to
refer to the goddess of love.

Blessing upon your vows, and in your bed
Find fairer fortune, if you ever wed!   85
LAFEW These boys are boys of ice, they'll none have her. Sure they are
   bastards to the English, the French ne'er got 'em.
HELENA [*To a fourth Lord*] You are too young, too happy, and too good,
   To make yourself a son out of my blood.
FOURTH LORD Fair one, I think not so.   90
LAFEW There's one grape yet; I am sure thy father drunk wine – but
   if thou be'st not an ass, I am a youth of fourteen. I have known
   thee already.
HELENA [*To Bertram*] I dare not say I take you, but I give
   Me and my service, ever whilst I live,   95
   Into your guiding power. – This is the man.
KING Why then, young Bertram, take her, she's thy wife.
BERTRAM My wife, my liege? I shall beseech your highness,
   In such a business, give me leave to use
   The help of mine own eyes.
KING   Know'st thou not, Bertram,   100
   What she has done for me?
BERTRAM   Yes, my good lord,
   But never hope to know why I should marry her.
KING Thou know'st she has raised me from my sickly bed.
BERTRAM But follows it, my lord, to bring me down
   Must answer for your raising? I know her well;   105
   She had her breeding at my father's charge –
   A poor physician's daughter my wife? Disdain
   Rather corrupt me ever!
KING 'Tis only title thou disdain'st in her, the which
   I can build up. Strange is it that our bloods,   110
   Of colour, weight, and heat, poured all together,

86 her] F2; heere F   88 SH HELENA] F3; *La.* F   88 SD] *Capell; not in* F   94 SD] *Rowe; not in* F
100–2 Know'st…her] *As verse, Pope; as prose,* F

87 **got** begot.
91 **grape** scion of a good stock.
91 **wine** Which, proverbially, makes good
blood. Compare Falstaff on the virtues of sherris
sack, *2H4* 4.3.89–125.
92 **known** seen through. Lafew may be covertly
addressing Bertram.
98 **liege** Sovereign lord to whom allegiance is
due.

104–5 **to…raising** With a sexual quibble,
which justifies the eccentric-seeming association, at
2.1.93, of Lafew with Pandarus.
106 **charge** expense.
107–8 **Disdain…ever** Instead let my disdain
of her ruin my fortunes forever.
109 **title** lack of title (as with 'name' at 116).

Would quite confound distinction, yet stands off
In differences so mighty. If she be
All that is virtuous – save what thou dislik'st,
A poor physician's daughter – thou dislik'st   115
Of virtue for the name. But do not so.
From lowest place, whence virtuous things proceed,
The place is dignified by th'doer's deed.
Where great additions swell's, and virtue none,
It is a dropsied honour. Good alone   120
Is good, without a name; vileness is so:
The property by what it is should go,
Not by the title. She is young, wise, fair,
In these to nature she's immediate heir;
And these breed honour. That is honour's scorn   125
Which challenges itself as honour's born
And is not like the sire. Honours thrive,
When rather from our acts we them derive
Than our foregoers. The mere word's a slave
Debauched on every tomb, on every grave   130
A lying trophy, and as oft is dumb
Where dust and damned oblivion is the tomb
Of honoured bones indeed. What should be said?
If thou canst like this creature as a maid,
I can create the rest. Virtue and she   135
Is her own dower; honour and wealth from me.
BERTRAM I cannot love her, nor will strive to do't.

117 place, whence] F; place when *Theobald, conj. Thirlby*   120–1 alone Is good, without a name; vileness] *Capell;* a
lone, Is good without a name? Vilenesse F   122 it is] F2; is is F   125 honour's] *Rowe³;* honours F   129 word's a]
F2; words, a F   130 Debauched] Deboshed F   130 grave] *Knight;* graue: F   132–3 tomb Of...indeed. What] *Theobald;*
Tombe. Of...indeed, what F

112 **confound distinction** i.e. could not be
distinguished in colour, weight and heat.
112–13 **stands...mighty** they stand separated
(in your judgement) by such great differences in
pedigree. The singular form 'stands' is influenced
by 'distinction'.
117 **whence** The Folio reading, generally
emended to 'when'.
117 **proceed** come forth.
119 **additions** titles.
119 **swell's** swell us up.
120 **dropsied** swollen unhealthily (by excess
fluid).
120 **alone** (1) lacking a title or 'name', (2) in
itself, (3) only (as opposed to all other things, except
'vileness').

121 **vileness is so** i.e. vileness is vile in itself.
122 **property** intrinsic nature.
122 **by** for (as at 123).
122 **go** be accepted.
124 She inherits these qualities directly from
nature.
125–7 **That...sire** That which proclaims itself
honourable by virtue of ancestry and does not
justify its claim by honourable behaviour is scorned
by true honour.
129 **foregoers** ancestors.
132–3 **Where...indeed** i.e. where truly honourable persons lie in (unremembered) death.
135 **she** i.e. her intrinsic qualities.
137 **strive** attempt.

KING Thou wrong'st thyself, if thou shouldst strive to choose.
HELENA That you are well restored, my lord, I'm glad.
　　　　Let the rest go.   140
KING My honour's at the stake, which to defeat,
　　　　I must produce my power. Here, take her hand,
　　　　Proud scornful boy, unworthy this good gift,
　　　　That dost in vile misprision shackle up
　　　　My love and her desert; that canst not dream,   145
　　　　We poising us in her defective scale,
　　　　Shall weigh thee to the beam; that wilt not know
　　　　It is in us to plant thine honour where
　　　　We please to have it grow. Check thy contempt;
　　　　Obey our will, which travails in thy good;   150
　　　　Believe not thy disdain, but presently
　　　　Do thine own fortunes that obedient right
　　　　Which both thy duty owes and our power claims;
　　　　Or I will throw thee from my care for ever
　　　　Into the staggers and the careless lapse   155
　　　　Of youth and ignorance, both my revenge and hate
　　　　Loosing upon thee, in the name of justice,
　　　　Without all terms of pity. Speak, thine answer.
BERTRAM Pardon, my gracious lord; for I submit
　　　　My fancy to your eyes. When I consider   160
　　　　What great creation and what dole of honour
　　　　Flies where you bid it, I find that she, which late
　　　　Was in my nobler thoughts most base, is now
　　　　The praisèd of the king, who so ennobled,
　　　　Is as 'twere born so.

155 careless] F; cureless *Dyce²,* conj. *W. S. Walker*   158 Speak, thine] F; Speak thine F3   160 eyes. When] *Rowe;* eies, when F

138 **choose** i.e. for yourself.
139 **restored** cured.
141 **at the stake** tied to the post (i.e. like a bear baited by dogs).
141 **which** i.e. which menace.
143 **boy** A term of contempt.
144 **misprision** (1) mistaking, (2) scorn (and with a quibble on 'false imprisonment', hence introducing 'shackle up').
146 **We** The royal pronoun, as the King puts on his power. So again at 148–9.
146 **poising...scale** adding in the balance our weight to her lightness (she having no title).
147 **weight...beam** outweigh you and tip your scale up to the cross-beam.

147 **that** thou that.
149 **Check** Restrain.
150 **travails in** works for.
151 **Believe not** Deny.
151 **presently** immediately (as again at 2.4.43).
152 Do right by your fortunes by being obedient.
155 **staggers** giddiness.
155 **careless lapse** fall into recklessness.
158 **all terms of pity** pity in any form.
160 **fancy** love.
161 **great creation** creation of greatness.
161 **dole** dealing out.
162 **which late** who recently.
164 **who** i.e. Helena.
164 **so** being so.

KING   Take her by the hand,   165
          And tell her she is thine; to whom I promise
          A counterpoise – if not to thy estate,
          A balance more replete.
BERTRAM   I take her hand.
KING Good fortune and the favour of the king
          Smile upon this contràct, whose ceremony   170
          Shall seem expedient on the now-born brief,
          And be performed tonight. The solemn feast
          Shall more attend upon the coming space,
          Expecting absent friends. As thou lov'st her,
          Thy love's to me religious; else, does err.   175

                                                              Exeunt

        Lafew and Parolles stay behind, commenting of this wedding
LAFEW Do you hear, monsieur? A word with you.
PAROLLES Your pleasure, sir?
LAFEW Your lord and master did well to make his recantation.
PAROLLES Recantation? My lord? My master?
LAFEW Ay; is it not a language I speak?   180
PAROLLES A most harsh one, and not to be understood without bloody
          succeeding. My master?
LAFEW Are you companion to the Count Rossillion?
PAROLLES To any count, to all counts: to what is man.
LAFEW To what is count's man. Count's master is of another style.   185
PAROLLES You are too old, sir; let it satisfy you, you are too old.
LAFEW I must tell thee, sirrah, I write man; to which title age cannot
          bring thee.

167–8 estate, A] F; estate A *Evans*   171 now-born] *Rowe*; now borne F

166 **whom** Presumably Helena, conceivably
Bertram.
167 **A counterpoise** An equal weight (recurring
to the image of balance, 146–7).
167–8 **if...replete** (1) which, if not greater than
your possessions, will be more fully matched; (2)
which will be, not equal to your possessions, but
more abundant. (*OED* supports both readings of
'replete'.)
170 **ceremony** marriage ceremony (which enacts
'this contract').
171 **seem...brief** This difficult passage may
mean: 'follow expeditiously on my royal command,
now uttered'. (*OED* sb 1.1 glosses 'brief' as 'royal
mandate'.)
172 **solemn** solemnising.
173–4 **more...friends** wait through a longer

interval for the arrival of expected friends now
absent.
175 **to me** as far as I'm concerned.
175 **religious** i.e. holy and true.
175 **does err** i.e. is errant and treacherous.
175 SD.2 **of** on.
179 Parolles is taken aback by Lafew's treatment
of Bertram both as a repentant heretic and as
Parolles's master.
182 **succeeding** consequences.
183 **companion** Lafew intends the old sense
'rascal' as well as the current one 'associate'.
185 **man** servant. Lafew sets aside Parolles's
claim to be on equal terms with all men.
187 **sirrah** Used to an inferior (as again at 222).
187 **write** call myself a.

PAROLLES What I dare too well do, I dare not do.

LAFEW I did think thee, for two ordinaries, to be a pretty wise fellow.   190
Thou didst make tolerable vent of thy travel; it might pass: yet the
scarfs and the bannerets about thee did manifoldly dissuade me
from believing thee a vessel of too great a burden. I have now found
thee. When I lose thee again, I care not; yet art thou good for
nothing but taking up, and that thou'rt scarce worth.   195

PAROLLES Hadst thou not the privilege of antiquity upon thee –

LAFEW Do not plunge thyself too far in anger, lest thou hasten thy trial;
which if – Lord have mercy on thee for a hen! So, my good window
of lattice, fare thee well. Thy casement I need not open, for I look
through thee. Give me thy hand.   200

PAROLLES My lord, you give me most egregious indignity.

LAFEW Ay, with all my heart, and thou art worthy of it.

PAROLLES I have not, my lord, deserved it.

LAFEW Yes, good faith, every dram of it, and I will not bate thee a
scruple.   205

PAROLLES Well, I shall be wiser.

LAFEW Even as soon as thou canst, for thou hast to pull at a smack
a'th'contrary. If ever thou be'st bound in thy scarf and beaten, thou
shalt find what it is to be proud of thy bondage. I have a desire
to hold my acquaintance with thee, or rather my knowledge, that   210

190 ordinaries,] *Theobald;* ordinaries: F; ordinaries F2   195 thou'rt] F3, th'ourt F   198 hen!] *Theobald;* hen, F;
hen; F3

189 i.e. I have courage enough to beat you only too well, but dare not because of your age.

190 for two ordinaries i.e. for two mealtimes spent in Parolles's company. An ordinary was a tavern.

191 make...of talk passably about.

192 scarfs...bannerets Denoting the military man and worn to excess by Parolles, so suggesting to Lafew an inconsiderable ship bedecked with pennants – like the 'scarfed bark' of *MV* 2.6.14–15.

193 of too...burden i.e. carrying a valuable cargo. Lafew means that Parolles would not advertise himself or show off if he had something precious to hide.

193 found found out. Introduces a quibble on 'lose' = 'get rid of'. Compare 2.4.25.

195 taking up picking up (in contrast to 'lose'); also 'calling to account'.

196 privilege of antiquity licence of age.

198 which if i.e. you are put to your trial or testing.

198 hen Perhaps alluding to Parolles's 'plumage' as well as to his fussiness and his timidity.

199 lattice With a possible suggestion of the red-lattice windows which denoted a common alehouse.

199 casement window.

201 egregious flagrant (but used here to exemplify Parolles's highfalutin diction).

204 bate abate.

205 scruple tiniest part (literally, one-third of a dram).

206 wiser i.e. by avoiding in future creatures like you. Lafew in his reply picks up the conventional sense.

207–8 pull...contrary swallow a large dose of your foolishness (before you grow wise).

209 bondage i.e. the scarves which he has bound about him.

210 hold continue.

I may say in the default, 'He is a man I know.'

PAROLLES My lord, you do me most insupportable vexation.

LAFEW I would it were hell-pains for thy sake, and my poor doing
eternal; for doing I am past, as I will by thee, in what motion age
will give me leave. *Exit* 215

PAROLLES Well, thou hast a son shall take this disgrace off me, scurvy,
old, filthy, scurvy lord! Well, I must be patient, there is no fettering
of authority. I'll beat him, by my life, if I can meet him with any
convenience, and he were double and double a lord. I'll have no
more pity of his age than I would have of – I'll beat him, and if 220
I could but meet him again.

Enter LAFEW

LAFEW Sirrah, your lord and master's married, there's news for you.
You have a new mistress.

PAROLLES I most unfeignedly beseech your lordship to make some
reservation of your wrongs. He is my good lord; whom I serve above 225
is my master.

LAFEW Who? God?

PAROLLES Ay, sir.

LAFEW The devil it is that's thy master. Why dost thou garter up thy
arms a'this fashion? Dost make hose of thy sleeves? Do other 230
servants so? Thou wert best set thy lower part where thy nose
stands. By mine honour, if I were but two hours younger, I'd beat
thee. Methink'st thou art a general offence, and every man should
beat thee. I think thou wast created for men to breathe themselves
upon thee. 235

PAROLLES This is hard and undeserved measure, my lord.

LAFEW Go to, sir, you were beaten in Italy for picking a kernel out of

211 **in the default** when you default (i.e. show yourself empty when you are brought to trial, 197). The Clarkes (cited Hunter) suggest a legal allusion: 'when you fail to appear in court'. Compare *MM* 5.1.126, 144.

211 **I know** i.e. know for what he is (compare *MM* 5.1.126).

213 **my...doing** i.e. my inadequate power to inflict vexation. Lafew would like to impose eternal damnation (with a quibble on 'do' = 'copulate').

214 **will by** will pass by (picking up 'past' in the preceding clause).

214–15 **motion...leave** movement my 'antiquity' permits.

216 **a son** Whom Parolles will beat in retaliation.

218–19 **with any convenience** on a suitable occasion.

219 **and** though.

220 **and if** if.

224–5 **make...wrongs** qualify your insults.

225 **good lord** patron (merely).

229–30 **garter...sleeves** i.e. Parolles wears scarves around his sleeves as others wear garters on their stockings.

233 **Methink'st** It seems to me that.

234 **breathe** exercise (by beating him).

236 **measure** treatment (meted out).

237–8 **picking...pomegranate** i.e. nothing at all; the most trivial kind of offence.

a pomegranate. You are a vagabond and no true traveller. You are
more saucy with lords and honourable personages than the
commission of your birth and virtue gives you heraldry. You are   240
not worth another word, else I'd call you knave. I leave you. *Exit*

Enter [BERTRAM] *Count Rossillion*

PAROLLES Good, very good, it is so then. Good, very good, let it be
    concealed awhile.
BERTRAM Undone, and forfeited to cares for ever!
PAROLLES What's the matter, sweet heart?   245
BERTRAM Although before the solemn priest I have sworn,
    I will not bed her.
PAROLLES What, what, sweet heart?
BERTRAM O my Parolles, they have married me!
    I'll to the Tuscan wars, and never bed her.   250
PAROLLES France is a dog-hole, and it no more merits
    The tread of a man's foot. To th'wars!
BERTRAM There's letters from my mother; what th'import is,
    I know not yet.
PAROLLES Ay, that would be known. To th'wars, my boy, to
    th'wars!   255
    He wears his honour in a box unseen,
    That hugs his kicky-wicky here at home,
    Spending his manly marrow in her arms,
    Which should sustain the bound and high curvet
    Of Mars's fiery steed. To other regions!   260
    France is a stable, we that dwell in't jades,
    Therefore to th'war!
BERTRAM It shall be so. I'll send her to my house,
    Acquaint my mother with my hate to her,
    And wherefore I am fled; write to the king   265

---

244 SH BERTRAM] *Rowe; Ros.* F *(and subst. through scene)*   246–7 Although…her] *As verse, Rowe³; as prose,* F

238 **vagabond** mere tramp, vagrant (as opposed
to a 'true traveller' who required a licence to travel).
240 **commission** warrant.
240 **heraldry** entitlement.
249 **Parolles** Trisyllabic.
253 **letters** a letter (Latin *litterae*).
256 **box unseen** With an allusion to the female
genital organs.
257 **kicky-wicky** Otherwise unknown but
meaning generically and jocosely 'mistress'.

258 **Spending** Expending, wasting.
258 **manly marrow** i.e. semen, but with a
general reference to the virile energies that 'sustain'
the soldier and his steed.
259 **curvet** A leap of a horse when all four legs
are off the ground at once.
261 **jades** inferior horses (as opposed to the 'fiery
steed' of 260).

That which I durst not speak. His present gift
Shall furnish me to those Italian fields
Where noble fellows strike. Wars is no strife
To the dark house and the detested wife.

PAROLLES Will this caprichio hold in thee, art sure?   270

BERTRAM Go with me to my chamber, and advise me.
I'll send her straight away. Tomorrow,
I'll to the wars, she to her single sorrow.

PAROLLES Why, these balls bound, there's noise in it. 'Tis hard!
A young man married is a man that's marred;   275
Therefore away, and leave her bravely; go.
The king has done you wrong; but hush, 'tis so.

                                                            Exeunt

[2.4] *Enter* HELENA *and* [LAVATCH, *the*] *Clown*

HELENA My mother greets me kindly. Is she well?

LAVATCH She is not well, but yet she has her health. She's very merry,
but yet she is not well; but thanks be given, she's very well, and
wants nothing i'th'world; but yet she is not well.

HELENA If she be very well, what does she ail that she's not very well?   5

LAVATCH Truly, she's very well indeed, but for two things.

HELENA What two things?

LAVATCH One, that she's not in heaven, whither God send her quickly!
the other, that she's in earth, from whence God send her quickly!

                         Enter PAROLLES

PAROLLES Bless you, my fortunate lady!   10

---

269 detested] *Rowe;* detected F   271 advise] F3; aduice F   277 SD *Exeunt*] *Rowe; Exit* F   Act 2, Scene 4   2.4] *Capell;*
not in F

266 present gift The 'counterpoise' of 167.
267 furnish me to equip me for.
269 To Compared to.
269 dark house (1) gloomy house, (2) lunatic asylum (like the 'hideous darkness' where Malvolio is laid: *TN* 4.2.30).
270 caprichio whim. Parolles again uses affected diction.
270 hold be maintained.
272 straight immediately.
274 balls tennis balls (stuffed with hair and covered with leather).
274 bound...hard Bertram is spirited, and

now playing the game properly, with bounding returns.
275 After the proverb 'Marrying is marring' (Tilley M701).
276 bravely with spirit.

Act 2, Scene 4
2.4 Editors, following Capell, locate the scene in the King's palace, Paris.
1 kindly affectionately.
2 not well i.e. 'not in heaven' (8).
4 wants lacks.
5 what in what.

HELENA I hope, sir, I have your good will to have mine own good
fortune.

PAROLLES You had my prayers to lead them on, and to keep them on,
have them still. O, my knave, how does my old lady?

LAVATCH So that you had her wrinkles and I her money, I would she   15
did as you say.

PAROLLES Why, I say nothing.

LAVATCH Marry, you are the wiser man; for many a man's tongue
shakes out his master's undoing. To say nothing, to do nothing, to
know nothing, and to have nothing, is to be a great part of your   20
title, which is within a very little of nothing.

PAROLLES Away, th'art a knave.

LAVATCH You should have said, sir, 'Before a knave th'art a knave',
that's 'Before me th'art a knave.' This had been truth, sir.

PAROLLES Go to, thou art a witty fool, I have found thee.   25

LAVATCH Did you find me in yourself, sir, or were you taught to find
me? The search, sir, was profitable, and much fool may you find
in you, even to the world's pleasure and the increase of laughter.

PAROLLES A good knave, i'faith, and well fed.

   Madam, my lord will go away tonight,   30
A very serious business calls on him.
The great prerogative and rite of love,
Which, as your due time claims, he does acknowledge,
But puts it off to a compelled restraint;
Whose want, and whose delay, is strewed with sweets,   35
Which they distil now in the curbèd time,
To make the coming hour o'erflow with joy,

---

12 fortune] F; fortunes *Evans, conj. Heath*   27 The search] *Rowe;* Clo. The search F

13 them i.e. her good fortune. Perhaps Heath's
conjecture 'fortunes' should be preferred.
  18 man (1) human being, (2) servant.
  19 shakes out causes.
  21 title status; and perhaps with a glance at the
name Parolles: (mere) words.
  23 Before In the presence of.
  24 Before me A mild oath: 'Upon my soul' (and
punning on 'Before', 23). Lavatch is saying that
Parolles is a knave.
  25 found thee i.e. seen you for what you are.
This is a significant expression in the play (see
3.6.73, 5.2.35).
  26 in yourself by your own efforts (but also with
the sense, which Parolles misses, 'by looking at
yourself').

27 The search The Folio introduces this line
with the speech heading *Clo.[wn]*, which may mean
that a reply by Parolles has dropped out.
  28 pleasure entertainment.
  29 well fed Resuming the proverb (2.2.3)
'Better fed than taught'.
  34 puts...to postpones it because of.
  35–8 Whose want...brim i.e. love's rite when
it comes will be sweeter and fuller for the delay, as
perfume is refined from flowers by distillation.
  35 sweets flowers.
  36 curbèd time time of restraint. The still
holding the distillate was sometimes called a
'cucurbit' (see *OED*).

And pleasure drown the brim.

HELENA   What's his will else?

PAROLLES That you will take your instant leave a'th'king,
And make this haste as your own good proceeding,   40
Strengthened with what apology you think
May make it probable need.

HELENA   What more commands he?

PAROLLES That having this obtained, you presently
Attend his further pleasure.

HELENA In every thing I wait upon his will.   45

PAROLLES I shall report it so.   *Exit Parolles*

HELENA   I pray you. Come, sirrah.

                                                Exeunt

[2.5] *Enter* LAFEW *and* BERTRAM

LAFEW But I hope your lordship thinks not him a soldier.

BERTRAM Yes, my lord, and of very valiant approof.

LAFEW You have it from his own deliverance.

BERTRAM And by other warranted testimony.

LAFEW Then my dial goes not true. I took this lark for a bunting.   5

BERTRAM I do assure you, my lord, he is very great in knowledge, and
accordingly valiant.

LAFEW I have then sinned against his experience, and transgressed
against his valour, and my state that way is dangerous, since I cannot
yet find in my heart to repent. Here he comes. I pray you make   10
us friends, I will pursue the amity.

Enter PAROLLES

PAROLLES [*To Bertram*] These things shall be done, sir.

46 you. Come] *Theobald*; you come F   46 *Exeunt*] *Pope*; *Exit* F   Act 2, Scene 5   2.5] *Capell*; *not in* F   12 SD] *Capell*; *not in* F

38 **else** besides.

40 **make...proceeding** represent your hasty departure as your own idea.

42 **it probable need** your hasty departure necessary and plausible.

44 **Attend** Await.

44 **pleasure** command.

Act 2, Scene 5

2.5 Editors, following Capell, locate the scene in the King's palace, Paris.

2 **valiant approof** demonstrated valour.

3 **deliverance** testimony.

5 **dial** pocket watch; as in *AYLI* 2.7.20.

5 **bunting** Which resembles the lark except in its singing. Lafew ironically reverses the proverb 'To take a bunting for a lark' (Tilley B722).

7 **accordingly** correspondingly.

8–10 **sinned...repent** Lafew again gives a religious account of his relationship with Parolles.

10 **find in** find it in.

LAFEW Pray you, sir, who's his tailor?

PAROLLES Sir!

LAFEW O, I know him well, I, sir, he, sir, 's a good workman, a very   15
good tailor.

BERTRAM [*Aside to Parolles*] Is she gone to the king?

PAROLLES She is.

BERTRAM Will she away tonight?

PAROLLES As you'll have her.   20

BERTRAM I have writ my letters, casketed my treasure,
          Given order for our horses, and tonight,
          When I should take possession of the bride,
          End ere I do begin.

LAFEW A good traveller is something at the latter end of a dinner, but   25
one that lies three thirds, and uses a known truth to pass a thousand
nothings with, should be once heard and thrice beaten. God save
you, captain.

BERTRAM Is there any unkindness between my lord and you, monsieur?

PAROLLES I know not how I have deserved to run into my lord's   30
displeasure.

LAFEW You have made shift to run into't, boots and spurs and all, like
him that leapt into the custard; and out of it you'll run again, rather
than suffer question for your residence.

BERTRAM It may be you have mistaken him, my lord.   35

LAFEW And shall do so ever, though I took him at's prayers. Fare you
well, my lord, and believe this of me: there can be no kernel in this
light nut; the soul of this man is his clothes. Trust him not in matter
of heavy consequence; I have kept of them tame, and know their
natures. Farewell, monsieur, I have spoken better of you than you   40

---

15 I, sir] I sir F; Ay, 'sir' *Hunter*   15 he, sir, 's] *Capell;* hee sirs F   17 SD] *Rowe; not in* F   24 End] *Collier;* And F
25 traveller] F3, Trauailer F   26 one] *Rowe³;* on F   27 heard] F2; hard F

13 **who's his tailor** Another reference to
Parolles's plumage (as in 2.3.192 and below,
38). Compare *Lear* 2.2.54–5: 'a tailor made
thee'.

15–16 Lafew pretends to take 'Sir' as the
tailor's name.

24 *****End** Collier's emendation of the Folio 'And'
is generally accepted. It is possible, however, that
the conjunction completes the thought of a line that
has dropped out.

25 **something** i.e. to amuse the table with tall
stories.

32 **made shift** contrived.

33 **him...custard** Referring to the jester who
leaped into an enormous custard pie at the annual
feast of the Lord Mayor of London.

34 **suffer...residence** tolerate enquiry as to
why you are there.

36 **took** Playing on 'mistaken' (35).

39 **heavy** important.

39 **of them tame** some of these creatures as
household pets.

have or will to deserve at my hand, but we must do good against
evil.   [*Exit*]

PAROLLES An idle lord, I swear.

BERTRAM I think so.

PAROLLES Why, do you not know him?   45

BERTRAM Yes, I do know him well, and common speech
   Gives him a worthy pass. Here comes my clog.

      Enter HELENA

HELENA I have, sir, as I was commanded from you,
   Spoke with the king, and have procured his leave
   For present parting; only he desires   50
   Some private speech with you.

BERTRAM   I shall obey his will.
   You must not marvel, Helen, at my course,
   Which holds not colour with the time, nor does
   The ministration and requirèd office
   On my particular. Prepared I was not   55
   For such a business; therefore am I found
   So much unsettled. This drives me to entreat you,
   That presently you take your way for home,
   And rather muse than ask why I entreat you,
   For my respects are better than they seem,   60
   And my appointments have in them a need
   Greater than shows itself at the first view
   To you that know them not. This to my mother.
      [*Giving a letter*]
   'Twill be two days ere I shall see you, so
   I leave you to your wisdom.

---

41 or will] F; or wit or will *conj. Singer* 42 SD] *Rowe; not in* F 44 I think so] F; I think not so *Singer²* 63 SD] *Rowe; not in* F

41 have...deserve have deserved or will deserve.

41 do good against return good for. See 1 Thess. 5.15.

43 idle foolish.

45 If Bertram's 'I think so' (44) is correct, Parolles's rejoinder is to be taken, not as a question, but as an intensifier: 'Come, we know what he is.'

47 worthy pass good reputation.

47 clog Wooden block tied to an animal to restrict its movement.

48 from by.

50 present parting immediate departure.

53 holds...time is not in keeping with a wedding-day.

53–5 nor...particular i.e. and does not fulfil my obligation as a husband.

59 muse wonder.

60 respects reasons.

61 appointments affairs.

HELENA   Sir, I can nothing say,   65
    But that I am your most obedient servant.

BERTRAM Come, come, no more of that.

HELENA   And ever shall
    With true observance seek to eke out that
    Wherein toward me my homely stars have failed
    To equal my great fortune.

BERTRAM   Let that go.   70
    My haste is very great. Farewell; hie home.

HELENA Pray, sir, your pardon.

BERTRAM   Well, what would you say?

HELENA I am not worthy of the wealth I owe,
    Nor dare I say 'tis mine; and yet it is;
    But like a timorous thief, most fain would steal   75
    What law does vouch mine own.

BERTRAM   What would you have?

HELENA Something, and scarce so much; nothing indeed.
    I would not tell you what I would, my lord.
    Faith, yes:
    Strangers and foes do sunder, and not kiss.   80

BERTRAM I pray you stay not, but in haste to horse.

HELENA I shall not break your bidding, good my lord.
    Where are my other men? Monsieur, farewell.   *Exit*

BERTRAM Go thou toward home, where I will never come
    Whilst I can shake my sword or hear the drum.   85
    Away, and for our flight.

PAROLLES   Bravely, *corragio*!

                                     Exeunt

70–1] *As verse, Pope; as prose,* F   78–9] *As Dyce²; as one line,* F   83 Where...men? Monsieur, farewell. *Exit*] F;
BERTRAM Where...Monsieur? – farewell. *Exit Helena* / *conj. Theobald*   86 SD] *Rowe; not in* F

68 **observance** dutiful service.
68 **eke out** supplement.
69 **my homely stars** i.e. my fate which denied me noble parents.
71 **hie** hasten.
73 **owe** own, possess.
75 **fain** willingly.
76 **vouch** affirm to be.

80 **sunder** separate from one another.
81 **stay** delay.
83 Theobald assigns this line to Bertram. But though Helena's stars are 'homely' she has status enough to be attended by a retinue (her 'other men').
86 **Bravely, *corragio*!** Bravo, courage (Italian).

3.[1] *Flourish. Enter the* DUKE OF FLORENCE, *the two Frenchmen* [*the*
FIRST *and* SECOND LORDS DUMAINE], *with a troop of soldiers*

DUKE So that from point to point now have you heard
        The fundamental reasons of this war,
        Whose great decision hath much blood let forth
        And more thirsts after.

FIRST LORD   Holy seems the quarrel
        Upon your grace's part; black and fearful   5
        On the opposer.

DUKE Therefore we marvel much our cousin France
        Would in so just a business shut his bosom
        Against our borrowing prayers.

SECOND LORD   Good my lord,
        The reasons of our state I cannot yield   10
        But like a common and an outward man
        That the great figure of a council frames
        By self-unable motion, therefore dare not
        Say what I think of it, since I have found
        Myself in my incertain grounds to fail   15
        As often as I guessed.

DUKE   Be it his pleasure.

FIRST LORD But I am sure the younger of our nature,
        That surfeit on their ease, will day by day
        Come here for physic.

DUKE   Welcome shall they be;

Act 3, Scene 1 3.1] *Rowe; Actus Tertius.* F   o SD *Frenchmen*] F; French *Lords / Rowe*   9 SH SECOND LORD] *Rowe;*
French E. F   13 self-unable] F4; selfe vnable F   17 SH FIRST LORD] *Cam.; Fren. G.* F   17 nature] F; Nation *Rowe*

Act 3, Scene 1
3.1 Editors, following Capell, locate the scene in
Florence, the Duke's palace.
    3 **Whose great decision** The violent deciding
of which.
    4 **more thirsts after** is still thirsty for more
(blood).
    4–9 **Holy...prayers** Shakespeare draws atten-
tion to the contrast between the aloof attitude of the
King of France to the Italian wars and that of his
committed nobles. Compare 1.2.1–17 and 2.1.1–5.
    6 **the opposer** the enemy's part.
    7 **cousin** fellow ruler.
    8 **bosom** heart.
    9 **borrowing prayers** entreaties for assistance.

10 **yield** produce.
    11 **Except** as a commoner who stands outside
(state councils).
    12 **figure** scheme.
    12 **frames** constructs.
    13 **self-unable motion** (his own) inadequate
thought. 'Motion' = 'agitation of the mind' (*OED*
Motion *sb* 4).
    16 **guessed** conjectured.
    16 **Be...pleasure** Let it be as he will.
    17 **nature** temperament.
    18 **surfeit on** grow sick with. Compare *MM*
1.2.126.
    19 **for physic** to be cured by bloodletting.

And all the honours that can fly from us   20
Shall on them settle. – You know your places well;
When better fall, for your avails they fell.
Tomorrow to th'field.

Flourish. [Exeunt]

[3.2] *Enter* COUNTESS *and* [LAVATCH, *the*] *Clown*

COUNTESS It hath happened all as I would have had it, save that he
    comes not along with her.
LAVATCH By my troth, I take my young lord to be a very melancholy
    man.
COUNTESS By what observance, I pray you?   5
LAVATCH Why, he will look upon his boot and sing, mend the ruff and
    sing, ask questions and sing, pick his teeth and sing. I know a man
    that had this trick of melancholy sold a goodly manor for a song.
COUNTESS Let me see what he writes, and when he means to come.
                        [*Opening the letter*]
LAVATCH I have no mind to Isbel since I was at court. Our old lings   10
    and our Isbels a'th'country are nothing like your old ling and your
    Isbels a'th'court. The brains of my Cupid's knocked out, and I
    begin to love, as an old man loves money, with no stomach.
COUNTESS What have we here?
LAVATCH E'en that you have there.   *Exit*   15

---

23 to th'] *After* F2 (to the); to'th the F   Act 3, Scene 2   3.2] *Pope; not in* F   8 sold] F3; hold F   9 SH COUNTESS]
Rowe; Lad. F *(and subst. through scene, with / Old La. / at 57)*   9 SD] *Capell; not in* F   10 lings] F; Ling F2
15 E'en] *Theobald; In* F

---

20 can...us i.e. we can bestow.
22 better fall better places fall vacant.
22 for...fell i.e. they will have become vacant
for you to fill. The Duke's words link this scene with
the opening of 3.3 on the battlefield, where the
'general of our horse' leaves a vacancy for Bertram.

Act 3, Scene 2
3.2 Editors, following Capell, locate the scene in
Rossillion, the Count's palace.
1 all altogether.
3 troth faith.
5 observance observation (of him).
6 mend adjust.
6 ruff Either the frilled collar worn by men and
women in Shakespeare's time, or the ruffle or
turned-over flap at the top of a boot.

7 pick his teeth Like the affected traveller
with his toothpick, 1.1.134.
8 trick quirk.
8 *sold The reading of F3 is supported by the
proverb, current in Shakespeare's time, 'sold for a
song' (Tilley s636).
10 old lings salt cod. 'Salt' can mean lecherous
and 'cod' (as in cod-piece) can mean scrotum; the
Clown's joke remains obscure, but it appears to
suggest that his own appetites have become more
mercenary since he was at court.
11 country Perhaps continuing the obscene
quibble. Compare *Ham.* 3.2.116.
12 brains...out i.e. my old love is finished.
13 stomach appetite.
15 E'en As Hunter remarks, F's 'In' appears to
be a variant spelling of 'E'en' (= even).

[COUNTESS] [*Reads*] *a letter* 'I have sent you a daughter-in-law; she
hath recovered the king, and undone me. I have wedded her, not
bedded her, and sworn to make the "not" eternal. You shall hear
I am run away; know it before the report come. If there be breadth
enough in the world, I will hold a long distance. My duty to you.   20
                                        Your unfortunate son,
                                                Bertram.'

This is not well, rash and unbridled boy,
To fly the favours of so good a king,
To pluck his indignation on thy head   25
By the misprising of a maid too virtuous
For the contempt of empire.

Enter [LAVATCH, *the*] *Clown*

LAVATCH O madam, yonder is heavy news within between two soldiers
    and my young lady!
COUNTESS What is the matter?   30
LAVATCH Nay, there is some comfort in the news, some comfort. Your
    son will not be killed so soon as I thought he would.
COUNTESS Why should he be killed?
LAVATCH So say I, madam, if he run away, as I hear he does. The
    danger is in standing to't; that's the loss of men, though it be the 35
    getting of children. Here they come will tell you more. For my part,
    I only hear your son was run away.

Enter HELENA *and two Gentlemen* [*the* FIRST *and* SECOND LORDS
                        DUMAINE]

SECOND LORD 'Save you, good madam.
HELENA Madam, my lord is gone, for ever gone.
FIRST LORD Do not say so.   40
COUNTESS Think upon patience. Pray you, gentlemen,
    I have felt so many quirks of joy and grief

---

16 SD COUNTESS *Reads*] Rowe³; *not in* F   37 SD *the French* LORDS] Neilson; *not in* F   38 SH SECOND LORD] Kittredge;
French E. F *(and subst. through scene)*   40 SH FIRST LORD] Kittredge; *French G.* F *(and subst. through scene, with* / 1.G. /
at 55*)*   41 patience.] Capell; patience, F; patience; F3

17 **recovered** cured.
18 **'not'** With a pun on the hymeneal knot.
25 **pluck** draw down.
26 **misprising** scorning (as at 2.3.144).
27 **the…empire** even an emperor to disdain
her.
28 **heavy** sad.

35 **standing to't** staying put (with a quibble on
tumescence, as in *TGV* 2.5.22–3).
36 **getting** begetting.
37 **run away** Most editors, beginning with
Capell, make the Clown leave at this point, though
there is no direction in the Folio.
42 **quirks** sudden strokes.

That the first face of neither on the start
Can woman me unto't. Where is my son, I pray you?
FIRST LORD Madam, he's gone to serve the Duke of Florence.   45
We met him thitherward, for thence we came;
And after some dispatch in hand at court,
Thither we bend again.
HELENA Look on his letter, madam, here's my passport.
[*Reads*] 'When thou canst get the ring upon my finger, which never   50
shall come off, and show me a child begotten of thy body that I
am father to, then call me husband; but in such a "then" I write
a "never".' This is a dreadful sentence.
COUNTESS Brought you this letter, gentlemen?
FIRST LORD Ay, madam, and for the contents' sake are sorry for our   55
pains.
COUNTESS I prithee, lady, have a better cheer;
If thou engrossest all the griefs are thine,
Thou robb'st me of a moiety. He was my son,
But I do wash his name out of my blood,   60
And thou art all my child. Towards Florence is he?
FIRST LORD Ay, madam.
COUNTESS   And to be a soldier?
FIRST LORD Such is his noble purpose, and believe't,
The duke will lay upon him all the honour
That good convenience claims.
COUNTESS   Return you thither?   65
SECOND LORD Ay, madam, with the swiftest wing of speed.
HELENA [*Reads*] 'Till I have no wife, I have nothing in France.'
'Tis bitter.
COUNTESS   Find you that there?
HELENA   Ay, madam.
SECOND LORD 'Tis but the boldness of his hand haply, which his heart
was not consenting to.   70

---

50 SD] *Capell; not in* F   58 engrossest all] F4; engrossest, *all* F   67 SD] *After Rowe; not in* F   68 'Tis...madam] *As verse, Var. 93; as prose,* F

43 face appearance.
43–4 first...unto't i.e. the startling first appearance of neither joy nor grief can surprise me into womanish weeping.
44 woman me unto't make me behave like a weeping woman.
46 thitherward on his way thither.
47 dispatch in hand urgent business.
49 passport licence to wander from home.

58 thou engrossest you monopolise.
58 are that are.
59 a moiety half. More generally, a part.
61 art all only are.
65 good convenience claims he can in propriety claim.
67 'Till...France' i.e. while Bertram has a wife living in France he will not return there.
69 haply perhaps.

COUNTESS Nothing in France, until he have no wife!
There's nothing here that is too good for him
But only she, and she deserves a lord
That twenty such rude boys might tend upon,
And call her hourly mistress. Who was with him? 75
SECOND LORD A servant only, and a gentleman
Which I have sometime known.
COUNTESS   Parolles, was it not?
SECOND LORD Ay, my good lady, he.
COUNTESS A very tainted fellow, and full of wickedness.
My son corrupts a well-derivèd nature 80
With his inducement.
SECOND LORD   Indeed, good lady,
The fellow has a deal of that too much,
Which holds him much to have.
COUNTESS   Y'are welcome, gentlemen.
I will entreat you, when you see my son,
To tell him that his sword can never win 85
The honour that he loses. More I'll entreat you
Written to bear along.
FIRST LORD   We serve you, madam,
In that and all your worthiest affairs.
COUNTESS Not so, but as we change our courtesies.
Will you draw near? 90
Exit [with the Lords Dumaine]
HELENA 'Till I have no wife, I have nothing in France.'
Nothing in France, until he has no wife!
Thou shalt have none, Rossillion, none in France;
Then hast thou all again. Poor lord, is't I
That chase thee from thy country, and expose 95
Those tender limbs of thine to the event
Of the none-sparing war? And is it I
That drive thee from the sportive court, where thou

81–8] *As verse, Capell; as prose,* F   82 that] *Rowe³; that,* F   90 SD *with Lords] Neilson, after Rowe; not in* F

79 **tainted** corrupt.
80 **a well-derivèd nature** i.e. the good nature
which he has inherited.
82 **that** power of inducement, persuasiveness.
83 **holds...have** i.e. stands him in good stead.
'Holds' = 'supports', 'maintains' (*OED v* 3d).
87 **Written** In writing.

89 i.e. you serve me only to the extent that we
exchange civilities.
90 **draw near** come along (with me).
93–4 **none in...again** Helena will not live in
France and Bertram will be free to come home (112).
96 **event** hazard.

Wast shot at with fair eyes, to be the mark
Of smoky muskets? O you leaden messengers,   100
That ride upon the violent speed of fire,
Fly with false aim, move the still-piercing air
That sings with piercing, do not touch my lord.
Whoever shoots at him, I set him there;
Whoever charges on his forward breast,   105
I am the caitiff that do hold him to't;
And though I kill him not, I am the cause
His death was so effected. Better 'twere
I met the ravin lion when he roared
With sharp constraint of hunger; better 'twere   110
That all the miseries which nature owes
Were mine at once. No, come thou home, Rossillion,
Whence honour but of danger wins a scar,
As oft it loses all. I will be gone.
My being here it is that holds thee hence.   115
Shall I stay here to do't? No, no, although
The air of paradise did fan the house,
And angels officed all. I will be gone,
That pitiful rumour may report my flight
To consolate thine ear. Come night, end day!   120
For with the dark, poor thief, I'll steal away.   *Exit*

102 still-piercing] F2; still-peering F; still-piecing *Var. 78*; still-'pearing *Delius*   118 angels] F2; Angles F

99 **mark** target.
100 **leaden messengers** i.e. bullets.
102 **move** (1) stir (to pity), (2) displace.
102 ***still-piercing**. The Folio text reads 'still-peering'. Among many emendations, the most popular is Steevens's 'still-piecing', i.e. always closing up again. Alternatively, the compound can mean 'always looking on' or 'still appearing'. But 'piercing' in the line that follows suggests a deliberate repetition of the gerund, with the emphatic word being 'sings'. It seems tenable, therefore, to read 'still-piercing', i.e. always invading to the quick, and this reading is supported by F2.
103 **sings with piercing** i.e. in token of its indifference or malignity; alternatively, as the bullets pierce it, or as it derides their piercing. Compare *Rom.* 1.1.111–12.

105 **forward** (1) facing the enemy, (2) pressing forward.
106 **caitiff** wretch.
106 **hold** compel.
109 **ravin** ravening.
111 **owes** owns, possesses.
113 **Whence** From the war (where).
113 **but...scar** (1) only from danger wins a scar, (2) wins from danger only a scar.
114 **As...all** And often loses life itself.
115 **holds** keeps.
116 **do't** i.e. keep thee hence.
118 **officed all** had the office of all the household duties.
119 **pitiful** full of pity (for Bertram).
121 **thief** Helena, who has 'stolen' the title of wife, and whose resolution recapitulates Bertram's at 2.1.33.

[3.3] *Flourish. Enter the* DUKE OF FLORENCE, [BERTRAM, *Count of*]
Rossillion, Drum and Trumpets, Soldiers, PAROLLES

DUKE The general of our horse thou art, and we,
     Great in our hope, lay our best love and credence
     Upon thy promising fortune.
BERTRAM   Sir, it is
     A charge too heavy for my strength, but yet
     We'll strive to bear it for your worthy sake   5
     To th'extreme edge of hazard.
DUKE   Then go thou forth,
     And Fortune play upon thy prosperous helm
     As thy auspicious mistress!
BERTRAM   This very day,
     Great Mars, I put myself into thy file;
     Make me but like my thoughts, and I shall prove   10
     A lover of thy drum, hater of love.

                                          Exeunt

[3.4] *Enter* COUNTESS *and* [RINALDO, *the*] *Steward*

COUNTESS Alas! and would you take the letter of her?
     Might you not know she would do as she has done
     By sending me a letter? Read it again.
[RINALDO] [*Reads*] *letter*
     'I am Saint Jaques' pilgrim, thither gone.

Act 3, Scene 3 3.3] Capell; *not in* F   o SD BERTRAM, *Count of*] *After Rowe; not in* F   Act 3, Scene 4 3.4] Capell;
not in F   1 SH COUNTESS] *Rowe; La.* F *(through scene)*   4 SD STEWARD *Reads*] Collier; *not in* F

Act 3, Scene 3
  3.3 Evidently located on a Florentine battlefield
(see 3.1.23).
  o SD The appearance of Parolles at the end of the
parade is probably calculated.
  o SD *Drum and Trumpets* Drummers and
trumpeters.
  2 **Great** in Swelling with (like a pregnant
woman).
  2 **lay** wager.
  2 **credence** trust.
  3 **promising fortune** promise of good fortune
to come.
  6 **extreme...hazard** utmost limit of danger.
'Hazard', signifying a game of chance, also picks up
the Duke's 'lay' at 2. See 2.1.49 n.
  7–8 **Fortune...mistress** For the play's concern
with Fortune see pp. 18–21 above.

  7 **helm** helmet.
  9 **file** ranks.

Act 3, Scene 4
  3.4 Editors, following Capell, locate the scene in
Rossillion, the Count's palace.
  4–17 **I...free** These fourteen lines make a
Shakespearean sonnet.
  4 **Saint Jaques' pilgrim** A pilgrim to the shrine
of Santiago de Compostella, a famous place of
pilgrimage in north-western Spain where St James
the Greater is buried. 'Jaques' is pronounced as a
disyllable. For the sense of 'pilgrim', see Dante,
Vita Nuova, XL: 'in a specific sense "pilgrim"
means only one who travels to or returns from the
house of St James'.

Ambitious love hath so in me offended   5
That barefoot plod I the cold ground upon
With sainted vow my faults to have amended.
Write, write, that from the bloody course of war
My dearest master, your dear son, may hie.
Bless him at home in peace, whilst I from far   10
His name with zealous fervour sanctify.
His taken labours bid him me forgive;
I, his despiteful Juno, sent him forth
From courtly friends, with camping foes to live,
Where death and danger dogs the heels of worth.   15
He is too good and fair for death and me,
Whom I myself embrace to set him free.'
COUNTESS Ah, what sharp stings are in her mildest words!
Rinaldo, you did never lack advice so much
As letting her pass so. Had I spoke with her,   20
I could have well diverted her intents,
Which thus she hath prevented.
RINALDO   Pardon me, madam,
If I had given you this at overnight,
She might have been o'erta'en; and yet she writes,
Pursuit would be but vain.
COUNTESS   What angel shall   25
Bless this unworthy husband? He cannot thrive,
Unless her prayers, whom heaven delights to hear
And loves to grant, reprieve him from the wrath
Of greatest justice. Write, write, Rinaldo,
To this unworthy husband of his wife.   30
Let every word weigh heavy of her worth,
That he does weigh too light. My greatest grief,

---

7 have] F2; *hane* F   10 peace, whilst] F3; peace. Whilst F   18 SH COUNTESS] *Capell; not in* F

7 **sainted** (1) holy, (2) made to a saint.
7 **to have amended** to cause to be amended (see Abbott 360).
8 **course** Possibly punning on 'curse'.
9 **hie** hasten.
10 **Bless him** Let him be blessed.
10 **in peace** i.e. both safe from the war and his unwanted wife.
11 **sanctify** invoke blessings on.
12 **His taken labours** As for the labours he has undertaken.
13 **despiteful** spiteful.

13 **Juno** Whose enmity imposed on Hercules his celebrated labours.
17 **Whom** i.e. death.
19 **advice** considered judgement.
22 **prevented** forestalled.
23 **at overnight** last evening.
27 **whom** i.e. both Helena and her prayers.
30 **unworthy...wife** husband unworthy of his wife.
31 **weigh heavy of** emphasise.
32 **greatest** very great.

Though little he do feel it, set down sharply.
Dispatch the most convenient messenger.
When haply he shall hear that she is gone,   35
He will return, and hope I may that she,
Hearing so much, will speed her foot again,
Led hither by pure love. Which of them both
Is dearest to me, I have no skill in sense
To make distinction. Provide this messenger.   40
My heart is heavy, and mine age is weak;
Grief would have tears, and sorrow bids me speak.

Exeunt

[3.5] *A tucket afar off. Enter old* WIDOW *of Florence, her daughter*
[DIANA], VIOLENTA, *and* MARIANA, *with other* CITIZENS

WIDOW Nay, come, for if they do approach the city, we shall lose all
the sight.
DIANA They say the French count has done most honourable service.
WIDOW It is reported that he has taken their great'st commander, and
that with his own hand he slew the duke's brother.   5
                    [*Tucket*]
We have lost our labour, they are gone a contrary way. Hark! you
may know by their trumpets.
MARIANA Come, let's return again and suffice ourselves with the report
of it. Well, Diana, take heed of this French earl. The honour of
a maid is her name, and no legacy is so rich as honesty.   10
WIDOW I have told my neighbour how you have been solicited by a
gentleman his companion.

Act 3, Scene 5 3.5] *Capell; not in* F   0 SD DIANA] *Rowe; not in* F   1–12] *As prose, Pope;* Nay…come, / …Citty,
/ …sight. / …done / …service. / …reported, / …Commander, / …slew / …labour, / …harke, / …Trumpets.
/ …againe, / …it. / …Earle, / …name, / …rich / …honestie. / …neighbour / …Gentleman /…Companion. F
5 SD] *Capell; not in* F

33 **sharply** emphatically, so that he will feel it.
35 **When haply** Perhaps when.
39 **skill in sense** ability in terms of what I feel.
40 **Provide** Equip.

Act 3, Scene 5
3.5 Editors, following Capell, locate the scene
outside Florence.
0 SD *tucket* A series of notes on the trumpet.
0 SD VIOLENTA This character does not speak.

Violenta appears in William Painter's *Palace of
Pleasure* (1566, 1569, 1575), in the 37th and 42nd
novelle, and may represent the name Shakespeare
originally intended for the Widow's daughter, or an
abandoned intention to create another character
here.
4 **their** i.e. the Senoys'.
8 **suffice** content.
10 **name** reputation (as maiden or virgin).
10 **honesty** chastity (as again at 55).

MARIANA I know that knave, hang him! one Parolles, a filthy officer
he is in those suggestions for the young earl. Beware of them, Diana;
their promises, enticements, oaths, tokens, and all these engines of   15
lust, are not the things they go under. Many a maid hath been
seduced by them, and the misery is, example, that so terrible shows
in the wrack of maidenhood, cannot for all that dissuade succession,
but that they are limed with the twigs that threatens them. I hope
I need not to advise you further, but I hope your own grace will   20
keep you where you are, though there were no further danger known
but the modesty which is so lost.
DIANA You shall not need to fear me.

Enter HELENA

WIDOW I hope so. Look, here comes a pilgrim. I know she will lie at
my house; thither they send one another. I'll question her. God   25
save you, pilgrim, whither are bound?
HELENA To Saint Jaques le Grand.
          Where do the palmers lodge, I do beseech you?
WIDOW At the Saint Francis here beside the port.
HELENA Is this the way?   30

A march afar

WIDOW Ay, marry, is't. Hark you, they come this way.
          If you will tarry, holy pilgrim,
          But till the troops come by,
          I will conduct you where you shall be lodged,
          The rather for I think I know your hostess   35
          As ample as myself.

17 is,] *Rowe³;* is F   23 SD *Enter* HELENA] F; *Enter* HELENA *disguised like a Pilgrim.* / *Rowe*   26 whither] F2; whether
F   26 are] F; are you F2   27 le] F3; la F

13 **officer** agent.
14 **suggestions** for solicitings on behalf of.
15 **engines** schemes.
16 **go under** pretend to be.
17–18 **example…maidenhood** that previous
examples will illustrate so terribly the ruin of
virginity.
18 **dissuade succession** prevent other maids
from taking the same course.
19 **but that** but for all that (wealth of example).
See Abbott 122 on 'but' as signifying prevention.
19 **limed…twigs** caught in the trap (as birds are
snared by birdlime smeared on twigs).
19 **threatens** Elizabethan usage sanctions a
singular verb with a plural subject.
23 **fear** fear for, worry about.

24 **lie** lodge.
26 **are** are you.
28 **palmers** Pilgrims who carried a palm leaf in
token of having visited the Holy Sepulchre in
Jerusalem.
29 **Saint Francis** An inn with the sign of St
Francis.
29 **port** city gate. It is likely that the main doors
of the façade of the tiring-house served to represent
it.
30–3 Hunter suggests that the short lines may
represent a compositor's attempt to regularise
confused copy. In any case, the dialogue is
punctuated by the sound of the approaching band.
36 **ample** amply.

HELENA   Is it yourself?

WIDOW If you shall please so, pilgrim.

HELENA I thank you, and will stay upon your leisure.

WIDOW You came, I think, from France?

HELENA   I did so.

WIDOW Here you shall see a countryman of yours   40
    That has done worthy service.

HELENA   His name, I pray you?

DIANA The Count Rossillion. Know you such a one?

HELENA But by the ear, that hears most nobly of him.
    His face I know not.

DIANA   Whatsome'er he is,
    He's bravely taken here. He stole from France,   45
    As 'tis reported, for the king had married him
    Against his liking. Think you it is so?

HELENA Ay, surely, mere the truth, I know his lady.

DIANA There is a gentleman that serves the count
    Reports but coarsely of her.

HELENA   What's his name?   50

DIANA Monsieur Parolles.

HELENA   O, I believe with him.
    In argument of praise, or to the worth
    Of the great count himself, she is too mean
    To have her name repeated. All her deserving
    Is a reservèd honesty, and that   55
    I have not heard examined.

DIANA   Alas, poor lady,
    'Tis a hard bondage to become the wife
    Of a detesting lord.

WIDOW I write 'good creature', wheresoe'er she is,
    Her heart weighs sadly. This young maid might do her   60
    A shrewd turn, if she pleased.

HELENA   How do you mean?

---

59 I write] F; I right F2; Ah! right *Rowe*; A right *Var. 78*; I warrant, *Globe*   59 'good creature',] *This edn*; good creature, F

38 stay upon await.
44 Whatsome'er Whatever.
45 bravely taken highly regarded.
46 for because.
48 mere absolutely.
52 In...or With respect to her merit, or in comparison.
53 mean low born.

54 **All her deserving** Her only merit.
55 **reservèd** strictly preserved.
56 **examined** called in question.
59 **write** style her. The Globe emendation 'warrant' is generally preferred to the Folio reading. But compare *MM* 2.4.16 and *Ado* 4.3.86–7.
60 **weighs sadly** is heavy.
61 **shrewd** (1) curst, (2) hurtful.

> May be the amorous count solicits her
> In the unlawful purpose?
WIDOW   He does indeed,
> And brokes with all that can in such a suit
> Corrupt the tender honour of a maid.   65
> But she is armed for him, and keeps her guard
> In honestest defence.

Drum and Colours. Enter [BERTRAM] *Count Rossillion,* PAROLLES,
and the whole army

MARIANA   The gods forbid else!
WIDOW So, now they come.
> That is Antonio, the duke's eldest son,
> That, Escalus.
HELENA   Which is the Frenchman?
DIANA   He,   70
> That with the plume; 'tis a most gallant fellow.
> I would he loved his wife. If he were honester
> He were much goodlier. Is't not a handsome gentleman?
HELENA I like him well.
DIANA 'Tis pity he is not honest. Yond's that same knave   75
> That leads him to these places. Were I his lady,
> I would poison that vile rascal.
HELENA   Which is he?
DIANA That jack-an-apes with scarfs. Why is he melancholy?
HELENA Perchance he's hurt i'th'battle.
PAROLLES Lose our drum! Well.   80
MARIANA He's shrewdly vexed at something. Look, he has spied us.
WIDOW Marry, hang you!
MARIANA And your courtesy, for a ring-carrier!
                              Exeunt [*Bertram, Parolles, and army*]

---

67 SD BERTRAM] *Rowe; not in* F   69 Antonio] F2; *Anthonio* F   75 Yond's] *Rowe;* yonds F   83 SD *Exeunt...army*]
After Rowe; Exit F

---

64 **brokes** bargains, like a go-between or bawd.
Compare *Tro.* 5.10.33.
66 **guard** ward. A term from weaponry
signifying defence. Compare *Tro.* 1.2.263.
67 **honestest** most chaste.
67 SD.1 *Colours* Colour-bearer (i.e.
standard-bearer).
67 **else** that it should be otherwise.
72 **honester** more honourable.
73 **were** would be.
75 **Yond's** Not an adverb but a demonstrative
pronoun: 'That one there is'.

78 **jack-an-apes** monkey.
80 **drum** As much a symbol of regimental honour
as the regiment's colours.
81 **shrewdly** keenly.
83 **courtesy** Alluding to the bow or curtsy
Parolles makes to the ladies.
83 **ring-carrier** Go-between who carries presents
or tenders of marriage between his master and the
woman marked down for prey.

WIDOW The troop is past. Come, pilgrim, I will bring you
　　　　 Where you shall host. Of enjoined penitents　　　　　　　85
　　　　 There's four or five, to great Saint Jaques bound,
　　　　 Already at my house.
HELENA　　　　　　　　　　　 I humbly thank you.
　　　　 Please it this matron and this gentle maid
　　　　 To eat with us tonight, the charge and thanking
　　　　 Shall be for me, and to requite you further,　　　　　　 90
　　　　 I will bestow some precepts of this virgin
　　　　 Worthy the note.
BOTH　　　　　　　　　　 We'll take your offer kindly.

Exeunt

[3.6] *Enter* [BERTRAM] *Count Rossillion and the Frenchmen* [*the* FIRST *and* SECOND LORDS DUMAINE], *as at first*

SECOND LORD Nay, good my lord, put him to't; let him have his way.
FIRST LORD If your lordship find him not a hilding, hold me no more
　　　　 in your respect.
SECOND LORD On my life, my lord, a bubble.
BERTRAM Do you think I am so far deceived in him?　　　　　　 5
SECOND LORD Believe it, my lord, in mine own direct knowledge,
　　　　 without any malice, but to speak of him as my kinsman, he's a most

Act 3, Scene 6　3.6] *Capell; not in* F　0 SD BERTRAM] *Rowe; not in* F　1 SH SECOND LORD] *Capell; Cap.E.* F *(and subst. through scene)*　2 SH FIRST LORD] *Capell; Cap.G.* F *(through scene)*　5] *As prose, Pope; Do...farre / Deceiued...him.* F

85 **host** lodge.
85 **enjoined penitents** Persons vowed to undertake a pilgrimage in penance for their sins.
88 **Please it** If it please.
89–90 **charge...me** i.e. I shall pay the bill and be grateful too.
91 **precepts** advice.
91 **of** on.
92 **Worthy the note** (1) 'worth listening to' (modifying 'precepts'), (2) 'worth looking at' (modifying 'virgin').
92 **kindly** gratefully.

Act 3, Scene 6
3.6 Editors, following Capell, locate the scene in the Florentine camp.
0 SD *as at first* Recalls their previous appearance at 3.2.37.
1 **to't** to the test.

2 *For SECOND LORD in the first speech heading and FIRST LORD in the second, F reads, respectively, 'Cap.E.' and 'Cap.G.' These F designations continue for SECOND LORD at 1, 4, 6, 31, 67, 77 and 85. At 17 he is simply 'C.E.' At 87 however, he becomes 'Cap.G.' FIRST LORD is designated 'Cap.G.' by F at 2, 11, 15, 26, 35, 39, 71 and 81, but becomes 'Cap.E.' at 89 and 95. In the text of the present scene all Es have, with three exceptions, been interpreted as SECOND LORD and all Gs as FIRST LORD. For the exceptions see notes on SHs 87, 89 and 95. For an account of the confusion between the two lords and their relation to the letters that designate them in F, see Textual Analysis, pp. 150–1 below.
2 **hilding** coward.
4 **bubble** glittering and empty cheat.
7 **as** as if he were.

notable coward, an infinite and endless liar, an hourly promise-
breaker, the owner of no one good quality worthy your lordship's
entertainment.   10

FIRST LORD It were fit you knew him, lest reposing too far in his virtue,
which he hath not, he might at some great and trusty business in
a main danger fail you.

BERTRAM I would I knew in what particular action to try him.

FIRST LORD None better than to let him fetch off his drum, which you   15
hear him so confidently undertake to do.

SECOND LORD I, with a troop of Florentines, will suddenly surprise him;
such I will have, whom I am sure he knows not from the enemy.
We will bind and hoodwink him so, that he shall suppose no other
but that he is carried into the leaguer of the adversaries, when we   20
bring him to our own tents. Be but your lordship present at his
examination, if he do not, for the promise of his life, and in the
highest compulsion of base fear, offer to betray you, and deliver all
the intelligence in his power against you, and that with the divine
forfeit of his soul upon oath, never trust my judgement in anything.   25

FIRST LORD O, for the love of laughter, let him fetch his drum; he says
he has a stratagem for't. When your lordship sees the bottom of
his success in't, and to what metal this counterfeit lump of ore will
be melted, if you give him not John Drum's entertainment, your
inclining cannot be removed. Here he comes.   30

Enter PAROLLES

SECOND LORD O, for the love of laughter, hinder not the honour of his
design. Let him fetch off his drum in any hand.

BERTRAM How now, monsieur? This drum sticks sorely in your
disposition.

FIRST LORD A pox on't, let it go, 'tis but a drum.   35

---

9 quality worthy] *Rowe;* qualitie, worthy F   28 his] *Rowe;* this F   28 ore] *Theobald;* ours F

10 **entertainment** patronage.
11 **reposing...in** depending too much on.
12 **trusty** needing trustworthiness.
14 **try** test.
15 **fetch off** retrieve.
17 **surprise** capture.
19 **hoodwink** blindfold.
20 **leaguer** camp.
24 **intelligence...power** information he possesses.
27 **bottom** extent.
28 ***his** F's 'this' looks like a misreading.

28 **counterfeit...ore** lump of counterfeit ore.
28 ***ore** F's 'ours' makes limp sense, and 'ore', as Hunter remarks, is a plausible misreading of the variant form 'oure'; here, as in *Ham.* 4.1.25, it means 'gold' (by confusion with 'or' in heraldry).
29 **John Drum's entertainment** Proverbial for being turned out of doors (Tilley J12).
30 **inclining** partiality (to Parolles).
32 **in any hand** in any case.
33–4 **sticks...disposition** annoys you sorely.
35 **pox on't** plague take it.

PAROLLES But a drum! Is't but a drum? A drum so lost! There was
    excellent command, to charge in with our horse upon our own
    wings, and to rend our own soldiers!

FIRST LORD That was not to be blamed in the command of the service;
    it was a disaster of war that Caesar himself could not have   40
    prevented, if he had been there to command.

BERTRAM Well, we cannot greatly condemn our success. Some dishonour
    we had in the loss of that drum, but it is not to be recovered.

PAROLLES It might have been recovered.

BERTRAM It might, but it is not now.   45

PAROLLES It is to be recovered. But that the merit of service is seldom
    attributed to the true and exact performer, I would have that drum
    or another, or *hic jacet*.

BERTRAM Why, if you have a stomach, to't, monsieur: if you think your
    mystery in stratagem can bring this instrument of honour again   50
    into his native quarter, be magnanimous in the enterprise and go
    on; I will grace the attempt for a worthy exploit. If you speed well
    in it, the duke shall both speak of it, and extend to you what further
    becomes his greatness, even to the utmost syllable of your
    worthiness.   55

PAROLLES By the hand of a soldier, I will undertake it.

BERTRAM But you must not now slumber in it.

PAROLLES I'll about it this evening, and I will presently pen down my
    dilemmas, encourage myself in my certainty, put myself into my
    mortal preparation; and by midnight look to hear further from me.   60

BERTRAM May I be bold to acquaint his grace you are gone about it?

PAROLLES I know not what the success will be, my lord, but the attempt
    I vow.

49 stomach, to't] F; stomack to't *Capell*   51 magnanimous] magnanimious F

38 **wings** flanks.
39 **command...service** military orders.
42 **greatly...success** feel too bad about the
outcome (as at 62).
46 **But** Were it not.
48 *hic jacet* here lies (the inscription on a
tombstone).
49 **a stomach** the courage.
50 **mystery** technical knowledge, as of a craft.
52 **grace** support.
52 **speed** succeed.
54 **becomes** does credit to.

54 **syllable** Perhaps Bertram is glancing
satirically at the name 'Parolles'.
58 **presently** immediately.
58 **pen down** (1) write out, (2) confine, as in a
pen.
59 **dilemmas** (1) alternative and equally
unfavourable arguments (whence the 'horns' of a
dilemma), (2) perplexities.
59 **certainty** i.e. of success (and opposing the
'dilemmas' of 59).
60 **mortal preparation** (1) preparation for my
death, (2) preparation for the deaths of others
(whom Parolles is about to slay).

BERTRAM I know th'art valiant, and to the possibility of thy soldiership
will subscribe for thee. Farewell. 65

PAROLLES I love not many words. *Exit*

SECOND LORD No more than a fish loves water. Is not this a strange
fellow, my lord, that so confidently seems to undertake this
business, which he knows is not to be done, damns himself to do,
and dares better be damned than to do't? 70

FIRST LORD You do not know him, my lord, as we do. Certain it is that
he will steal himself into a man's favour, and for a week escape a
great deal of discoveries, but when you find him out, you have him
ever after.

BERTRAM Why, do you think he will make no deed at all of this that 75
so seriously he does address himself unto?

SECOND LORD None in the world, but return with an invention, and
clap upon you two or three probable lies. But we have almost
embossed him, you shall see his fall tonight; for indeed he is not
for your lordship's respect. 80

FIRST LORD We'll make you some sport with the fox ere we case him.
He was first smoked by the old Lord Lafew. When his disguise and
he is parted, tell me what a sprat you shall find him, which you
shall see this very night.

SECOND LORD I must go look my twigs. He shall be caught. 85

BERTRAM Your brother, he shall go along with me.

SECOND LORD As't please your lordship. I'll leave you. *[Exit]*

BERTRAM Now will I lead you to the house, and show you
The lass I spoke of.

FIRST LORD But you say she's honest.

64–5] *As prose, Pope;* I…valiant, / And…souldiership, / Will…Farewell. F   87 SH SECOND LORD] *Rowe; Cap.G.*
F; FIRST LORD *Malone*   87 SD] *Theobald; not in* F   89, 95 SH FIRST LORD] *Rowe³; Cap.E.* F; SECOND LORD *Malone*

---

64 possibility utmost capacity.
65 subscribe vouch.
69 damns swears (perjured) oaths.
73 have him perceive his true character.
75 make no deed perform no part.
77 an invention a fabricated tale.
78 probable plausible.
79 embossed him (1) driven him into a corner, (2) made him foam at the mouth like an exhausted animal. (It seems likely that the verb conflates both meanings.)
80 respect regard.
81 case skin (hence 'unmask').
82 smoked (1) smelled out, (2) driven out of his hole by smoke (as again at 4.1.21).

83 sprat small fry, contemptible creature.
85 look overlook.
· **85 twigs** i.e. trap (the twigs being smeared with birdlime as a snare).
87 SH •SECOND LORD F's assignment of this line to *Cap.G.* (usually signifying the FIRST LORD) is inconsistent with 17 SH and 85 SH, which require the initiative in the plot against Parolles to be taken by *Cap.E.* (the SECOND LORD).
89 SH, 95 SH •FIRST LORD F's assignment of these lines to the SECOND LORD (*Cap.E.*) is inconsistent with 17, 85 and 86.
89 honest chaste.

BERTRAM That's all the fault. I spoke with her but once,   90
    And found her wondrous cold, but I sent to her,
    By this same coxcomb that we have i'th'wind,
    Tokens and letters which she did re-send,
    And this is all I have done. She's a fair creature;
    Will you go see her?
FIRST LORD   With all my heart, my lord.   95

                                        Exeunt

[3.7] *Enter* HELENA *and* WIDOW

HELENA If you misdoubt me that I am not she,
    I know not how I shall assure you further
    But I shall lose the grounds I work upon.
WIDOW Though my estate be fall'n, I was well born,
    Nothing acquainted with these businesses,   5
    And would not put my reputation now
    In any staining act.
HELENA   Nor would I wish you.
    First give me trust, the count he is my husband,
    And what to your sworn counsel I have spoken
    Is so from word to word; and then you cannot,   10
    By the good aid that I of you shall borrow,
    Err in bestowing it.
WIDOW   I should believe you,
    For you have showed me that which well approves
    Y'are great in fortune.
HELENA   Take this purse of gold,
    And let me buy your friendly help thus far,   15
    Which I will over-pay and pay again

Act 3, Scene 7   3.7] *Capell; not in* F

92 **coxcomb** fool.
92 **have…wind** are to the windward of (i.e. we can track him without being scented by him).

Act 3, Scene 7
3.7 Editors, following Capell, locate the scene in Florence, the Widow's house.
1 **misdoubt** doubt.
3 **But…lose** Without losing. Helena fears she might give away her position ('grounds').

4 **estate be fall'n** worldly fortune has declined.
8 **trust** belief.
9 **sworn counsel** private hearing, backed by a vow to be secret.
10 **from…word** word by word.
11 **By** With regard to.
13 **approves** proves.
16 **over-pay…again** doubly recompense.

When I have found it. The count he woos your daughter,
Lays down his wanton siege before her beauty,
Resolved to carry her. Let her in fine consent,
As we'll direct her how 'tis best to bear it.   20
Now his important blood will naught deny
That she'll demand. A ring the county wears,
That downward hath succeeded in his house
From son to son, some four or five descents,
Since the first father wore it. This ring he holds   25
In most rich choice; yet in his idle fire,
To buy his will, it would not seem too dear,
Howe'er repented after.

WIDOW   Now I see
The bottom of your purpose.

HELENA You see it lawful then. It is no more   30
But that your daughter, ere she seems as won,
Desires this ring; appoints him an encounter;
In fine, delivers me to fill the time,
Herself most chastely absent. After,
To marry her, I'll add three thousand crowns   35
To what is passed already.

WIDOW   I have yielded.
Instruct my daughter how she shall persèver,
That time and place with this deceit so lawful
May prove coherent. Every night he comes
With musics of all sorts, and songs composed   40
To her unworthiness. It nothing steads us
To chide him from our eaves, for he persists
As if his life lay on't.

19 Resolved] *Collier;* Resolue F; Resolves F2   28–9 Now...purpose] *As Capell; as one line,* F   34 After,] *Hunter;* after
F; after this F2   41 steads] F4; steeds F

17 **found** received.
18 **wanton** lecherous.
19 **carry** conquer (the looked-for result of the siege).
19 **fine** so many words (as again at 33).
20 **bear it** conduct the business.
21 **important** importunate.
21 **blood** passion.
22 **That** That which.
26 **rich choice** high regard.
26 **idle fire** worthless passion.
27 **buy his will** achieve the object of his lust.
29 **bottom** extent.

30 **lawful** i.e. to be lawful.
32 **encounter** assignation.
35 **marry her** enable her to get married (by furnishing her with a dowry).
36 **is passed** has been given.
37 **persèver** carry herself.
39 **coherent** in accord.
40 **musics** musicians.
40–1 **composed...unworthiness** (1) leading to her disrepute, (2) addressed to her (socially) inferior person.
41 **nothing steads us** does us no good.
43 **lay** depended.

HELENA   Why then tonight
　　　Let us assay our plot, which if it speed,
　　　Is wicked meaning in a lawful deed,   45
　　　And lawful meaning in a lawful act,
　　　Where both not sin, and yet a sinful fact.
　　　But let's about it.

                                                                    [*Exeunt*]

4.[1] *Enter one of the Frenchmen [the* SECOND LORD DUMAINE], *with five or six other* SOLDIERS *in ambush*

SECOND LORD He can come no other way but by this hedge corner.
　　　When you sally upon him, speak what terrible language you will.
　　　Though you understand it not yourselves, no matter; for we must
　　　not seem to understand him, unless some one among us, whom we
　　　must produce for an interpreter.   5
FIRST SOLDIER Good captain, let me be th'interpreter.
SECOND LORD Art not acquainted with him? Knows he not thy voice?
FIRST SOLDIER No, sir, I warrant you.
SECOND LORD But what linsey-woolsey hast thou to speak to us again?
FIRST SOLDIER E'en such as you speak to me.   10
SECOND LORD He must think us some band of strangers i'th'adversary's
　　　entertainment. Now he hath a smack of all neighbouring languages;
　　　therefore we must every one be a man of his own fancy, not to know
　　　what we speak to one another; so we seem to know, is to know

---

48 SD] *Rowe; not in* F   Act 4, Scene 1 4.1] *Rowe; Actus Quartus.* F   0 SD *the* SECOND LORD] *After Cam; not in* F
1 SH SECOND LORD] *Cam.; 1.Lord E.* F *(and subst. through scene)*   6 captain] F3; Captaiue F

44 **assay** try.
44 **speed** succeed.
45 **meaning** intention (on Bertram's part).
45 a **lawful deed** i.e. Helena cohabiting with her husband.
46 **meaning** intention (on Helena's part).
47 In which, notwithstanding Bertram's conviction that he is committing adultery, neither party is guilty of adulterous behaviour.
47 **fact** act, deed.

Act 4, Scene 1
4.1. Editors, following Capell, locate the scene outside the Florentine camp. In 1 'this hedge corner' reminds us that the stage was provided with hiding-places for the soldiers who enter 'in ambush'.

1 SH SECOND LORD F in this scene uses the anomalous SH *1.Lord E* at 1, 7, 9, 11, and *Lor.E, Lo.E.* or *L.E.* to the end of the scene. For consistency with 3.6, all Es in the present scene have been interpreted as SECOND LORD.
2 **terrible** ferocious.
4 **unless** except for.
9 **linsey-woolsey** hodgepodge (of words). Literally, cloth made of a mixture of linen and wool.
11–12 **some...entertainment** foreign troops in the service of the enemy.
12 **smack** smattering.
13 **to know** knowing.
14–15 **know...purpose** see our intention effected at once.

straight our purpose: choughs' language, gabble enough, and good   15
enough. As for you, interpreter, you must seem very politic. But
couch ho, here he comes, to beguile two hours in a sleep, and then
to return and swear the lies he forges.

Enter PAROLLES

PAROLLES Ten a'clock: within these three hours 'twill be time enough
to go home. What shall I say I have done? It must be a very plausive   20
invention that carries it. They begin to smoke me, and disgraces
have of late knocked too often at my door. I find my tongue is too
foolhardy, but my heart hath the fear of Mars before it, and of his
creatures, not daring the reports of my tongue.

SECOND LORD This is the first truth that e'er thine own tongue was   25
guilty of.

PAROLLES What the devil should move me to undertake the recovery
of this drum, being not ignorant of the impossibility, and knowing
I had no such purpose? I must give myself some hurts, and say
I got them in exploit. Yet slight ones will not carry it. They will   30
say, 'Came you off with so little?' And great ones I dare not give;
wherefore what's the instance? Tongue, I must put you into a
butter-woman's mouth, and buy myself another of Bajazeth's mule,

15 choughs'] *Dyce*, Choughs F   33 Bajazeth's] *Baiazeths* F; Bajazet's *Rowe*; Balaam's *Lowes, conj. Addis*   33 mule]
F; mute *Hanmer, conj. Warburton*

15 **choughs'** jackdaws'.

17 **couch** lie down. (Presumably the soldiers
conceal themselves about the stage.)

17 **beguile** idle away.

20 **plausive** plausible.

21 **carries it** i.e. makes my lies believable (as
again at 30).

23–4 **his creatures** i.e. soldiers (Mars being the
god of war).

24 **not...tongue** being afraid to bear out my
bragging.

32 **instance** (1) motive (i.e. 'What the devil
should move me...?'), (2) proof (of my sufficient
'hurts...in exploit').

33 **butter-woman's** dairy-woman's. Some editors (e.g. Evans, Kittredge) associate this with
garrulity. A 'butter-whore' is a scolding butter-
woman (*OED* Butter *sb*[1] 5). Parolles, wanting to get
rid of his prattling tongue, will give it to a
loquacious butter-woman who can make better use
of it.

33 **Bajazeth's mule** Bajazeth defies Tamburlaine
when he is taken prisoner (in Marlowe's *Tamburlaine*), and perhaps Parolles is thinking of the mule's

defiance of any master, and associates Bajazeth and
the mule. Inconsequently, he himself is found out
to be an ass at 4.3.282–3. Steevens notes (Var. 73):
'In one of our old Turkish histories, there is a
pompous description of Bajazet riding on a mule in
Divan.' None of these associations is inevitable or
fully clarifies an allusion to Bajazeth's mule. It is
possible, however, that Shakespeare is remembering,
not Marlowe's Bajazeth, but Bajazeth the son of
Suleyman the Magnificent, who was strangled by
the royal mutes with their bowstrings at the order
of his father, 25 September 1561. If it is this event
that Shakespeare is remembering, Hanmer's emendation of F 'mule' to 'mute' will be the preferred
reading. Painter, in the penultimate tale (34) in
Volume II of his *Palace of Pleasure*, tells how
Suleyman had the mutes strangle his eldest son
Mustapha, and Painter recalls in passing the murder
of Sultan Bajazeth by his son Selim the Grim, the
father of Suleyman. These atrocities, perhaps
conflated or confused and engendering the image of
the 'malignant and turbaned Turk', were notorious
in sixteenth-century England, and their currency in
the literature of the period has been documented by

if you prattle me into these perils.

SECOND LORD Is it possible he should know what he is, and be that 35
he is?

PAROLLES I would the cutting of my garments would serve the turn,
or the breaking of my Spanish sword.

SECOND LORD We cannot afford you so.

PAROLLES Or the baring of my beard, and to say it was in stratagem. 40

SECOND LORD 'Twould not do.

PAROLLES Or to drown my clothes, and say I was stripped.

SECOND LORD Hardly serve.

PAROLLES Though I swore I leapt from the window of the citadel –

SECOND LORD How deep? 45

PAROLLES Thirty fathom.

SECOND LORD Three great oaths would scarce make that be believed.

PAROLLES I would I had any drum of the enemy's. I would swear I
recovered it.

SECOND LORD You shall hear one anon. 50

PAROLLES A drum now of the enemy's –

Alarum within

SECOND LORD *Throca movousus, cargo, cargo, cargo.*

ALL *Cargo, cargo, cargo, villianda par corbo, cargo.*

PAROLLES O ransom, ransom! Do not hide mine eyes.

[They blindfold him]

INTERPRETER *Boskos thromuldo boskos.* 55

PAROLLES I know you are the Muskos' regiment,
And I shall lose my life for want of language.
If there be here German, or Dane, Low Dutch,
Italian, or French, let him speak to me,
I'll discover that which shall undo the Florentine. 60

INTERPRETER *Boskos vauvado.* I understand thee, and can speak thy
tongue. *Kerelybonto*, sir, betake thee to thy faith, for seventeen
poniards are at thy bosom.

PAROLLES O!

---

46 fathom] fadom F 48, 51 enemy's] *Malone;* enemies F 54] *As one line, Pope;* O...ransome, / Do...eyes. F
54 SD] *After Rowe; not in* F 55 SH INTERPRETER] F; *First Soldier / Capell* 56 Muskos'] *Capell;* Muskos F

Samuel C. Chew, *The Crescent and the Rose*, 1937.
The Turk was evidently in Shakespeare's mind
when he wrote this play. See e.g. 2.3.80 and
4.4.7. For the conjunction of mutes and Turks, see
TN 1.2.62: 'Be you his eunuch, and your mute I'll
be.'
  35 **that** what.
  37 **serve the turn** suffice.
  39 **afford you so** let you off like that.

40 **baring** shaving.
40 **in stratagem** an act of cunning.
46 **fathom** A measure of six feet.
52 'Choughs' language'.
56 **Muskos'** Muscovites'.
60 **discover** reveal.
62 **betake...faith** fall to your prayers.
63 **poniards** daggers.

INTERPRETER O, pray, pray, pray! *Manka revania dulche.*   65
SECOND LORD *Oscorbidulchos volivorco.*
INTERPRETER The general is content to spare thee yet,
    And hoodwinked as thou art, will lead thee on
    To gather from thee. Haply thou mayst inform
    Something to save thy life.
PAROLLES   O, let me live,   70
    And all the secrets of our camp I'll show,
    Their force, their purposes; nay, I'll speak that
    Which you will wonder at.
INTERPRETER   But wilt thou faithfully?
PAROLLES If I do not, damn me.
INTERPRETER   *Acordo linta.*
    Come on, thou art granted space.   75
                              Exit [with Parolles]
            A short alarum within
SECOND LORD Go tell the Count Rossillion, and my brother,
    We have caught the woodcock, and will keep him muffled
    Till we do hear from them.
SOLDIER   Captain, I will.
SECOND LORD 'A will betray us all unto ourselves:
    Inform on that.
SOLDIER   So I will, sir.   80
SECOND LORD Till then I'll keep him dark and safely locked.
                              Exeunt

[4.2] *Enter* BERTRAM *and the maid called* DIANA

BERTRAM They told me that your name was Fontybell.
DIANA No, my good lord, Diana.
BERTRAM   Titled goddess,

65] *As Staunton; Oh…pray, / Manka reuania dulche.* F   **75** art] F3; *are* F   **75** SD *with Parolles] After Capell; not in* F
78, 80 SH SOLDIER] *Sol.* F; *Second Soldier / Capell*   **81** SD] *Rowe; not in* F   **Act 4, Scene 2**   **4.2]** *Pope; not in* F

68 hoodwinked blindfolded; with residual sense of 'deceived', as in *Mac.* 4.3.72.

69 gather get information.

69 Haply Perhaps.

73 faithfully truthfully; with the ironic sense of 'loyally'.

75 space a reprieve.

77 woodcock A proverbially foolish bird. Compare *Ham.* 5.2.306.

77 muffled blindfolded.

80 Inform on Report.

Act 4, Scene 2

1 They…Fontybell A haunting line. The name Fontybell means 'beautiful fountain'.

2–3 Titled…addition! You bear the name of the goddess (of chastity), and deserve the name, with additional marks of distinction.

> And worth it, with addition! But, fair soul,
> In your fine frame hath love no quality?
> If the quick fire of youth light not your mind,   5
> You are no maiden, but a monument.
> When you are dead, you should be such a one
> As you are now; for you are cold and stern,
> And now you should be as your mother was
> When your sweet self was got.   10

DIANA   She then was honest.

BERTRAM   So should you be.

DIANA   No;

> My mother did but duty, such, my lord,
> As you owe to your wife.

BERTRAM   No more a' that.

> I prithee do not strive against my vows.
> I was compelled to her, but I love thee   15
> By love's own sweet constraint, and will for ever
> Do thee all rights of service.

DIANA   Ay, so you serve us

> Till we serve you; but when you have our roses,
> You barely leave our thorns to prick ourselves,
> And mock us with our bareness.

BERTRAM   How have I sworn!   20

DIANA   'Tis not the many oaths that makes the truth,

> But the plain single vow that is vowed true.
> What is not holy, that we swear not by,
> But take the High'st to witness. Then pray you tell me,
> If I should swear by Jove's great attributes   25
> I loved you dearly, would you believe my oaths
> When I did love you ill? This has no holding,

---

6 monument.] F2 *(subst.)*; monument F

4 **quality** part.
5 **quick** lively.
6 **monument** lifeless effigy.
10 **got** begotten.
14 **vows** i.e. resolution to live apart from Helena.
16 **constraint** compulsion which wedded him to Helena.
18 **serve** gratify (sexually).
19 i.e. once you have denuded us of roses you leave our thorns exposed to prick us.
22 **single** As opposed to 'double' = 'equivocal'.
23–4 **What...witness** A self-evident observation, perhaps meant in ironic response to Bertram's 'How have I sworn!' (20): 'We do not swear

(whatever our vicious purpose) by the devil but by God' – with the implication: 'So much for your pious asseverations!'
24 **High'st** F does not capitalise the name of God here, or the pronoun 'Him' at 28 and 29.
25 **Jove's** Perhaps replacing 'God's' to accord with the statute of 1606 which forbade the profane use of the Lord's name in plays. However, Shakespeare and his contemporaries routinely allow Christian attributes to pagan deities.
27 **ill** (1) indifferently (as opposed to 'dearly', 26), (2) wickedly.
27 **has no holding** is not tenable.

To swear by Him whom I protest to love
That I will work against Him. Therefore your oaths
Are words and poor conditions, but unsealed –   30
At least in my opinion.
BERTRAM   Change it, change it!
Be not so holy-cruel. Love is holy,
And my integrity ne'er knew the crafts
That you do charge men with. Stand no more off,
But give thyself unto my sick desires,   35
Who then recovers. Say thou art mine, and ever
My love, as it begins, shall so persèver.
DIANA I see that men make rope's in such a scarre,
That we'll forsake ourselves. Give me that ring.
BERTRAM I'll lend it thee, my dear; but have no power   40
To give it from me.
DIANA   Will you not, my lord?
BERTRAM It is an honour 'longing to our house,
Bequeathèd down from many ancestors,
Which were the greatest obloquy i'th'world
In me to lose.
DIANA   Mine honour's such a ring,   45
My chastity's the jewel of our house,
Bequeathèd down from many ancestors,
Which were the greatest obloquy i'th'world
In me to lose. Thus your own proper wisdom
Brings in the champion Honour on my part,   50
Against your vain assault.
BERTRAM   Here, take my ring!
My house, mine honour, yea, my life, be thine,
And I'll be bid by thee.

28, 29 Him...Him] *Neilson;* him...him F   42 'longing] *Rowe;* longing F

28 **protest** profess.
30 **words** mere words.
30 **poor...unsealed** (1) a worthless contract, simply unsealed (i.e. without the seal that would make it valid), (2) but (i.e. only) a worthless unsealed contract.
32 **holy-cruel** cruel in your holiness.
33 **crafts** craftiness.
36 **Who then recovers** Which then recover.
38 **make...scarre** This, perhaps the most notorious crux in the Folio, has been frequently emended, e.g. 'make Hopes in such Affairs' (Rowe); 'make hopes in such a scene' (Malone);

'may cope's in such a stir' (Tannenbaum). The best emendation seems that proposed by P. A. Daniel in 1870 and followed by Sisson in his edition, 'may rope's in such a snare' (i.e. may rope us in such a snare). The text, however, is probably irrecoverably corrupt.
41 **from** away from.
42 **honour 'longing** source or token of honour belonging.
45 **honour's** chastity's.
49 **proper** personal (peculiar to you).
50 **part** side.
53 **bid** commanded.

DIANA When midnight comes, knock at my chamber window;
　　　　I'll order take my mother shall not hear.　　　　　　　　55
　　　　Now will I charge you in the band of truth,
　　　　When you have conquered my yet maiden bed,
　　　　Remain there but an hour, nor speak to me.
　　　　My reasons are most strong, and you shall know them
　　　　When back again this ring shall be delivered;　　　　　60
　　　　And on your finger in the night I'll put
　　　　Another ring, that what in time proceeds
　　　　May token to the future our past deeds.
　　　　Adieu till then, then fail not. You have won
　　　　A wife of me, though there my hope be done.　　　　　65
BERTRAM A heaven on earth I have won by wooing thee.　　　　*Exit*
DIANA For which live long to thank both heaven and me!
　　　　You may so in the end.
　　　　My mother told me just how he would woo,
　　　　As if she sat in's heart. She says all men　　　　　70
　　　　Have the like oaths. He had sworn to marry me
　　　　When his wife's dead; therefore I'll lie with him
　　　　When I am buried. Since Frenchmen are so braid,
　　　　Marry that will, I live and die a maid.
　　　　Only in this disguise I think't no sin　　　　　75
　　　　To cozen him that would unjustly win.　　　　*Exit*

---

57 maiden bed] *Theobald;* maiden-bed F　　66 SD] F2; *not in* F　　70 sat] *Warburton;* sate F

55 **order take** insure that.
56 **band** bond.
57 **yet** still.
62 **Another ring** By exchanging rings, Diana means to signify their betrothal.
62 **what...proceeds** whatever may fall out in future.
63 **token** betoken.
64–5 **You...done** Diana is deliberately cryptic. She may mean 'You have made me yield to you as a wife when I cannot hope to marry you'; but her first words could mean 'You have won a wife through my agency' and her last could allude to the

forfeiture of her chastity, spoiling her hope of wedlock.
71–2 **had...dead** We do not hear him so swear, but it appears at 5.3.139–40 and 166–73 that he does so when they exchange rings; 'had' could mean 'would have', but some have emended to 'has'.
73 **braid** twisted, like plaited braid.
74 **that** who.
75 **disguise** assumed role. Compare *MM* 3.2.262–3.
76 **cozen** deceive.

[4.3] *Enter the two French Captains [the* FIRST *and* SECOND LORDS
DUMAINE] *and some two or three* SOLDIERS

FIRST LORD You have not given him his mother's letter?

SECOND LORD I have delivered it an hour since. There is something
in't that stings his nature; for on the reading it he changed almost
into another man.

FIRST LORD He has much worthy blame laid upon him for shaking off   5
so good a wife and so sweet a lady.

SECOND LORD Especially he hath incurred the everlasting displeasure
of the king, who had even tuned his bounty to sing happiness to
him. I will tell you a thing, but you shall let it dwell darkly with
you.   10

FIRST LORD When you have spoken it, 'tis dead, and I am the grave
of it.

SECOND LORD He hath perverted a young gentlewoman here in
Florence, of a most chaste renown, and this night he fleshes his will
in the spoil of her honour. He hath given her his monumental ring,   15
and thinks himself made in the unchaste composition.

FIRST LORD Now God delay our rebellion! As we are ourselves, what
things are we!

SECOND LORD Merely our own traitors. And as in the common course
of all treasons, we still see them reveal themselves, till they attain   20
to their abhorred ends, so he that in this action contrives against
his own nobility in his proper stream o'erflows himself.

Act 4, Scene 3   4.3] *Pope; not in* F   0 SD *Captains]* F; *Lords Rowe*   1 SH FIRST LORD] *Rowe; Cap.G* F *(through
scene, except 70, 104)*   1 letter?] *Rowe;* letter. F   2 SH SECOND LORD] *Rowe; Cap.E.* F *(through scene, except 263, 265)*
22 stream o'erflows] *Theobald;* streame, ore-flowes F

Act 4, Scene 3

4.3 Apparently a street scene, as suggested
by another encounter reported in 65, but
editors, following Capell, locate it in the Florentine
camp.

2 since ago.

4 another man i.e. his mood completely
changed.

5 worthy deserved.

9 darkly secretly.

13 perverted corrupted (i.e. seduced).

14 renown reputation.

14 fleshes his will rewards and so stimulates his
lust (as hounds or hawks are fleshed or fed with a
piece of meat from the animal they have hunted
down).

15 spoil Concretely, 'the dead prey'; by analogy,
'the entity (honour) that has been destroyed'.

15 monumental i.e. which serves as a token of
his identity (see *OED adj* 2b).

16 made a made man.

16 composition bargain (with a play on
'composition' as something made).

17 delay our rebellion quench our rebellious
appetites. See *OED* Delay v². The modern sense of
'delay' as 'postpone' is also quite possible, a mere
postponing being the best human nature can look
for.

17 ourselves i.e. not supported by God's grace.

19 Merely Simply.

20 still always.

21 abhorred ends damnable objectives; i.e. their
deaths, which put an end to their revelations.

21–2 contrives...nobility is a traitor to his
station.

22 his proper...himself This may mean

FIRST LORD Is it not meant damnable in us, to be trumpeters of our unlawful intents? We shall not then have his company tonight?

SECOND LORD Not till after midnight; for he is dieted to his hour. 25

FIRST LORD That approaches apace. I would gladly have him see his company anatomised, that he might take a measure of his own judgements, wherein so curiously he had set this counterfeit.

SECOND LORD We will not meddle with him till he come; for his presence must be the whip of the other. 30

FIRST LORD In the mean time, what hear you of these wars?

SECOND LORD I hear there is an overture of peace.

FIRST LORD Nay, I assure you a peace concluded.

SECOND LORD What will Count Rossillion do then? Will he travel higher, or return again into France? 35

FIRST LORD I perceive by this demand, you are not altogether of his council.

SECOND LORD Let it be forbid, sir. So should I be a great deal of his act.

FIRST LORD Sir, his wife some two months since fled from his house. 40 Her pretence is a pilgrimage to Saint Jaques le Grand, which holy undertaking with most austere sanctimony she accomplished; and there residing, the tenderness of her nature became as a prey to her grief; in fine, made a groan of her last breath, and now she sings in heaven. 45

SECOND LORD How is this justified?

FIRST LORD The stronger part of it by her own letters, which makes her story true, even to the point of her death. Her death itself, which

---

27 anatomised] *Rowe;* anathomiz'd F   37 council] *Rowe³;* councell F; counsel *Rowe*

---

either (1) his self-revealing discourse is like a body of water which exceeds its appointed limit and so forfeits its integrity; or (2) he does not confine himself to the proper course of his own nobility but allows the treacheries of his nature to overflow. For (1) compare *Ham.* 4.5.100–1.

23–4 **Is it...intents** Is it not meant to be damnable sin in us to proclaim our unlawful intentions?

25 **dieted...hour** restricted to his appointed time; continuing residually the play at 14 on eating or fleshing.

27 **company** companion.

27 **anatomised** dissected, laid open to inspection.

28 **curiously** carefully.

28 **set this counterfeit** i.e. as a fake stone is placed in an elaborate setting or foil.

29 **him...he** Parolles...Bertram.

29–30 **his...the other** Bertram's...Parolles.

33 **Nay** i.e. more than an overture.

35 **higher** farther; perhaps into the mountains. See 2.1.12 n.

36 **demand** question.

36–7 **of his council** in his confidence. The spelling of Rowe³, followed here, conveys either 'council' (a deliberative body) or 'counsel' (confidence).

38–9 **a great...act** deeply involved as an accessory in his affairs (with a play on 'act' and 'council' as in 'acts of the Council').

41 **pretence** intention.

41 **is** i.e. was.

42 **sanctimony** sanctity.

44 **fine** sum.

46 **justified** proved.

could not be her office to say is come, was faithfully confirmed by
the rector of the place.   50
SECOND LORD Hath the count all this intelligence?
FIRST LORD Ay, and the particular confirmations, point from point, to
the full arming of the verity.
SECOND LORD I am heartily sorry that he'll be glad of this.
FIRST LORD How mightily sometimes we make us comforts of our   55
losses!
SECOND LORD And how mightily some other times we drown our gain
in tears! The great dignity that his valour hath here acquired for
him shall at home be encountered with a shame as ample.
FIRST LORD The web of our life is of a mingled yarn, good and ill   60
together: our virtues would be proud, if our faults whipped them
not, and our crimes would despair, if they were not cherished by
our virtues.

Enter a [SERVANT *as*] *Messenger*

How now? where's your master?
SERVANT He met the duke in the street, sir, of whom he hath taken   65
a solemn leave. His lordship will next morning for France. The duke
hath offered him letters of commendations to the king.
SECOND LORD They shall be no more than needful there, if they were
more than they can commend.

Enter [BERTRAM] *Count Rossillion*

FIRST LORD They cannot be too sweet for the king's tartness. Here's   70
his lordship now. How now, my lord, is't not after midnight?
BERTRAM I have tonight dispatched sixteen businesses, a month's
length apiece, by an abstract of success: I have congied with the

---

63 SD SERVANT *as*] *Kittredge; not in* F   65 SH SERVANT] F; *Messenger / Neilson*   69 SD BERTRAM] *Rowe; not in* F
70 SH FIRST LORD] *Rowe; Ber.* F; *Cap.G.* F3

49 **office** function (she being dead).
50 **rector** priest (recalling 'office' in the
preceding line).
51 **intelligence** information.
53 **arming...verity** strengthening of the truth
against attack.
58 **dignity** honour.
59 **encountered** met.
62 **crimes** sins.
62 **cherished** entertained kindly (i.e. palliated).
But carries also the sense of 'accommodation', or
happy mingling.

66 **solemn** formal.
66 **will** i.e. will depart.
67 **offered** given.
68–9 **if...commend** even if they commended
Bertram more strongly than he deserves.
70 **for** i.e. to balance.
73 **by...success** Meaning either (1) summarily
and successfully, or (2) to give a brief account of my
success – or a brief account of the successive items.
(The account then follows.)
73 **congied with** taken leave of.

duke, done my adieu with his nearest; buried a wife, mourned for
her, writ to my lady mother I am returning, entertained my convoy, 75
and between these main parcels of dispatch effected many nicer
needs. The last was the greatest, but that I have not ended yet.

SECOND LORD If the business be of any difficulty, and this morning
your departure hence, it requires haste of your lordship.

BERTRAM I mean the business is not ended, as fearing to hear of it 80
hereafter. But shall we have this dialogue between the fool and the
soldier? Come, bring forth this counterfeit module, h'as deceived
me like a double-meaning prophesier.

SECOND LORD Bring him forth.

[Exeunt Soldiers]

H'as sat in th'stocks all night, poor gallant knave. 85

BERTRAM No matter, his heels have deserved it, in usurping his spurs
so long. How does he carry himself?

SECOND LORD I have told your lordship already: the stocks carry him.
But to answer you as you would be understood, he weeps like a
wench that had shed her milk. He hath confessed himself to 90
Morgan, whom he supposes to be a friar, from the time of his
remembrance to this very instant disaster of his setting i'th'stocks;
and what think you he hath confessed?

BERTRAM Nothing of me, has'a?

SECOND LORD His confession is taken, and it shall be read to his face. 95
If your lordship be in't, as I believe you are, you must have the
patience to hear it.

Enter PAROLLES *with his* INTERPRETER

BERTRAM A plague upon him! Muffled! He can say nothing of me.

FIRST LORD Hush, hush! Hoodman comes! *Portotartarossa.*

---

76 effected] F3; affected F   82 h'as] *Rowe*³, ha s F   84 SD] *Capell; not in* F   85 H'as] *Rowe*, Ha's F   99 SH FIRST
LORD] *Rann; not in* F

<table>
<tr><td>

75 **entertained my convoy** seen to my escort.
Compare 4.4.10.

76 **between. . .dispatch** in between these major
items of business.

76 **nicer** more delicate.

77 **The last** i.e. his supposed conquest of Diana.

80–1 **as. . .hereafter** Bertram fears that Diana
may in future claim him for a husband.

82 **module** model (of a soldier).

83 **double meaning prophesier** equivocal
oracle. see *Mac.* 5.8.19–22.

85 **gallant** showy in appearance.

86 **usurping his spurs** wrongly laying claim
to the trappings of knightly valour.

</td><td>

87 **carry** comport (with a play on 'carry', 88)

90 **shed** spilled.

91–2 **from. . .remembrance** as far back as he can
remember.

92 **very instant disaster** misfortune in the
immediate present.

98 **Muffled** Blindfolded.

99 ***Hush, hush** Assigned to Bertram in F, but
an interruption is more probable.

99 **Hoodman** The blindfolded player in the
game of hoodman blind (blind man's buff).

</td></tr>
</table>

INTERPRETER He calls for the tortures. What will you say without 'em? 100
PAROLLES I will confess what I know without constraint. If ye pinch
    me like a pasty, I can say no more.
INTERPRETER *Bosko chimurcho.*
FIRST LORD *Boblibindo chicurmurco.*
INTERPRETER You are a merciful general. Our general bids you answer 105
    to what I shall ask you out of a note.
PAROLLES And truly, as I hope to live.
INTERPRETER *[Reads]* 'First demand of him, how many horse the duke
    is strong.' What say you to that?
PAROLLES Five or six thousand, but very weak and unserviceable. The 110
    troops are all scattered, and the commanders very poor rogues, upon
    my reputation and credit, and as I hope to live.
INTERPRETER Shall I set down your answer so?
PAROLLES Do, I'll take the sacrament on't, how and which way you
    will. 115
BERTRAM All's one to him. What a past-saving slave is this!
FIRST LORD Y'are deceived, my lord, this is Monsieur Parolles, the
    gallant militarist – that was his own phrase – that had the whole
    theoric of war in the knot of his scarf, and the practice in the chape
    of his dagger. 120
SECOND LORD I will never trust a man again for keeping his sword
    clean, nor believe he can have everything in him by wearing his
    apparel neatly.
INTERPRETER Well, that's set down.
PAROLLES 'Five or six thousand horse', I said – I will say true – 'or 125
    thereabouts', set down, for I'll speak truth.
FIRST LORD He's very near the truth in this.
BERTRAM But I con him no thanks for't, in the nature he delivers it.
PAROLLES 'Poor rogues', I pray you say.

---

104 SH FIRST LORD] *Rowe; Cap.* F   108, 133, 146, 175 SD *Reads*] *Cam.; not in* F   116 SD BERTRAM] *Capell; not in* F

102 **pasty** A kind of pie which has the crusts
pinched together.
106 **note** list (of questions).
108 **horse** horsemen.
114–15 **how…will** according to whatever rite
you choose.
116 ***All's…him** It's all the same to him. These
words are assigned to Parolles in F.
118 **militarist** expert in military affairs.
119 **theoric…practice** Hunter, citing
Hoby's *Theorique and Practice of Warre* (1597) and
Barret's *The Theorike and Practice of Modern*

Warres (1598), sees these words as technical terms
for the division of military (and other) science.
119 **chape** The metal plate covering the point of
a scabbard.
121–3 W. S. Walker suggests that these lines
should be assigned to Bertram.
121 **for keeping** because he keeps.
122 **clean** polished.
123 **neatly** elegantly.
128 **I con…it** I know no reason to thank him
for speaking that manner of truth.

INTERPRETER Well, that's set down. 130

PAROLLES I humbly thank you, sir. A truth's a truth, the rogues are marvellous poor.

INTERPRETER [*Reads*] 'Demand of him, of what strength they are afoot.' What say you to that?

PAROLLES By my troth, sir, if I were to live this present hour, I will 135 tell true. Let me see: Spurio, a hundred and fifty; Sebastian, so many; Corambus, so many; Jaques, so many; Guiltian, Cosmo, Lodowick, and Gratii, two hundred fifty each; mine own company, Chitopher, Vaumond, Bentii, two hundred fifty each; so that the muster-file, rotten and sound, upon my life, amounts not to fifteen 140 thousand pole, half of the which dare not shake the snow from off their cassocks, lest they shake themselves to pieces.

BERTRAM What shall be done to him?

FIRST LORD Nothing, but let him have thanks. Demand of him my condition, and what credit I have with the duke. 145

INTERPRETER Well, that's set down. [*Reads*] 'You shall demand of him, whether one Captain Dumaine be i'th'camp, a Frenchman; what his reputation is with the duke; what his valour, honesty, and expertness in wars; or whether he thinks it were not possible with well-weighing sums of gold to corrupt him to a revolt.' What say 150 you to this? What do you know of it?

PAROLLES I beseech you let me answer to the particular of the inter'gatories. Demand them singly.

INTERPRETER Do you know this Captain Dumaine?

PAROLLES I know him. 'A was a botcher's prentice in Paris, from 155 whence he was whipped for getting the shrieve's fool with child, a dumb innocent that could not say him nay.

BERTRAM Nay, by your leave, hold your hands – though I know his brains are forfeit to the next tile that falls.

INTERPRETER Well, is this captain in the Duke of Florence's camp? 160

PAROLLES Upon my knowledge, he is, and lousy.

---

135 **live** i.e. live only until.
136–7 **so many** as many.
140 **muster-file** total roll.
140 **rotten and sound** sick (with disease) and well.
141 **pole** poll (i.e. heads).
142 **cassocks** military cloaks.
145 **condition** military character.
150 **well-weighing** (1) heavy, (2) influential.
152 **particular** particular items.

153 **inter'gatories** interrogatories. A syncopated form, now obsolete.
155 **botcher's** patcher's. Referring to a tailor or cobbler who does rough repair work.
156 **shrieve's fool** idiot girl ('innocent') in the care of the sheriff.
158 Bertram addresses the First Lord ('Captain Dumaine').
158–9 **his...falls** i.e. he is in danger of death from the next accident.

FIRST LORD Nay, look not so upon me; we shall hear of your lordship
    anon.
INTERPRETER What is his reputation with the duke?
PAROLLES The duke knows him for no other but a poor officer of mine,   165
    and writ to me this other day to turn him out a'th'band. I think
    I have his letter in my pocket.
INTERPRETER Marry, we'll search.
PAROLLES In good sadness, I do not know. Either it is there, or it is
    upon a file with the duke's other letters in my tent.   170
INTERPRETER Here 'tis, here's a paper. Shall I read it to you?
PAROLLES I do not know if it be it or no.
BERTRAM Our interpreter does it well.
FIRST LORD Excellently.
INTERPRETER [*Reads*] 'Dian, the count's a fool, and full of gold' –   175
PAROLLES That is not the duke's letter, sir; that is an advertisement
    to a proper maid in Florence, one Diana, to take heed of the
    allurement of one Count Rossillion, a foolish idle boy, but for all
    that very ruttish. I pray you, sir, put it up again.
INTERPRETER Nay, I'll read it first, by your favour.   180
PAROLLES My meaning in't, I protest, was very honest in the behalf
    of the maid; for I knew the young count to be a dangerous and
    lascivious boy, who is a whale to virginity, and devours up all the
    fry it finds.
BERTRAM Damnable both-sides rogue!   185
INTERPRETER [*Reads the*] *letter*
    'When he swears oaths, bid him drop gold, and take it;
    After he scores, he never pays the score.
    Half won is match well made; match, and well make it;
    He ne'er pays after-debts, take it before,
    And say a soldier, Dian, told thee this: 190
    Men are to mell with, boys are not to kiss;

162 lordship] *Pope;* Lord F   186 SD *Reads the*] *Rowe; not in* F

169 **good sadness** all seriousness.
176 **advertisement** advice, warning.
177 **proper** respectable.
179 **ruttish** lustful.
179 **up again** back.
180 **favour** leave.
184 **fry** small fish.
187 **scores** (1) hits the mark, (2) incurs (scores
up) a debt.
187 **score** bill.

188 **Half...made** i.e. a bargain will turn out
successfully in so far as the conditions are agreed
in advance. The 'match' is the prospective union
of Diana and Bertram.
189 **after-debts** obligations still outstanding
(after the goods have been delivered).
191 **mell** meddle (in the sense of sexual
intercourse).
191 **boys** i.e. like Bertram as opposed to Parolles.

> For count of this, the count's a fool, I know it,
> Who pays before, but not when he does owe it.
>   Thine, as he vowed to thee in thine ear,
>   Parolles.'   195

BERTRAM He shall be whipped through the army with this rhyme in's forehead.

SECOND LORD This is your devoted friend, sir, the manifold linguist and the armipotent soldier.

BERTRAM I could endure anything before but a cat, and now he's a cat   200
to me.

INTERPRETER I perceive, sir, by the general's looks, we shall be fain to hang you.

PAROLLES My life, sir, in any case! Not that I am afraid to die, but that my offences being many, I would repent out the remainder of   205
my nature. Let me live, sir, in a dungeon, i'th'stocks, or anywhere, so I may live.

INTERPRETER We'll see what may be done, so you confess freely; therefore once more to this Captain Dumaine. You have answered to his reputation with the duke, and to his valour. What is his   210
honesty?

PAROLLES He will steal, sir, an egg out of a cloister. For rapes and ravishments he parallels Nessus. He professes not keeping of oaths; in breaking 'em he is stronger than Hercules. He will lie, sir, with such volubility, that you would think truth were a fool. Drunkenness   215
is his best virtue, for he will be swine-drunk, and in his sleep he does little harm, save to his bed-clothes about him; but they know his conditions, and lay him in straw. I have but little more to say,

---

199 armipotent] *Capell*, army-potent F   202 the] F3; your F

---

192 **For count** Therefore take note.

193 **pays before** i.e. if you can compel him to make prior payment.

193 **when...it** (1) after he owes payment for his debt, (2) after he has possessed the desired thing (Diana's virginity).

196 **in** on.

198 **manifold linguist** speaker of many languages.

199 **armipotent** powerful in action.

202 *the F reads 'your', which could mean 'the general concerned' (*OED* Your 5). Compare 1.1.135–6 n.

202 **fain** obliged.

205–6 **would...nature** want to devote the rest of my life to repenting.

207 **so** provided that.

212 **an...cloister** 'He will steal anything, however trifling, from any place, however holy' (Johnson).

213 **Nessus** The Centaur, half-man, half-horse, who tried to rape Hercules' wife Dejanira. The Centaurs, ravishers of the women at the Feast of the Lapithae, figure as an emblem of lust.

213 **professes not** makes no practice of.

214 **stronger** i.e. however strong the oaths.

215 **volubility** facility in expression.

215 **a fool** i.e. because so easily put down or discredited.

217 **they** i.e. the attendants who put him to bed.

218 **conditions** habits.

sir, of his honesty. He has everything that an honest man should
not have; what an honest man should have, he has nothing.   220
FIRST LORD I begin to love him for this.
BERTRAM For this description of thine honesty? A pox upon him for
me, he's more and more a cat.
INTERPRETER What say you to his expertness in war?
PAROLLES Faith, sir, h'as led the drum before the English tragedians.   225
To belie him I will not, and more of his soldiership I know not,
except in that country he had the honour to be the officer at a place
there called Mile-end, to instruct for the doubling of files. I would
do the man what honour I can, but of this I am not certain.
FIRST LORD He hath out-villained villainy so far, that the rarity   230
redeems him.
BERTRAM A pox on him, he's a cat still.
INTERPRETER His qualities being at this poor price, I need not to ask
you if gold will corrupt him to revolt.
PAROLLES Sir, for a cardecue he will sell the fee-simple of his   235
salvation, the inheritance of it, and cut th'entail from all remainders,
and a perpetual succession for it perpetually.
INTERPRETER What's his brother, the other Captain Dumaine?
SECOND LORD Why does he ask him of me?
INTERPRETER What's he?   240
PAROLLES E'en a crow a'th'same nest; not altogether so great as the
first in goodness, but greater a great deal in evil. He excels his
brother for a coward, yet his brother is reputed one of the best that
is. In a retreat he outruns any lackey; marry, in coming on he has
the cramp.   245
INTERPRETER If your life be saved, will you undertake to betray the
Florentine?
PAROLLES Ay, and the captain of his horse, Count Rossillion.
INTERPRETER I'll whisper with the general, and know his pleasure.

225 h'as] *Rowe;* ha's F   235 cardecue] F2; Cardceue F

225 **drum** Which went before troops of actors
advertising their performances; i.e. so much for his
'expertness in war'.
226 **To...not** I will not belie him. An old use
of 'to'; see Abbott 357.
228 **Mile-end** An open field east of the City of
London where the citizen-militia, an inconsiderable
force, received its training.
228 **doubling of files** A simple kind of military
marching drill.

235 **cardecue** *quart d'écu.* A French coin of slight
value.
235 **fee-simple** absolute possession (of land).
236–7 **cut...perpetually** break the reversion
of property rights ('remainders') not only to his
immediate heir but to all heirs to the end of time.
244 **lackey** servant who ran errands.
244 **coming on** advancing.
246 **undertake** commit yourself.

PAROLLES I'll no more drumming, a plague of all drums! Only to seem   250
to deserve well, and to beguile the supposition of that lascivious
young boy the count, have I run into this danger. Yet who would
have suspected an ambush where I was taken?

INTERPRETER There is no remedy, sir, but you must die. The general
says, you that have so traitorously discovered the secrets of your   255
army, and made such pestiferous reports of men very nobly held,
can serve the world for no honest use; therefore you must die.
Come, headsman, off with his head.

PAROLLES O Lord, sir, let me live, or let me see my death!

INTERPRETER That shall you, and take your leave of all your friends.   260
[*Unmuffling him*]
So, look about you. Know you any here?

BERTRAM Good morrow, noble captain.

SECOND LORD God bless you, Captain Parolles.

FIRST LORD God save you, noble captain.

SECOND LORD Captain, what greeting will you to my Lord Lafew? I   265
am for France.

FIRST LORD Good captain, will you give me a copy of the sonnet you
writ to Diana in behalf of the Count Rossillion? And I were not
a very coward, I'd compel it of you, but fare you well.
Exeunt [*Bertram and Lords*]

INTERPRETER You are undone, captain, all but your scarf; that has a   270
knot on't yet.

PAROLLES Who cannot be crushed with a plot?

INTERPRETER If you could find out a country where but women were
that had received so much shame, you might begin an impudent
nation. Fare ye well, sir, I am for France too. We shall speak of   275
you there.
Exit [*with Soldiers*]

PAROLLES Yet am I thankful. If my heart were great,
'Twould burst at this. Captain I'll be no more,
But I will eat, and drink, and sleep as soft

---

260 SD] *Var. 93; not in* F   263, 265 SH SECOND LORD] *Rowe; Lo.E.* F   269 SD *Bertram and Lords*] *After Capell; not in* F
276 SD *with Soldiers*] *Cam.; not in* F

251 **beguile the supposition** deceive the
opinion.
  255 **discovered** revealed.
  256 **pestiferous** pernicious.
  256 **held** esteemed.
  265 **will you** do you wish to send.

266 **for off to.**
269 **very absolute.**
270 **undone** (1) ruined, (2) undressed.
273 **but** only.
274 **impudent** shameless.

As captain shall. Simply the thing I am   280
Shall make me live. Who knows himself a braggart,
Let him fear this; for it will come to pass
That every braggart shall be found an ass.
Rust sword, cool blushes, and, Parolles, live
Safest in shame! Being fooled, by fool'ry thrive!   285
There's place and means for every man alive.
I'll after them.   *Exit*

[4.4] *Enter* HELENA, WIDOW, *and* DIANA

HELENA That you may well perceive I have not wronged you,
One of the greatest in the Christian world
Shall be my surety; 'fore whose throne 'tis needful,
Ere I can pèrfect mine intents, to kneel.
Time was, I did him a desirèd office,   5
Dear almost as his life, which gratitude
Through flinty Tartar's bosom would peep forth,
And answer thanks. I duly am informed
His grace is at Marseilles, to which place
We have convenient convoy. You must know   10
I am supposèd dead. The army breaking,
My husband hies him home, where heaven aiding,
And by the leave of my good lord the king,
We'll be before our welcome.
WIDOW   Gentle madam,
You never had a servant to whose trust   15
Your business was more welcome,
HELENA   Nor you, mistress,
Ever a friend whose thoughts more truly labour
To recompense your love. Doubt not but heaven

Act 4, Scene 4   4.4] *Capell; not in* F   3 'fore] F3; *for* F; *fore* F2   9 Marseilles] *Pope; Marcellæ* F   16 you] F4; *your* F

284 Parolles Trisyllabic.
285 fooled gulled.

Act 4, Scene 4
  4.4 Editors, following Capell, locate the scene in Florence, the Widow's house.
  3 surety guarantee.
  6 which gratitude gratitude for which.
  7 Tartar's Whose heart ('bosom') was prover-

bially hard. This reference to the Tartars is perhaps evoked unconsciously by association with Bajazeth (4.1.33), and hence with Tamburlaine, countryman of Genghis Khan.
  9 Marseilles Pronounced as three syllables, and spelt 'Marcellus' in F at 4.5.64.
  10 convenient convoy suitable transport.
  11 breaking disbanding.
  14 our welcome i.e. we are expected.

Hath brought me up to be your daughter's dower,
As it hath fated her to be my motive 20
And helper to a husband. But O, strange men,
That can such sweet use make of what they hate,
When saucy trusting of the cozened thoughts
Defiles the pitchy night; so lust doth play
With what it loathes for that which is away – 25
But more of this hereafter. You, Diana,
Under my poor instructions yet must suffer
Something in my behalf.

DIANA   Let death and honesty
Go with your impositions, I am yours
Upon your will to suffer.

HELENA   Yet, I pray you: 30
But with the word the time will bring on summer,
When briers shall have leaves as well as thorns,
And be as sweet as sharp. We must away:
Our wagon is prepared, and time revives us.
All's well that ends well; still the fine's the crown. 35
Whate'er the course, the end is the renown.

Exeunt

35 fine's] *Theobald;* fines F

20 **motive** Probably 'means', though this sense is not recorded elsewhere.

23 **saucy...thoughts** wanton abandonment to deluded appetites.

24 **Defiles...night** Blackens even pitch-black night, being blacker than it. See *1H4* 2.4.410–13, where Falstaff quotes the proverb 'Pitch doth defile' (from Ecclus. 13.1).

25 **for** in place of.

27 **yet** still for a while (as again at 30).

28 **death and honesty** an honest death; i.e. I am willing to die for you provided I remain chaste.

29 **impositions** The 'instructions' of 27.

30 **Upon your will** At your pleasure.

31 **the word** Variously glossed: 'in a word'; 'as the proverb has it'; 'as I have promised'. It is hard not to feel that there are deeper intimations here, and that 'the word' is analogous in power to Holy Writ.

32 **leaves** petals.

33 **sweet** sweet-smelling.

34 **revives** i.e. will revive.

35 **All's...well** Proverbial from at least the beginning of the fourteenth century.

35 **the...crown** Also proverbial and a familiar commonplace to Shakespeare, e.g. in *Tro.* 4.5.224.

35 **fine's** end's.

36 **is the renown** determines the praise.

[4.5] *Enter* [LAVATCH, *the*] *Clown, old Lady* [COUNTESS], *and* LAFEW

LAFEW No, no, no, your son was misled with a snipped-taffeta fellow
there, whose villainous saffron would have made all the unbaked
and doughy youth of a nation in his colour. Your daughter-in-law
had been alive at this hour, and your son here at home, more
advanced by the king than by that red-tailed humble-bee I speak   5
of.

COUNTESS I would I had not known him; it was the death of the most
virtuous gentlewoman that ever nature had praise for creating. If
she had partaken of my flesh, and cost me the dearest groans of a
mother, I could not have owed her a more rooted love.   10

LAFEW 'Twas a good lady, 'twas a good lady. We may pick a thousand
sallets ere we light on such another herb.

LAVATCH Indeed, sir, she was the sweet marjoram of the sallet, or rather
the herb of grace.

LAFEW They are not herbs, you knave, they are nose-herbs.   15

LAVATCH I am no great Nebuchadnezzar, sir, I have not much skill in
grace.

LAFEW Whether dost thou profess thyself – a knave or a fool?

LAVATCH A fool, sir, at a woman's service, and a knave at a man's.

LAFEW Your distinction?   20

LAVATCH I would cozen the man of his wife and do his service.

Act 4, Scene 5   0 SD COUNTESS] *Rowe; not in* F   7 SH COUNTESS] *Rowe; La.* F *(and subst. through scene)*   17 grace]
F; grass *Rowe*

Act 4, Scene 5
4.5 Editors, following Capell, locate the scene in
Rossillion, the Count's palace.
  1 with by.
  1 snipped-taffeta flashy. Literally, silk slashed
to allow the rich underlining to show through.
  2 saffron A yellow dye (yellow denoting
cowards) used to colour the starch of ruffs and
collars, also to colour pastries.
  2–3 unbaked and doughy immature and
unformed. Continuing the culinary figure suggested
by 'saffron'.
  5 red-tailed humble-bee brightly coloured
insect, showy fellow of no consequence (with an
allusion to Parolles's gaudy apparel). Elsewhere
Shakespeare calls the humble-bee 'red-hipped'
(*MND* 4.1.11).

  9 dearest direst, but with suggestion of 'most
precious'.
  12 sallets salads.
  14 herb of grace rue (not marjoram), signifying
repentance.
  15 herbs salad herbs.
  15 nose-herbs Cultivated for their fragrance
rather than for eating.
  16 Nebuchadnezzar The Babylonian king who
ate grass like the oxen. See Dan. 4.
  17 grace Picking up 14, also punning on 'grass'
(the pronunciation being presumably the same), and
introducing the graceless cozenage Lavatch
imputes to himself in the lines that follow.
  18 Whether Which.
  19 service With the sense of sexual intercourse.
  21 cozen cheat.

LAFEW So you were a knave at his service indeed.

LAVATCH And I would give his wife my bauble, sir, to do her service.

LAFEW I will subscribe for thee, thou art both knave and fool.

LAVATCH At your service.   25

LAFEW No, no, no.

LAVATCH Why, sir, if I cannot serve you, I can serve as great a prince as you are.

LAFEW Who's that? A Frenchman?

LAVATCH Faith, sir, 'a has an English maine, but his fisnomy is more   30
hotter in France than there.

LAFEW What prince is that?

LAVATCH The black prince, sir, alias the prince of darkness, alias the devil.

LAFEW Hold thee, there's my purse. I give thee not this to suggest thee   35
from thy master thou talk'st of; serve him still.

LAVATCH I am a woodland fellow, sir, that always loved a great fire,
and the master I speak of ever keeps a good fire. But sure he is the
prince of the world; let his nobility remain in's court. I am for the
house with the narrow gate, which I take to be too little for pomp   40
to enter. Some that humble themselves may, but the many will be
too chill and tender, and they'll be for the flowery way that leads
to the broad gate and the great fire.

LAFEW Go thy ways, I begin to be aweary of thee, and I tell thee so
before, because I would not fall out with thee. Go thy ways, let my   45
horses be well looked to, without any tricks.

30 maine] F; name *Rowe*   36 of] F3; off F

23 bauble The Fool's staff, topped with a knob, and suggesting an obscene quibble on 'penis'. See *Rom.* 2.3.91–3.

24 subscribe vouch.

30 maine Of doubtful meaning. Variously glossed as: (1) retinue, (2) domicile, (3) quality. Most editors, following Rowe, emend to 'name'. *OED* allows the first two readings, however, under 'meinie', and the third under 'maine', as in the collocation 'main bread' or 'pain-demaine'. See 41 n.

30 fisnomy In Shakespeare's time an acceptable (not illiterate) form of 'physiognomy', here meaning the characteristic expression of the face.

30–1 more hotter (1) because inflamed by the 'French disease', (2) because Edward, the Black Prince (33) of England, was such a scourge to the French.

35 suggest tempt.

39 prince...world A familiar appellation for the devil. See John 12.31, 14.30.

40 narrow gate A reminiscence of Matt. 7.13.

41 many multitude. 'Many' and 'meiny' are interchangeable in this sense.

42 chill and tender sensitive to cold (so preferring the 'good fire' of hell) and loving their comfort.

42 flow'ry way As in *Mac* 2.3.19: 'the primrose way to th'everlasting bonfire'.

44 Go thy ways Go along.

45 before i.e. before quarrelling.

46 tricks Like that practised by the ostler in *Lear* (2.4.125–6) who buttered his horse's hay to make his teeth shine.

LAVATCH If I put any tricks upon 'em, sir, they shall be jades' tricks, which are their own right by the law of nature.   *Exit*

LAFEW A shrewd knave and an unhappy.

COUNTESS So 'a is. My lord that's gone made himself much sport out   50
of him. By his authority he remains here, which he thinks is a patent for his sauciness, and indeed he has no pace, but runs where he will.

LAFEW I like him well, 'tis not amiss. And I was about to tell you, since I heard of the good lady's death, and that my lord your son was   55
upon his return home, I moved the king my master to speak in the behalf of my daughter, which in the minority of them both, his majesty, out of a self-gracious remembrance, did first propose. His highness hath promised me to do it, and to stop up the displeasure he hath conceived against your son, there is no fitter matter. How   60
does your ladyship like it?

COUNTESS With very much content, my lord, and I wish it happily effected.

LAFEW His highness comes post from Marseilles, of as able body as when he numbered thirty. 'A will be here tomorrow, or I am   65
deceived by him that in such intelligence hath seldom failed.

COUNTESS It rejoices me, that I hope I shall see him ere I die. I have letters that my son will be here tonight. I shall beseech your lordship to remain with me till they meet together.

LAFEW Madam, I was thinking with what manners I might safely be   70
admitted.

COUNTESS You need but plead your honourable privilege.

LAFEW Lady, of that I have made a bold charter, but I thank my God it holds yet.

---

64 Marseilles] *Pope; Marcellus* F; *Marsellis* F2   67 It] F3; Ir F

---

47 jades' tricks i.e. the tricks played by ill-bred or exhausted horses. Lavatch sees himself as 'jaded' like his charges.

49 shrewd curst, biting.

49 unhappy sharp, mischievous (inflicting unhappiness with his keen wit).

51 patent warrant.

52 has no pace will not move as the reins direct him. The Countess reverts to the horse-talk of 45–8. See 2.1.49 n.

54 'tis not amiss there's no harm done.

56 upon his return returning.

57 in...both when they were children.

58 self-gracious remembrance a kindness which needed no prompting.

64 post speedily.

65 numbered thirty was thirty years old.

66 him i.e. an unnamed intelligencer or supplier of information.

67 I hope I can hope.

70 with...safely how I might properly.

71 admitted i.e. presumably to the castle of the Countess, not the presence of the King.

72 your honourable privilege the privilege done to your honoured self.

73 made...charter too boldly put forward my claim.

Enter [LAVATCH, *the*] *Clown*

LAVATCH O madam, yonder's my lord your son with a patch of velvet   75
on's face. Whether there be a scar under't or no, the velvet knows,
but 'tis a goodly patch of velvet. His left cheek is a cheek of two
pile and a half, but his right cheek is worn bare.

LAFEW A scar nobly got, or a noble scar, is a good livery of honour;
so belike is that.   80

LAVATCH But it is your carbonadoed face.

LAFEW Let us go see your son, I pray you. I long to talk with the young
noble soldier.

LAVATCH Faith, there's a dozen of 'em, with delicate fine hats, and most
courteous feathers, which bow the head, and nod at every man.   85

Exeunt

5.[1] *Enter* HELENA, WIDOW, *and* DIANA, *with two* ATTENDANTS

HELENA But this exceeding posting day and night
        Must wear your spirits low; we cannot help it.
        But since you have made the days and nights as one,
        To wear your gentle limbs in my affairs,
        Be bold you do so grow in my requital   5
        As nothing can unroot you.

Enter [GENTLEMAN,] *a* GENTLE ASTRINGER

                In happy time!
        This man may help me to his majesty's ear,

79–80] *As prose, Pope;* A...got, / Or...honor, / So...that. F   79 livery] liv'ry F   82–3] *As prose, Pope;* Let...see
/ your...talke / With...souldier. F   **Act 5, Scene 1   5.1**] *Rowe; Actus Quintus.* F   6 SD] *Placed as Kittredge; follows*
6 *in* F   6 SD *a* GENTLE ASTRINGER] F; *a gentle Astranger* F2; *a Gentleman a stranger* F3; *a Gentleman* / *Rowe*

75 **patch of velvet** Used impartially to cover
honourable wounds and the carbonadoes or
incisions which were supposed to relieve syphilis.
Hence the joke at 81.
  76 **scar** wound.
  77–8 **two...half** i.e. thickly bandaged (the
thickest velvet being three-piled).
  78 **is worn bare** has no patch.
  79 **livery** Distinctive costume or insignia.
  80 **belike** probably.

Act 5, Scene 1
  5.1 Editors, following Capell, locate the scene in
Marseilles.
  1 **posting** speedy travelling.

4 **wear** weary.
  5 **bold** assured.
  5 **requital** obligation to requite you.
  6 SD *a* GENTLE ASTRINGER a gentleman
falconer (literally, a keeper of goshawks). See
illustration 6, p. 25 above. Why this character's
occupation is stipulated has never been obvious to
editors, who frequently emend to 'a Gentleman, a
stranger'. The only warrant for this, however, is F2's
corrupt reading 'Astranger'. It seems best, then, to
stay with the Folio text – not least because the noun,
being so eccentric a word, probably reflects
deliberate intention.
  6 **In happy time!** Most opportunely!

          If he would spend his power. God save you, sir.
GENTLEMAN And you.
HELENA Sir, I have seen you in the court of France.   10
GENTLEMAN I have been sometimes there.
HELENA I do presume, sir, that you are not fall'n
          From the report that goes upon your goodness,
          And therefore goaded with most sharp occasions,
          Which lay nice manners by, I put you to   15
          The use of your own virtues, for the which
          I shall continue thankful.
GENTLEMAN   What's your will?
HELENA That it will please you
          To give this poor petition to the king,
          And aid me with that store of power you have   20
          To come into his presence.
GENTLEMAN The king's not here.
HELENA   Not here, sir?
GENTLEMAN   Not indeed.
          He hence removed last night, and with more haste
          Than is his use.
WIDOW   Lord, how we lose our pains!
HELENA All's well that ends well yet,   25
          Though time seem so adverse and means unfit.
          I do beseech you, whither is he gone?
GENTLEMAN Marry, as I take it, to Rossillion,
          Whither I am going.
HELENA   I do beseech you, sir,
          Since you are like to see the king before me,   30
          Commend the paper to his gracious hand,
          Which I presume shall render you no blame,
          But rather make you thank your pains for it.
          I will come after you with what good speed
          Our means will make us means.
GENTLEMAN   This I'll do for you.   35
HELENA And you shall find yourself to be well thanked,

8 **spend** expend.

12–13 **are…goodness** have not changed in your behaviour from your reputation for goodness.

14 **sharp occasions** urgent necessities. See illustration 7, p. 26 above.

15 **lay…by** put aside finicking politeness.

15 **put** press.

16 **virtues** powers.

23 **removed** departed.

24 **use** custom.

35 **Our means…means** Our resources will facilitate.

Whate'er falls more. We must to horse again.
Go, go, provide.

[*Exeunt*]

[5.2] *Enter* [LAVATCH, *the*] *Clown and* PAROLLES

PAROLLES Good Master Lavatch, give my Lord Lafew this letter. I
have ere now, sir, been better known to you, when I have held
familiarity with fresher clothes; but I am now, sir, muddied in
Fortune's mood, and smell somewhat strong of her strong
displeasure.   5

LAVATCH Truly, Fortune's displeasure is but sluttish if it smell so
strongly as thou speak'st of. I will henceforth eat no fish of
Fortune's buttering. Prithee allow the wind.

PAROLLES Nay, you need not to stop your nose, sir; I spake but by
a metaphor.   10

LAVATCH Indeed, sir, if your metaphor stink, I will stop my nose, or
against any man's metaphor. Prithee get thee further.

PAROLLES Pray you, sir, deliver me this paper.

LAVATCH Foh, prithee stand away. A paper from Fortune's close-stool
to give to a nobleman! Look here he comes himself.   15

Enter LAFEW

Here is a purr of Fortune's, sir, or of Fortune's cat – but not a
musk-cat – that has fall'n into the unclean fishpond of her
displeasure, and as he says, is muddied withal. Pray you, sir, use
the carp as you may, for he looks like a poor, decayed, ingenious,

---

38 SD] F2; *not in* F 1 Master] *Neilson;* Mʳ F; M. F2 8 buttering] butt'ring F
16 Here] *Theobald;* Clo. Heere F 17 musk-cat] *Theobald;* Muscat F 19 ingenious] F; ingenerous *NS. conj.*
Brigstocke

---

37 **falls more** else should happen.

Act 5, Scene 2
5.2 Editors, following Capell, locate the scene in
Rossillion, the Count's palace.

1 **Lavatch** No one has explained why the Clown
should be named here for the first and only time in
the play. His name suggests French *la vache* =
'cow', or Italian *lavaccio* = 'lavage' or 'slop'.

4 **mood** displeasure (perhaps with a play on
'muddied', 'mood' being pronounced 'mud').

7–8 **of Fortune's buttering** prepared by
Fortune (see Tilley F305).

8 **allow the wind** stand to the windward of me
(so I don't smell you).

14 **close-stool** privy.

16 **purr** (1) the knave or jack in the card-game
of post and pair (see *OED* Pur), (2) piece of animal
excrement, (3) the sound made by a cat.

17 **musk-cat** Perfume was made from secretions
of the civet cat and musk deer. Lavatch,
conflating them, says that Parolles' is not
sweet-smelling.

18 **withal** with it.

19 **carp** (1) a fish raised in manured ponds, (2)
a person who carps or chatters.

19 **ingenious** An unexpectedly generous word in
the context and Hunter may be right to interpret
as 'un-genious', i.e. without intellectual capacity.
But Parolles, like Helena, is in many things
contradictory, and Lafew may be commending
Parolles as a resourceful rascal.

foolish, rascally knave. I do pity his distress in my similes of comfort,   20
and leave him to your lordship.   [*Exit*]

PAROLLES My lord, I am a man whom Fortune hath cruelly scratched.

LAFEW And what would you have me to do? 'Tis too late to pare her
nails now. Wherein have you played the knave with Fortune that
she should scratch you, who of herself is a good lady, and would   25
not have knaves thrive long under her? There's a cardecue for you.
Let the justices make you and Fortune friends; I am for other
business.

PAROLLES I beseech your honour to hear me one single word.

LAFEW You beg a single penny more. Come, you shall ha't; save your   30
word.

PAROLLES My name, my good lord, is Parolles.

LAFEW You beg more than 'word' then. Cox my passion! give me your
hand. How does your drum?

PAROLLES O my good lord, you were the first that found me!   35

LAFEW Was I, in sooth? And I was the first that lost thee.

PAROLLES It lies in you, my lord, to bring me in some grace, for you
did bring me out.

LAFEW Out upon thee, knave! Dost thou put upon me at once both the
office of God and the devil? One brings thee in grace, and the other   40
brings thee out.

[*Trumpets sound*]

The king's coming, I know by his trumpets. Sirrah, enquire further
after me. I had talk of you last night; though you are a fool and
a knave, you shall eat. Go to, follow.

PAROLLES I praise God for you.   45

[*Exeunt*]

---

20 similes] *Theobald, conj. Warburton;* smiles F   21 SD] *Capell; not in* F   26 her] F2; *not in* F   33 than] F4; then F
33 'word'] *Cam.;* word F; one word F3   39 Dost] *Rowe,* doest F   41 SD] *After Theobald; not in* F   42 coming,] F3,
comming F   45 SD] *Rowe; not in* F

20 *similes Because Parolles is said to be 'like'   33 more than 'word' more than one word (since
a knave rather than the thing itself. F's reading is   your name signifies 'words').
indefensible and looks like a minim error.   33 Cox Cock's (God's). A casual oath.
22 scratched Fortune has become the cat.   35 found me found me out.
26 cardecue The small coin of 4.3.235.   36 lost See 2.3.193–4.
27 justices i.e. justices of the peace, who were   37 in some grace into some favour. Lafew in
responsible for beggars under the Elizabethan poor   rejoining plays on 'grace' as the grace of God.
law.   42–3 enquire further after come later to see.

[5.3] *Flourish. Enter* KING, *old Lady* [COUNTESS], LAFEW, *the two French Lords* [*the* FIRST *and* SECOND LORDS DUMAINE], *with* ATTENDANTS

KING We lost a jewel of her, and our esteem
    Was made much poorer by it; but your son,
    As mad in folly, lacked the sense to know
    Her estimation home.

COUNTESS   'Tis past, my liege,
    And I beseech your majesty to make it   5
    Natural rebellion, done i'th'blade of youth,
    When oil and fire, too strong for reason's force,
    O'erbears it, and burns on.

KING   My honoured lady,
    I have forgiven and forgotten all,
    Though my revenges were high bent upon him,   10
    And watched the time to shoot.

LAFEW   This I must say –
    But first I beg my pardon – the young lord
    Did to his majesty, his mother, and his lady
    Offence of mighty note; but to himself
    The greatest wrong of all. He lost a wife   15
    Whose beauty did astonish the survey
    Of richest eyes, whose words all ears took captive,
    Whose dear perfection hearts that scorned to serve
    Humbly called mistress.

KING   Praising what is lost
    Makes the remembrance dear. Well, call him hither,   20
    We are reconciled, and the first view shall kill
    All repetition. Let him not ask our pardon,

Act 5, Scene 3   5.3] *Pope; not in* F   0 SD COUNTESS] *Rowe; not in* F   4 SH COUNTESS] *Rowe; Old La.* F *(through scene except 193)*   6 blade] F; blaze *Capell, conj. Theobald*

Act 5, Scene 3
  5.3 Editors locate the scene as 5.2.
  1 **of** in.
  1 **our esteem** my value.
  3 **As** Being.
  4 **estimation home** worth to the full.
  6 **Natural rebellion** i.e. of the natural passions against 'reason's force' (7).
  6 **blade** green shoot (i.e. immaturity).
  10 **high bent** i.e. like a tautened bow.

  11 **watched** waited for.
  12 **But...pardon** Perhaps recurring to the excessive boldness Lafew acknowledges in himself at 4.5.73
  16–17 **astonish...eyes** dumbfound the gazing of even those most experienced in beholding beautiful women.
  21–2 **kill...repetition** cancel any reviewing of past wrongs.

The nature of his great offence is dead,
And deeper than oblivion we do bury
Th'incensing relics of it. Let him approach   25
A stranger, no offender; and inform him
So 'tis our will he should.
GENTLEMAN   I shall, my liege.   [*Exit*]
KING What says he to your daughter? Have you spoke?
LAFEW All that he is hath reference to your highness.
KING Then shall we have a match. I have letters sent me   30
That sets him high in fame.

Enter COUNT BERTRAM

LAFEW   He looks well on't.
KING I am not a day of season,
For thou mayst see a sunshine and a hail
In me at once. But to the brightest beams
Distracted clouds give way, so stand thou forth,   35
The time is fair again.
BERTRAM   My high-repented blames,
Dear sovereign, pardon to me.
KING   All is whole,
Not one word more of the consumèd time.
Let's take the instant by the forward top;
For we are old, and on our quick'st decrees   40
Th'inaudible and noiseless foot of time
Steals ere we can effect them. You remember
The daughter of this lord?
BERTRAM Admiringly, my liege. At first

---

27 SD] *Capell; not in* F   28] *As Theobald;* What...daughter. / Haue...spoke? F   30–1] *As verse, Pope; as prose,* F
44 Admiringly, my liege.] *Rowe;* Admiringly my Liege, F

---

23 **nature...dead** i.e. just what it was the king has already forgotten.

25 **incensing relics** reminders that would rekindle anger. With an unexpected quibble on perfuming or censing, the offence being understood as somehow palliating itself.

26 **stranger** i.e. one newly arrived, his past unknown.

29 **hath reference** to is at the disposal of.

30 **letters** a letter (as at 2.3.253).

31 **on't** i.e. after his recent experience.

32 **of season** of one season (i.e. I am not altogether a summer's or a winter's day).

34 **at once** simultaneously.

35 **Distracted** Broken (i.e. the clouds will break when the sun shines).

36 **high-repented blames** deeply repented sins.

37 **to** in.

39 **forward top** forelock. The only way to grasp Opportunity or Occasion, who is generally figured as being bald behind. See illustration 7, p. 26 above.

40 **quick'st** (1) most urgent, (2) most quick with life.

44 **Admiringly** With wonder.

I stuck my choice upon her, ere my heart   45
Durst make too bold a herald of my tongue;
Where the impression of mine eye infixing,
Contempt his scornful pèrspective did lend me,
Which warped the line of every other favour,
Scorned a fair colour, or expressed it stol'n,   50
Extended or contracted all proportions
To a most hideous object. Thence it came
That she whom all men praised, and whom myself,
Since I have lost, have loved, was in mine eye
The dust that did offend it.

KING   Well excused.   55
That thou didst love her, strikes some scores away
From the great compt; but love that comes too late,
Like a remorseful pardon slowly carried,
To the great sender turns a sour offence,
Crying, 'That's good that's gone.' Our rash faults   60
Make trivial price of serious things we have,
Not knowing them until we know their grave.
Oft our displeasures, to ourselves unjust,
Destroy our friends, and after weep their dust;
Our own love waking cries to see what's done,   65
While shameful hate sleeps out the afternoon.
Be this sweet Helen's knell, and now forget her.
Send forth your amorous token for fair Maudlin.

58 carried,] *Rowe;* carried F   59 sender turns] *Theobald;* sender, turnes F   65 done] F2; don,e F

45 **stuck** fixed.

45–6 ere…tongue (1) before I dared say what I feel in my heart (for Lafew's daughter), (2) before I, in my rashness, allowed my tongue to say what I felt (about Helena).

47 Where i.e. in the heart.

47 impression…infixing image beheld by my eye impressing itself.

48 pèrspective The ordinary perspective glass was a convex mirror bringing a whole scene into view and helping the artist to compose it. But this is 'Contempt's perspective'. See M. M. Martinet, *Le Miroir de l'esprit dans le théâtre Elisabéthain*, 1981, p. 317 n. 29 (discussion of 'le prisme de Dédain').

49 favour face.

50 fair colour beautiful complexion.

50 expressed it stol'n said that it was painted on.

51–2 Extended…object Distorted all shapes,

as by elongating or shortening them, so that they became an ugly sight.

53 she i.e. Helena.

56 scores debts. In alehouses they were scored up on a slate.

57 compt account (with a residual suggestion of the Day of Judgement).

59 turns…offence becomes offensive to, goes sour on – the pardon arriving too late to save the victim whom 'the great sender' wished to save.

61 Make…of Put a trifling value on.

62 know their grave have lost them forever.

64 weep their dust mourn over their remains.

65 cries to see i.e. is saddened by seeing.

66 sleeps…afternoon enjoys an untroubled repose.

68 Maudlin So pronounced but signifying 'Magdalen'. Perhaps an unconscious reminiscence of Mary Magdalene. See p. 6 above.

The main consents are had, and here we'll stay
To see our widower's second marriage day.   70
COUNTESS Which better than the first, O dear heaven, bless!
      Or, ere they meet, in me, O nature, cesse!
LAFEW Come on, my son, in whom my house's name
      Must be digested; give a favour from you
      To sparkle in the spirits of my daughter,   75
      That she may quickly come.
                  [*Bertram gives a ring*]
                              By my old beard,
      And every hair that's on't, Helen, that's dead,
      Was a sweet creature; such a ring as this,
      The last that e'er I took her leave at court,
      I saw upon her finger.
BERTRAM   Hers it was not.   80
KING Now pray you let me see it; for mine eye,
      While I was speaking, oft was fastened to't.
      This ring was mine, and when I gave it Helen,
      I bade her, if her fortunes ever stood
      Necessitied to help, that by this token   85
      I would relieve her. Had you that craft to reave her
      Of what should stead her most?
BERTRAM   My gracious sovereign,
      Howe'er it pleases you to take it so,
      The ring was never hers.
COUNTESS   Son, on my life,
      I have seen her wear it, and she reckoned it   90
      At her life's rate.
LAFEW   I am sure I saw her wear it.
BERTRAM You are deceived, my lord, she never saw it.
      In Florence was it from a casement thrown me,
      Wrapped in a paper, which contained the name

---

71 SH COUNTESS] *Theobald; not in* F   72 meet,...nature,] *Rowe;* meete...Nature F   76 SD] *Hanmer; not in* F
91 life's] liues F

69 **The...had** i.e. all the interested parties have agreed to the marriage.

71–2 *Given by F to the King, but most follow Theobald and reassign to the Countess. The King has already spoken the couplet that signals the conclusion of his speech (69–70).

72 **cesse** cease.

74 **digested** absorbed (since his daughter's name will be lost in marriage).

74 **favour** love-token.

79 **last** last time.

79 **took her leave** took leave of her.

85 **Necessitied to** In need of.

86 **reave** deprive.

87 **stead** benefit.

90 **reckoned** esteemed.

91 **At** As highly as.

Of her that threw it. Noble she was, and thought   95
I stood ingaged; but when I had subscribed
To mine own fortune, and informed her fully
I could not answer in that course of honour
As she had made the overture, she ceased
In heavy satisfaction, and would never   100
Receive the ring again.

KING   Plutus himself,
That knows the tinct and multiplying med'cine,
Hath not in nature's mystery more science
Than I have in this ring. 'Twas mine, 'twas Helen's,
Whoever gave it you. Then if you know   105
That you are well acquainted with yourself,
Confess 'twas hers, and by what rough enforcement
You got it from her. She called the saints to surety
That she would never put it from her finger,
Unless she gave it to yourself in bed,   110
Where you have never come, or sent it us
Upon her great disaster.

BERTRAM   She never saw it.

KING Thou speak'st it falsely, as I love mine honour,
And mak'st conjectural fears to come into me,
Which I would fain shut out. If it should prove   115
That thou art so inhuman – 'twill not prove so;
And yet I know not: thou didst hate her deadly,
And she is dead, which nothing but to close
Her eyes myself could win me to believe,
More than to see this ring. Take him away.   120
My fore-past proofs, howe'er the matter fall,

---

101 Plutus] *Rowe³, Platus* F   113 falsely,] *Rowe;* falsely: F   114 conjectural] F2 *(subst.);* connecturall F
115 out.] *Singer²;* out, F; out; F4   116–17 inhuman–...not:] *After Rowe;* inhumane,...not, F

96 **ingaged** pledged (to her), as by giving his gage. The figure, continued with 'subscribed' and 'course of honour', is from duelling.

96–7 **subscribed To** given her an account of.

98–9 **in...As** with the like honour with which.

100 **heavy satisfaction** sad conviction.

101 **Plutus** The god of riches and skilled in alchemical lore (102).

102 **tinct...med'cine** tincture and elixir which (as the alchemists supposed) converted base metals to gold, thus multiplying gold indefinitely.

103 **science** knowledge.

105–6 **if...yourself** This contingent phrase is ironic, for Bertram does not know himself.

108 **surety** bear witness.

112 **Upon...disaster** In the event of some great misfortune overtaking her.

114 **conjectural fears** surmises full of foreboding.

121 **My fore-past proofs** The evidence I have had already.

121 **fall** turn out.

Shall tax my fears of little vanity,
Having vainly feared too little. Away with him!
We'll sift this matter further.

BERTRAM   If you shall prove
This ring was ever hers, you shall as easy   125
Prove that I husbanded her bed in Florence,
Where yet she never was.

                                            [*Exit guarded*]

                    Enter GENTLEMAN

KING I am wrapped in dismal thinkings.
GENTLEMAN   Gracious sovereign,
Whether I have been to blame or no, I know not.
Here's a petition from a Florentine,   130
Who hath for four or five removes come short
To tender it herself. I undertook it,
Vanquished thereto by the fair grace and speech
Of the poor suppliant, who by this I know
Is here attending. Her business looks in her   135
With an importing visage, and she told me,
In a sweet verbal brief, it did concern
Your highness with herself.
[KING] [*Reads*] *a letter* 'Upon his many protestations to marry me when
his wife was dead, I blush to say it, he won me. Now is the Count   140
Rossillion a widower, his vows are forfeited to me, and my honour's
paid to him. He stole from Florence, taking no leave, and I follow
him to his country for justice. Grant it me, O king, in you it best
lies; otherwise a seducer flourishes, and a poor maid is undone.
                              Diana Capilet.'   145

---

122 tax] F3; taze F; taxe F2   127 SD *Exit guarded*] *Rowe; not in* F   139 SD KING *Reads*] *Rowe; not in* F   141 honour's]
Rowe³; honors F

122–3 **Shall…little** Will suffice to show that my
fears were not foolish; my foolishness consists
rather in not having feared enough.
124 **sift** examine.
127 SD GENTLEMAN Presumably the astringer
of 5.1.6 SD.
131 **removes** Stopping-places in a royal progress.
Helena has just missed or come short of the King
at each of these places.
133 **Vanquished thereto** Won to the
undertaking.

134 **by this** by this time.
135 **looks** shows itself.
136 **importing** (1) importunate, (2) important.
137 **sweet verbal brief** summary recital, sweetly
delivered.
140–1 **Now…Rossillion** Now that the Count
Rossillion is.
141 **vows…me** promises of marriage are debts
which I may legitimately claim.

LAFEW I will buy me a son-in-law in a fair, and toll for this. I'll none
    of him.
KING The heavens have thought well on thee, Lafew,
        To bring forth this discovery. Seek these suitors.
        Go speedily, and bring again the count.   150
                                            [*Exeunt Attendants*]
        I am afear'd the life of Helen, lady,
        Was foully snatched.
COUNTESS   Now, justice on the doers!

                    Enter BERTRAM [*guarded*]

KING I wonder, sir, since wives are monsters to you,
        And that you fly them as you swear them lordship,
        Yet you desire to marry. What woman's that?   155

                    Enter WIDOW, DIANA

DIANA I am, my lord, a wretched Florentine,
        Derivèd from the ancient Capilet.
        My suit, as I do understand, you know,
        And therefore know how far I may be pitied.
WIDOW I am her mother, sir, whose age and honour   160
        Both suffer under this complaint we bring,
        And both shall cease, without your remedy.
KING Come hither, count, do you know these women?
BERTRAM My lord, I neither can nor will deny
        But that I know them. Do they charge me further?   165
DIANA Why do you look so strange upon your wife?
BERTRAM She's none of mine, my lord.
DIANA   If you shall marry,

---

146 toll] *Rowe,* toule F   150 SD] *After Capell; not in* F   152 SD *Enter* BERTRAM] *Placed as Capell; after 150* F
152 SD *guarded*] *Capell; not in* F   153 sir, since wives] *Var. 93, conj. Tyrwhitt;* sir, sir, wiues F; sir, wiues F2; sir, sith
wiues *Dyce*   155 SD DIANA] *Rowe;* Diana, and Parrolles. F

146 **in** at.
146 **a fair** Which offers the chance of buying a
better husband than Bertram, though sleazy or
stolen goods were often sold there.
146 **toll for this** register Bertram for sale in
the toll-book (where merchandise offered at a
market had to be entered for a fee).
149 **suitors** i.e. the wronged women who sue for
justice, and Bertram, suitor for Lafew's daughter.
153 *****since** F's reading is a compositor's slip,
possibly for MS. form 'sith' = 'since'.
154 **that** since.

154 **as** as soon as.
154 **swear them lordship** promise them
marriage.
155 SD *****Enter** WIDOW, DIANA F adds '*and
Parrolles*'. Does Parolles enter here and sneak away?
Presumably not, since he is summoned for the first
time at 202. Perhaps the confusion represents
an original intention of Shakespeare's preserved in
his working copy but not carried through.
157 **Derivèd** Descended.
162 **both** i.e. age and honour.

You give away this hand, and that is mine;
You give away heaven's vows, and those are mine;
You give away myself, which is known mine;   170
For I by vow am so embodied yours,
That she which marries you must marry me,
Either both or none.

LAFEW Your reputation comes too short for my daughter, you are no
    husband for her.   175

BERTRAM My lord, this is a fond and desperate creature,
Whom sometime I have laughed with. Let your highness
Lay a more noble thought upon mine honour
Than for to think that I would sink it here.

KING Sir, for my thoughts, you have them ill to friend   180
Till your deeds gain them; fairer prove your honour
Than in my thought it lies.

DIANA   Good my lord,
Ask him upon his oath, if he does think
He had not my virginity.

KING What say'st thou to her?

BERTRAM   She's impudent, my lord,   185
And was a common gamester to the camp.

DIANA He does me wrong, my lord; if I were so,
He might have bought me at a common price.
Do not believe him. O, behold this ring,
Whose high respect and rich validity   190
Did lack a parallel; yet for all that
He gave it to a commoner a'th'camp,
If I be one.

COUNTESS   He blushes, and 'tis hit.
Of six preceding ancestors, that gem,
Conferred by testament to th'sequent issue,   195

---

181 them; fairer] *Theobald*[2]; them fairer: F

168 **this hand** i.e. Bertram's.
171 **embodied yours** made a part of your body.
176 **fond and desperate** foolish and reckless.
177 **sometime** formerly.
179 **sink** degrade.
180 **you...friend** they are not friendly to you.
181 **them; fairer** This emending by Theobald of F's 'them fairer' is generally accepted. Hunter, who accepts it, suggests, however, that F will make sense if we read '...them fairer. Prove your honour; Then' ('then' and 'than' being interchangeable Elizabethan spellings).

181 **gain them** win their friendship.
185 **impudent** shameless.
186 **gamester** whore.
190 **high...validity** great honour in his regard and high value.
191 **Did...parallel** Was without equal.
193 **'tis hit** Diana has hit the mark.
194 **Of** By.
195 **testament...issue** will to the succeeding heir.

Hath it been owed and worn. This is his wife,
That ring's a thousand proofs.

KING   Methought you said
You saw one here in court could witness it.

DIANA I did, my lord, but loath am to produce
So bad an instrument. His name's Parolles.   200

LAFEW I saw the man today, if man he be.

KING Find him, and bring him hither.

                                        [*Exit an Attendant*]

BERTRAM   What of him?
He's quoted for a most perfidious slave,
With all the spots a'th'world taxed and debauched,
Whose nature sickens but to speak a truth.   205
Am I or that or this for what he'll utter,
That will speak any thing?

KING   She hath that ring of yours.

BERTRAM I think she has. Certain it is I liked her,
And boarded her i'th'wanton way of youth.
She knew her distance, and did angle for me,   210
Madding my eagerness with her restraint,
As all impediments in fancy's course
Are motives of more fancy, and in fine,
Her insuite cunning, with her modern grace,
Subdued me to her rate. She got the ring,   215
And I had that which any inferior might
At market-price have bought.

---

202 SD] *Dyce; not in* F   202 SH BERTRAM] *Rowe; Ros.* F *(through scene)*   205 sickens but...truth.] *Staunton;* sickens: but...truth, F   214 insuite cunning] *This edn;* insuite comming F; insuit comming F2; insuit coming F4; in suit coming *Hanmer;* inf'nite cunning *conj. W. S. Walker*   215 rate.] rate; F3; rate, F

---

196 **owed** possessed.

197–8 **Methought...it** We do not hear Diana say this.

203 **quoted for** set down as.

204 **With...debauched** Censured for being debauched with every vice.

205 **but** only.

206 **or...this** either that or this (i.e. anything).

206 **for** by virtue of.

207 **That** Who.

209 **boarded** went aboard (i.e. had intercourse with).

210 **knew her distance** (1) understood the difference in our stations (which might properly have kept her aloof), (2) understood how to keep a teasing distance (the better to draw me on).

211 **Madding** Maddening.

211 **eagerness** sharpness (i.e. of his sexual edge).

212 **fancy's** love's.

213 **motives** occasions.

213 **in fine** to sum up.

214 **insuite cunning** If this reading of F is correct, it represents a Shakespearean coinage from Latin *insuetus*. Compare English 'insuetude' = 'the quality of being unusual', not in use, a rare substantive but not cited by *OED* before 1824. Editors generally emend to read 'inf'nite'.

214 **modern** commonplace, ordinary. This adjective is conventionally pejorative in Shakespeare and supports the antithesis with 'insuite'.

215 **Subdued...rate** Made me submit to her price.

DIANA   I must be patient.
    You that have turned off a first so noble wife,
    May justly diet me. I pray you yet
    (Since you lack virtue, I will lose a husband)   220
    Send for your ring, I will return it home,
    And give me mine again.
BERTRAM   I have it not.
KING What ring was yours, I pray you?
DIANA   Sir, much like
    The same upon your finger.
KING Know you this ring? This ring was his of late.   225
DIANA And this was it I gave him, being abed.
KING The story then goes false, you threw it him
    Out of a casement.
DIANA   I have spoke the truth.

Enter PAROLLES

BERTRAM My lord, I do confess the ring was hers.
KING You boggle shrewdly, every feather starts you.   230
    Is this the man you speak of?
DIANA   Ay, my lord.
KING Tell me, sirrah – but tell me true, I charge you,
    Not fearing the displeasure of your master,
    Which on your just proceeding I'll keep off –
    By him and by this woman here what know you?   235
PAROLLES So please your majesty, my master hath been an honourable
    gentleman. Tricks he hath had in him, which gentlemen have.
KING Come, come, to th'purpose. Did he love this woman?
PAROLLES Faith, sir, he did love her, but how?
KING How, I pray you?   240
PAROLLES He did love her, sir, as a gentleman loves a woman.
KING How is that?
PAROLLES He loved her, sir, and loved her not.
KING As thou art a knave, and no knave. What an equivocal companion
    is this!   245

223–4 Sir...finger] *As Capell; as one line,* F   226 abed] a-bed *Rowe;* a bed F   241 gentleman] *Rowe;* Gent. F
244 knave.] *Rowe (*knave;)*;* knave, F

218 a...noble so noble a first.
219 diet me confine me to a lean regimen.
230 boggle shrewdly are quick to shy (like a
skittish horse).
230 starts agitates.
235 By...by About...about.

236–7 honourable gentleman True when
reductively interpreted – honourable because he is
touchy about his reputation and status, a gentleman
because he behaves like others of his class.
244 companion fellow (pejorative).

PAROLLES I am a poor man, and at your majesty's command.

LAFEW He's a good drum, my lord, but a naughty orator.

DIANA Do you know he promised me marriage?

PAROLLES Faith, I know more than I'll speak.

KING But wilt thou not speak all thou know'st?   250

PAROLLES Yes, so please your majesty. I did go between them as I said,
    but more than that, he loved her, for indeed he was mad for her,
    and talked of Satan and of Limbo and of furies, and I know not
    what. Yet I was in that credit with them at that time that I knew
    of their going to bed, and of other motions, as promising her   255
    marriage, and things which would derive me ill will to speak of;
    therefore I will not speak what I know.

KING Thou hast spoken all already, unless thou canst say they are
    married. But thou art too fine in thy evidence, therefore stand aside.
    This ring you say was yours?

DIANA   Ay, my good lord.   260

KING Where did you buy it? Or who gave it you?

DIANA It was not given me, nor I did not buy it.

KING Who lent it you?

DIANA   It was not lent me neither.

KING Where did you find it then?

DIANA   I found it not.

KING If it were yours by none of all these ways,   265
    How could you give it him?

DIANA   I never gave it him.

LAFEW This woman's an easy glove, my lord, she goes off and on at
    pleasure.

KING This ring was mine, I gave it his first wife.

DIANA It might be yours or hers for aught I know.   270

KING Take her away, I do not like her now,
    To prison with her; and away with him.
    Unless thou tell'st me where thou hadst this ring,
    Thou diest within this hour.

DIANA   I'll never tell you.

KING Take her away.

DIANA   I'll put in bail, my liege.   275

KING I think thee now some common customer.

252 that,] F3; that F

247 **drum** drummer.
247 **naughty** no good.
254 **credit** confidence.

255 **motions** proposals.
259 **fine** subtle.
276 **common customer** prostitute.

DIANA By Jove, if ever I knew man, 'twas you.
KING Wherefore hast thou accused him all this while?
DIANA Because he's guilty, and he is not guilty.
　　　　He knows I am no maid, and he'll swear to't;   280
　　　　I'll swear I am a maid, and he knows not.
　　　　Great king, I am no strumpet, by my life;
　　　　I am either maid, or else this old man's wife.
　　　　　　　　　　[*Pointing to Lafew*]
KING She does abuse our ears. To prison with her!
DIANA Good mother, fetch my bail.
　　　　　　　　　　　　　　　[*Exit Widow*]
　　　　　　　　　　Stay, royal sir.   285
　　　　The jeweller that owes the ring is sent for,
　　　　And he shall surety me. But for this lord,
　　　　Who hath abused me, as he knows himself,
　　　　Though yet he never harmed me, here I quit him.
　　　　He knows himself my bed he hath defiled,   290
　　　　And at that time he got his wife with child.
　　　　Dead though she be, she feels her young one kick.
　　　　So there's my riddle: one that's dead is quick –
　　　　And now behold the meaning.

　　　　　　　　Enter HELENA *and* WIDOW

KING   Is there no exorcist
　　　　Beguiles the truer office of mine eyes?   295
　　　　Is't real that I see?
HELENA   No, my good lord,
　　　　'Tis but the shadow of a wife you see,
　　　　The name and not the thing.
BERTRAM   Both, both. O, pardon!
HELENA O my good lord, when I was like this maid,
　　　　I found you wondrous kind. There is your ring,   300
　　　　And look you, here's your letter. This it says:
　　　　'When from my finger you can get this ring,
　　　　And are by me with child, etc.' This is done.
　　　　Will you be mine now you are doubly won?

283 SD] *Rowe; not in* F   285 SD] *Pope (after 285), placed as Craig; not in* F   303 are] *Rowe; is* F

277 **knew** knew sexually.
289 **quit** (1) acquit, (2) requite.
293 **quick** alive.
294 **exorcist** raiser of spirits.

295 Deceives my eyes' true sight?
297 **shadow** (1) ghost, shade, (2) imitation.
299 **was like** appeared to you as.

BERTRAM If she, my liege, can make me know this clearly,   305
    I'll love her dearly, ever, ever dearly.
HELENA If it appear not plain and prove untrue,
    Deadly divorce step between me and you!
    O my dear mother, do I see you living?
LAFEW Mine eyes smell onions, I shall weep anon.   310
    [*To Parolles*] Good Tom Drum, lend me a handkercher. So, I thank
    thee; wait on me home, I'll make sport with thee. Let thy curtsies
    alone, they are scurvy ones.
KING Let us from point to point this story know,
    To make the even truth in pleasure flow.   315
    [*To Diana*] If thou beest yet a fresh uncroppèd flower,
    Choose thou thy husband, and I'll pay thy dower.
    For I can guess that by thy honest aid
    Thou kept'st a wife herself, thyself a maid.
    Of that and all the progress, more and less,   320
    Resolvedly more leisure shall express.
    All yet seems well, and if it end so meet,
    The bitter past, more welcome is the sweet.
                      Flourish

[EPILOGUE]

    The king's a beggar, now the play is done;
    All is well ended, if this suit be won,
    That you express content; which we will pay,
    With strife to please you, day exceeding day.
    Ours be your patience then, and yours our parts;   5
    Your gentle hands lend us, and take our hearts.
                      Exeunt

---

311 SD] *Rowe; not in* F   311 Good...handkercher.] *As prose, Capell; as verse,* F   316 SD] *Rowe; not in* F   321 Resolvedly] F4; Resolduedly F; Resolv'dly F3   Epilogue EPILOGUE] *Rowe; not in* F   4 strife] F2; strift F   6 SD *Exeunt*] Exeunt omn. FINIS. F

308 **Deadly divorce** Divorcing death.
312 **wait on me** accompany me (as a servant).
312–13 **Let...ones** Parolles is bowing and scraping.
315 **even** plain, exact.
320 **more and less** both greater and lesser details.
321 **Resolvedly** In a manner which will resolve all questions.
322 **meet** fitly.
323 **past** being past.

Epilogue
1 **king's a beggar** 'Perhaps there is some allusion to the old tale of The King and the Beggar, which was the subject of a ballad' (Malone).
3 **express content** show your satisfaction (by applauding).
4 **strife** striving.
5 Reversing roles, we will be the patient spectators and listen to your applause, you applauding will be the actors.
6 **Your...us** i.e. applaud.
6 **hearts** gratitude.

TEXTUAL ANALYSIS

There are no editions in quarto of *All's Well That Ends Well*, and the basis for any edition of the play is that of its first publication in the Folio of 1623. The Folio text is sometimes carelessly printed, and there are stumbling-places or cruces that require an editor's intervention. (This intervention is not invariably successful.) Examples are Helena musing on her virginity (1.1.140), the King referring cryptically to those who 'inherit but the fall of the last monarchy' (2.1.13–14), Helena on the 'still-peering' air (3.2.102), Parolles invoking 'Bajazeth's mule' (4.1.33), Bertram thinking he knows Diana as 'Fontybell' (4.2.1), and Diana fearing that women will forsake themselves, seeing that men 'make rope's in such a scarre' (4.2.38).

The printing of the Folio text has been assigned by modern editors, such as Hunter, to two compositors, designated A and B, with the latter doing the bulk of the work. Hinman, building on spelling preferences (in *The Printing and Proof-Reading of the First Folio of Shakespeare*, 2 vols., 1963), saw three compositors at work, and he divided the assignment of Compositor A between him and a colleague designated C. Failing a correct discrimination of the parts of the text set by each compositor, it is difficult to speak of compositorial influence on textual readings. But if this discrimination depends on spelling, as it does in the work of Hinman and Alice Walker (*Textual Problems of the First Folio*, 1953), it will necessarily be open to query. The point is made emphatically by T. H. Howard-Hill in an article on 'The compositors of Shakespeare's Folio comedies' (*SB* 26 (1973), 61–106): 'without precise knowledge of the spellings of the copy from which the compositors set their Folio pages, it is hard to identify their shares of text printed from manuscript copy of unknown character'.

How many compositors worked on *All's Well* is uncertain, and so is the order in which they set the play. Shakespeare's great Folio is a 'Folio-in-sixes': three folded sheets are placed one within another at the fold and sewn together to make a quire or gathering of six leaves or twelve pages. In such a gathering, leaves 1 and 6, 2 and 5, and 3 and 4 will be conjugate, i.e. part of the same sheet joined at the fold. According to Hinman (in *SQ* 6 (1955), 259–73), the compositor set the text not by pages but by formes (a unit of two type-pages printed on the same sheet and subsequently locked in the metal rectangular frame that enclosed them). Generally the compositor worked from the inside out, first setting pages 6 and 7, then 5 and 8, then 4 and 9, and continuing in this sequence until he had set 11 and 12. This done, he proceeded to pages 6 and 7 of the next quire. If two compositors were involved, A set page 6 while B set 7, and they continued to divide the work between them, following the sequence outlined above.

In the Folio, *All's Well* extends over 25 pages, encompassing three gatherings which bear the signatures V, X and Y. The text begins on the verso of sig. V1 and continues through the verso of Y1. In gathering V (according to Hunter), Compositor A set sigs. V3^v, V4, and probably V3 and V4^v. (Hinman gives V4 and V4^v to Compositor C.) Compositor B set sigs. V1^v, V2 and V2^v. The composition of gathering X and the two pages of gathering Y devoted to *All's Well* are also assigned to Compositor B.

Compositor A (Hinman's A and C), though generally characterised as more meticulous than his colleague, is not especially meticulous. For example, he drops words (at 1.3.89), or transposes letters (1.3.143, 2.1.151), or garbles the text (reading ''ton tooth' at 1.3.149), and sometimes his punctuation involves us in difficulties (2.1.3). Compositor B also punctuates carelessly, distorting the sense (2.3.64, 121, 133, 160, 5.3.181). He alters words (4.3.202, 5.3.303), or omits or repeats them (2.3.122, 5.2.26), or he repeats speech headings (2.2.31, 2.4.27), or assigns them incorrectly (4.3.99, 116, 5.3.71). He misreads letters in his copy (2.5.24, 3.2.8, 3.6.28, 3.7.19), or adds letters (3.6.28) or omits letters (5.2.20, 5.3.153).

Compositor B has an indifferent eye for calculating the relation of copy to type. Occasionally the foot of the Folio pages is marred by 'space-losing', as if the compositor had not enquired beforehand how much manuscript copy he needed to fill the printed page. Illustrations of this occur at the foot of sig. V2^v (1.3.12), where the Clown's dialogue is widely spaced to no purpose except to eke out the available space, and the foot of the first column on X5^v (4.5.79–83) where the prose is printed in short lines, presumably to fill the column and allow the second column to begin with Act 5. This makes trouble in the second column, where crowding is apparent. There is crowding again on X6^v and Y1 (5.3.76–296). On X1 at the bottom of the second column, four lines of verse assigned to the Countess are contracted to three lines of prose (3.2.83–6), while on X1^v towards the end of the second column, the prose is printed in short lines as if it were verse (3.5.1–12), probably because the compositor lacked sufficient copy to finish his stint. These examples of maladroit composition are described by bibliographers as 'bad casting-off'. Not only do they comment on the compositor: perhaps they attest to the provisional state of the copy from which he was working. In the first column of X2, for instance, short lines recur again (3.5.30–3), and scholars, including Hunter, conjecture that the compositor is seeking to regularise confused copy.

The nature of this copy has been variously described. Arthur Quiller-Couch and J. Dover Wilson, in the New Shakespeare edition of the play (1929), emphasised a mingling of consistency with inconsistency, like our mingled yarn, and they supposed that the Folio text depended on a prompt-book prepared by the company's book-keeper. W. W. Greg detected the book-keeper's intervention in the presence of stage directions such as *Flourish cornets* (1.2 and 2.1) and *Alarum within* (4.1), but he thought that a prompt-copy, being valuable, would have stayed in the archives rather than gone to the printer. Conceivably it was the book-keeper who divided the Folio text into acts, not a rarity in Shakespeare but not customary practice either. The act-division carries right through the Comedies section of the Folio, however, and is more likely to be the work of the Folio editors.

Hypothetically, the prompt-book theory takes support from the use of the letters 'E' and 'G' by which Shakespeare's First and Second Lord are designated throughout. E. K. Chambers (in *William Shakespeare*, 1930) attributed these letters to the book-keeper, who is assumed to have made a transcript of Shakespeare's manuscript. The argument here is that the book-keeper is indicating the names of the actors – Ecclestone and Gough, or Gilburne for Gough – who played the parts in question. It is true that Shakespeare designed his parts, or some of them, for specific members of the company, and in *Much Ado* the first speech of the Constable Verges in 4.2 is assigned in the Folio to 'Cowley', the actor who took this part. But nowhere in Shakespeare, unless in *All's Well*, does a single letter denote a particular actor. Also, the letters 'E' and 'G' seem to be used indifferently for First and Second Lord, an intolerable confusion with which editors must cope but with which the book-keeper, whose intervention used to be hypothesised, evidently declined to cope.

Spelling in the Folio text is not notably peculiar, and this might support the hypothesising of a scribe (whether the book-keeper or somebody else), intervening between the manuscript and printed text. Shakespeare's spelling, as represented in the autograph customarily attributed to him (Hand D of the play of *Sir Thomas More*), is certainly peculiar. Final consonants are often doubled, final 'e' is omitted after 'c' ('obedyenc' for 'obedience'), 'straing' does duty for 'strange', and 'how' for 'ho', 'deule' for 'devil', 'on' for 'one'. G. Blakemore Evans in *The Riverside Shakespeare* (1974) found traces of this spelling in the Folio ('on' for 'one' at 2.5.26, 'Angles' for 'angels' at 3.2.118, 'In' for 'E'en' at 3.2.15), and Shakespeare, said Dover Wilson, was consistent in this latter eccentricity, spelling 'England' with an 'I'. By and large, however, the Folio text does not exhibit what are called Shakespearean spellings, and this has prompted some scholars to suppose that a scribe whose spelling was less eccentric than Shakespeare's had made a transcript of the manuscript. Greg, who took this position, also argued paradoxically (in *The Shakespeare First Folio*, 1955) that the supposed transcript was not an improvement but a debasing, and that Jaggard's compositors would have done a better job had they had the manuscript before them. Hunter, for whom the evidence leaves 'little doubt that the copy for the Folio text was Shakespeare's foul papers', is willing to entertain the alternative that copy was furnished by a transcript. Evans follows suit. The alternative seems not worth invoking, however. Inconsistencies in the text are dramatic enough to point away from a scribe or book-keeper, whose labours would have been too servile to accomplish any useful purpose. The E/G designations, though singular, seem explicable only as they indicate an author writing with specific players in mind. And if characteristic Shakespearean spellings do not much survive the compositors, that is not necessarily surprising. As Dover Wilson pointed out, the compositors themselves might have normalised spelling routinely.

The view of most recent scholarship, beginning with R. B. McKerrow in 1935, is that the author's manuscript or 'foul papers' stands behind the Folio. Fredson Bowers defines these 'foul papers' as 'the author's last complete draft in a shape satisfactory to him for transfer to fair copy', and the supposition that they furnished copy for the printer is made more plausible by virtue of the inconsistency which marks the use of speech headings. The hero appears variously as *Ber.*, *Count.* and *Ros.*, while his mother the Countess is *Mo.*, *Cou.*, *Old Cou.* or *La.* The courtier Lafew is introduced as *Laf.*, *Ol. Laf.* and *Ol. Lord.* The interpreter of 4.1 is initially I. *Sol.*, subsequently *Inter.* Though the writer of the play might not be perplexed by these differing descriptions, actors would certainly find them confusing, and presumably the keeper of a prompt-copy would have made it his business to rationalise them all for performance. McKerrow's argument seems conclusive: 'a copy intended for use in the theatre would surely, of necessity, be accurate and unambiguous in the matter of character-names'.

In fact, the text as we have it is characterised by apparent errors and confusions that cannot be ascribed to the compositors and that suggest work in progress, Shakespeare clarifying or more fully realising his fiction in the course of writing. Not only are speech headings subject to change but stage directions are suspiciously permissive, as if the author had not made up his mind or didn't care to. 'Divers' attendants enter at 1.2, and 'divers' lords take leave at 2.1. At 2.3.45 'three or four' lords enter, and at 4.3 'some two or three soldiers'. As 4.1 begins, 'five or six' of these soldiers lie in ambush. A character called Violenta is named in 3.5 but makes no appearance; in any case she has nothing to say. Lafew at 4.5.66 refers to an unnamed intelligencer, and this may be the 'astringer' who enters at 5.1.6 and who (presumably) appears again at 5.3.127. An astringer is a falconer, but why his occupation is specified remains mysterious. In the course of the play, generic characters are particularised. The Widow is named Capilet and the Clown is named Lavatch. The anonymous French lords are displaced by the brothers Dumaine. A person hitherto called Steward is abruptly called Rinaldo. Shakespeare, said H. F. Brooks, 'was finding out, in the course of composition, what to call these characters'.

Loose ends or frayed ends are apparent. Lafew at 2.3.79 ff. seems not to know what is going on, and editors are unsuccessful in explaining away his confusion. Later in the same scene, he is give a son (216), otherwise unknown to the play. The Clown, who ought to leave the stage at 3.2.37, is left on stage but has nothing to do. At 4.3.136–8 we hear of characters called Sebastian, Jacques and Lodowick, familiar to us from other plays of Shakespeare's, and also of one Corambus, the name given to Polonius in the first quarto of *Hamlet*. These names which mean nothing for Shakespeare's play perhaps had some private and occult meaning for Shakespeare, and they seem to bring us close to the writer. The stage direction at 5.3.155 indicates an entrance for Parolles, who is summoned on stage more than 40 lines later. The confusion here and elsewhere suggests an original intention of Shakespeare's, preserved in his foul papers but not carried through.

Here and there, unlikely speech headings which most editors attribute to a compositor's error – as in the assigning of a speech to Bertram at 4.3.99 or to Parolles at 4.3.116 – may quite as tenably represent the author's aborted idea. Working through the text, I take the impression that the copy for the Folio is probably autograph and that its confusions are to be explained largely as authorial inconsistencies or changes of mind. I conclude that Shakespeare's manuscript lies behind the Folio text of the play.

READING LIST

Adams, J. F. '*All's Well That Ends Well*: the paradox of procreation', *SQ* 12 (1961), 261–70

Arthos, J. 'The comedy of generation', *EIC* 5 (1955), 97–117 (a fine defence of the play)

Baldwin, T. W. *Shakespeare's Love's Labor's Won*, 1957

Barnet, S. (ed.). *All's Well That Ends Well* (Signet Shakespeare), 1965

Bennett, J. W. 'New techniques of comedy in *All's Well That Ends Well*', *SQ* 18 (1967), 337–62

Bergeron, D. 'The mythical structure of *All's Well That Ends Well*', *TSLL* 14 (1972), 559–68

Bradbrook, M. C. *Shakespeare and Elizabethan Poetry*, 1951 (expands on argument that 'Virtue is the true nobility', *RES* 26 (1950), 289–301)

Calderwood, J. L. 'The mingled yarn of *All's Well*', *JEGP* 62 (1963), 61–76 'Styles of knowing in *All's Well*', *MLQ* 25 (1964), 272–94

Carter, A. H. 'In defence of Bertram', *SQ* 7 (1956), 21–31 (compare Schoff)

Chambers, E. K. *Shakespeare: A Survey*, 1925

Cole, Howard C. *The '*All's Well*' Story from Boccaccio to Shakespeare*, 1981

Craig, H. *An Interpretation of Shakespeare*, 1948

Donaldson, I. '*All's Well That Ends Well*: Shakespeare's play of endings', *EIC* 27 (1977), 34–55

Dowden, E. *Shakespere: A Critical Study of His Mind and Art*, 1875

Fripp, E. *Shakespeare, Man and Artist*, 1938

Goldsmith, R. *Wise Fools in Shakespeare*, 1955

Greg, W. W. *The Editorial Problem in Shakespeare*, 1942

Halio, J. L. '*All's Well That Ends Well*', *SQ* 15 (1964), 33–45

Hapgood, R. 'The life of shame: Parolles and *All's Well That Ends Well*', *EIC* 15 (1965), 269–78

Hunter, G. K. (ed.). *All's Well That Ends Well* (Arden Shakespeare), 1959 (valuable introduction to the play)

Hunter, R. G. *Shakespeare and the Comedy of Forgiveness*, 1965

Huston, J. D. 'The function of Parolles', *SQ* 21 (1970), 431–8

King, W. N. 'Shakespeare's "mingled yarn"', *MLQ* 21 (1959), 33–44

Knight, G. W. *The Sovereign Flower*, 1958

Krapp, G. 'Parolles', in B. Matthews and A. Thorndike (eds.), *Shakesperian Studies*, 1916

Lawrence, W. W. *Shakespeare's Problem Comedies*, 1931 (expands on argument of 'The meaning of *All's Well That Ends Well*', *PMLA* 37 (1922), 418–69; compare Murry)

Leech, C. 'The theme of ambition in *All's Well*', *ELH* 21 (1954), 17–29

Legouis, E. 'La Comtesse de Roussillon', *English* 1 (1937), 399–404

Murry, J. M. *Shakespeare*, 1936 (refutes Lawrence)

Nagarajan, S. 'The structure of *All's Well That Ends Well*', *EIC* 10 (1960), 24–31

Price, J. G. *The Unfortunate Comedy*, 1968 (the first book devoted solely to *All's Well*; contains a comprehensive stage history of the play)

Ranald, M. L. 'The betrothals of *All's Well That Ends Well*', *HLQ* 26 (1963), 179–92

Rossiter, A. P. *Angel with Horns*, 1961

Rothman, J. 'A vindication of Parolles', *SQ* 23 (1972), 183–96

Salingar, L. *Shakespeare and the Traditions of Comedy*, 1974

Schoff, F. G. 'Claudio, Bertram, and a note on interpretation', *SQ* 10 (1959), 11–23 (refutes Carter)

Shaw, G. B. *Our Theatres in the Nineties*, I, 1932
Pen Portraits, I, 1932

Sisson, C. J. 'Shakespeare's Helena and Dr William Harvey', *E&S* (1960), 1–20

Smallwood, R. L. 'The design of *All's Well That Ends Well*', *S.Sur.* 25 (1972), 45–61

Spencer, H. *The Art and Life of William Shakespeare*, 1940

Stoll, E. E. *From Shakespeare to Joyce*, 1944

Styan, J. B. *All's Well That Ends Well* (Shakespeare in Performance), Manchester, 1984

Tillyard, E. M. W. *Shakespeare's Problem Plays*, 1949

Toole, W. B. *Shakespeare's Problem Plays*, 1966

Turner, R. Y. 'Dramatic conventions in *All's Well That Ends Well*', *PMLA* 75 (1960), 497–502

Van Doren, M. *Shakespeare*, 1939

Vickers, B. *The Artistry of Shakespeare's Prose*, 1968

Warren, R. 'Why does it end well? Helena, Bertram, and the sonnets', *S.Sur.* 22 (1969), 79–92

Wilson, H. S. 'Dramatic emphasis in *All's Well*', *HLQ* 13 (1949–50), 217–40

Wilson, J. D. (ed.). *All's Well That Ends Well* (New Shakespeare), 1929 (proposes an elaborate theory of revision)